VANCOUVER AND VICTORIA

A COLOURGUIDE

Edited by Constance Brissenden
Photography by Hamid Attie

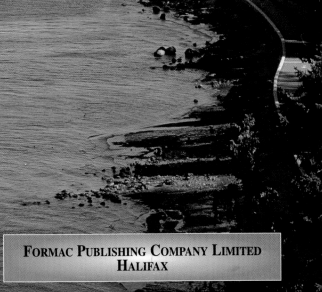

FORMAC PUBLISHING COMPANY LIMITED
HALIFAX

CONTENTS

MAPS   4
Greater Vancouver Map   4
Locator Map   6
Vancouver Dining Map   7
Vancouver Accommodation Map   8
About This Guide   9

VANCOUVER   11
Exploring Vancouver   12
A Brief History   15
Top Attractions   20
Dining   40
Shopping   49
Entertainment   56
Galleries   61
Parks & Gardens   64
Sports & Activities   69
Kids' Stuff   75
Annual Events   81

VANCOUVER NEIGHBOURHOODS   85
Downtown   86
West End   92
Gastown   97
Chinatown   101
Commercial Drive   105

For photo credits and acknowledgements, see page 216.

CONTENTS

Granville Island and False Creek	107
Kitsilano	111
UBC	115
North Shore	119
VICTORIA	**125**
Map	126
Exploring Victoria	127
A Brief History	128
Top Attractions	130
Shopping	149
Dining	153
EXCURSIONS	**157**
Whistler	158
Gulf Islands	163
Sunshine Coast	167
LISTINGS	**169**
INDEX	**211**

Canadian Cataloguing in Publication Data

Main entry under title:

Vancouver & Victoria: A Colourguide

(Colourguide series)
Includes index.
ISBN 0-88780-520-5

1. Vancouver (B.C.) — Guidebooks. 2. Victoria (B.C.) — Guidebooks. I. Brissenden, Connie, 1947- . II. Attie, Hamid. III. Title: Vancouver and Victoria. IV. Series.

FC3847.18.V34 2000   917.11'33044   C00-931480-6
F1089.5.V22V335 2000

Formac Publishing Company Limited
5502 Atlantic Street
Halifax, Nova Scotia B3H 1G4

Printed and bound in Canada

Distributed in the United States by:
Seven Hills Book Distributors
1531 Tremont Street
Cincinnati, Ohio 45214

Distributed in the United Kingdom by:
World Leisure Marketing
9 Downing Road
West Meadows Industrial Estate
Derby, DE216HA
England

Horseshoe Bay

Howe Sound

To Nanaimo,
Sunshine Coast
& Bowen Island

Cypress Prov. Park

①

99

WEST
VANCOUVER

Lighthouse Park

NORTH SHORE

N

Burrard Inlet

STANLEY PARK →

5 km/3 mi

WEST END —

⑧ N.W. Marine Dr.

Pacific Spirit
Regional Park

4th Ave.
KITSILANO

Strait of Georgia

UNIVERSITY OF
BRITISH COLUMBIA

VANCOUVER

Pacific Spirit
Regional Park

S.W. Marine Dr.

41st Ave.

North Arm

Vancouver
International
Airport

RICHMOND

Fraser River

1 Canada Place
2 Capilano Suspension Bridge
3 Dr. Sun Yat-Sen Classical
Chinese Garden
4 Grouse Mountain
5 Vanier Park location includes;
Pacific Space Centre, Vancouver
Maritime Museum & Vancouver
Museum
6 Science World
7 Stanley Park
8 UBC Museum of Anthropology
9 Vancouver Aquarium
10 Vancouver Art Gallery

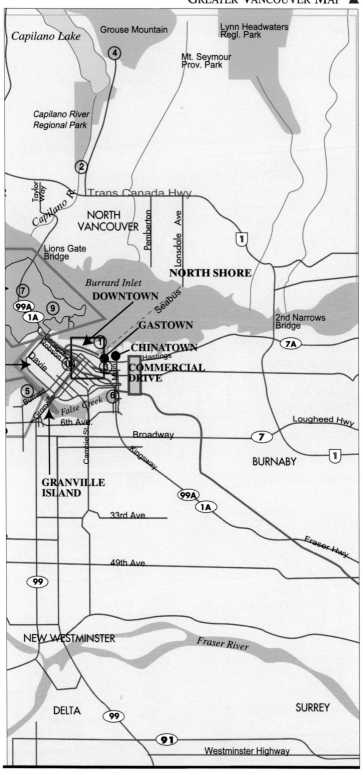

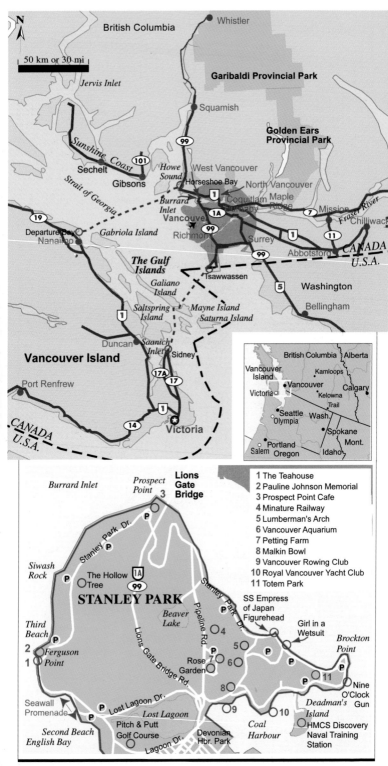

British Columbia

Whistler

N

50 km or 30 mi

Jervis Inlet

Garibaldi Provincial Park

Squamish

Golden Ears Provincial Park

99

Sunshine Coast

101

Sechelt

Gibsons

Howe Sound

West Vancouver

Horseshoe Bay

North Vancouver

Maple Ridge

Mission

Chilliwack

Fraser River

7

Burrard Inlet

Vancouver

1A

Coquitlam

Burnaby

19

Departure Bay

Nanaimo

Gabriola Island

Richmond

99

Surrey

11

Abbotsford

CANADA

U.S.A.

Strait of Georgia

The Gulf Islands

Galiano Island

Tsawwassen

99

5

Washington

Duncan

1

Saltspring Island

Mayne Island

Saturna Island

Bellingham

Vancouver Island

Saanich Inlet

Sidney

17A

17

Port Renfrew

1

14

★ **Victoria**

CANADA

U.S.A.

British Columbia | **Alberta**

Vancouver Island

Vancouver

Kamloops

Victoria

Kelowna

Calgary

Trail

Seattle

Olympia

Wash.

Spokane

Mont.

Portland

Salem

Oregon

Idaho

Burrard Inlet

Prospect Point

Lions Gate Bridge

3

P

P

Stanley Park Dr.

1 The Teahouse
2 Pauline Johnson Memorial
3 Prospect Point Cafe
4 Minature Railway
5 Lumberman's Arch
6 Vancouver Aquarium
7 Petting Farm
8 Malkin Bowl
9 Vancouver Rowing Club
10 Royal Vancouver Yacht Club
11 Totem Park

Siwash Rock

The Hollow Tree

1A
99

STANLEY PARK

Beaver Lake

SS Empress of Japan Figurehead

Stanley Park Dr.

Girl in a Wetsuit

Brockton Point

Third Beach

2

1

Ferguson Point

P

Pipeline Rd.

4

5

P

11

Nine O'Clock Gun

Lions Gate Bridge Rd.

Rose Garden

7

6

P

P

Deadman's Island

8

Seawall Promenade

P

Lost Lagoon Dr.

P

9

10

Coal Harbour

HMCS Discovery Naval Training Station

Second Beach

English Bay

Pitch & Putt Golf Course

Lost Lagoon

Devonian Hbr. Park

Lagoon Dr.

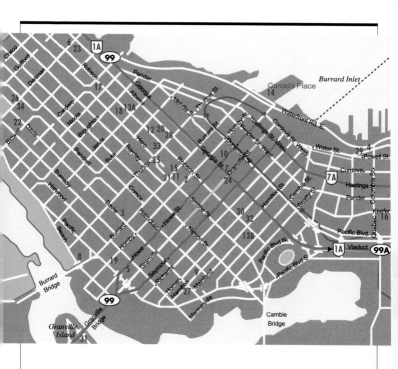

1. 900 West Restaurant and Wine Bar
2. Bacchus Ristorante
3. Bin 941 Tapas Parlour
4. Borgo Antico
5. C
6. Café de Paris
7. Chartwell
8. Chili Club Thai Restaurant
9. Cioppino's
10. Diva at the Met
11. Dynasty Chinese Seafood Restaurant
12. Earl's Restaurants
13. Ezogiku Noodle Café
14. Five Sails Restaurant
15. Fleuri Restaurant
16. Floata Seafood Restaurant
17. Gyoza King
18. Hon's Wun Tun House
19. Il Giardino di Umberto
20. Kirin Mandarin Restaurant
21. Le Crocodile
22. Liliget Feast House
23. Musashi Japanese Restaurant
24. Nottes Bon Ton Bakery and Confectionary
25. Piccolo Mondo
26. Raincity Grill
27. Rodney's Oyster House
28. Shanghai Chinese Bistro
29. Steamworks Brewing Co.
30. Subeez
31. The Creek Restaurant Brewery and Bar
32. Villa Del Lupo
33. White Spot Triple O's
34. Won More Szechuan Cuisine

▲ VANCOUVER ACCOMMODATION MAP

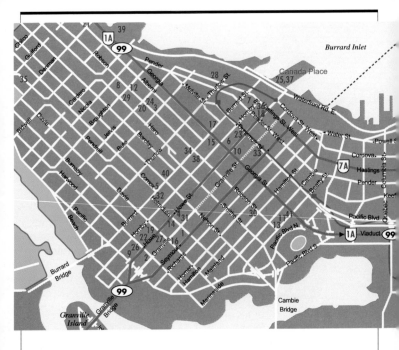

1. Best Western Chateau Granville Hotel
2. Best Western Downtown Vancouver
3. Blue Horizon Hotel
4. Bosman's Hotel
5. Century Plaza Hotel and Spa
6. Crowne Plaza Hotel Georgia Vancouver
7. Days Inn Vancouver Downtown
8. Empire Landmark Hotel and Conference Centre
9. Executive Inn Hotel Downtown Vancouver
10. Four Seasons Hotel
11. Georgian Court Hotel
12. Greenbrier Hotel
13. Hampton Inn and Suites
14. Holiday Inn Vancouver Downtown Hotel and Suites
15. Hotel Vancouver
16. Howard Johnson Hotel
17. Hyatt Regency Vancouver
18. Jolly Taxpayer Hotel
19. Landis Hotel and Suites
20. Listel Vancouver
21. Lord Stanley Suites on the Park
22. Marriott Residence Inn
23. Metropolitan Hotel
24. Pacific Palisades Hotel
25. Pan Pacific Hotel
26. Quality Hotel The Inn at False Creek
27. Ramada Inn and Suites Downtown Vancouver
28. Renaissance Vancouver Harbourside
29. Robsonstrasse Hotel
30. Rosedale on Robson
31. Royal Hotel
32. Sheraton Vancouver Wall Centre Hotel
33. St. Regis Hotel
34. Sutton Place Hotel
35. Sylvia Hotel
36. Terminal City Club Tower Hotel
37. Waterfront Centre Hotel
38. Wedgewood Hotel
39. Westin Bayshore Resort and Marina Vancouver
40. YMCA Hotel
41. YWCA Hotel/Residence

ABOUT THIS GUIDE

This guide has been written to help you get the most out of your stay in Vancouver and Victoria, two favourite West Coast destinations. It will enrich your stay by directing you to the top attractions in both cities as well as to places off the beaten track. The contributors to this book are people who know and love these cities and want to share their knowledge with you.

The guide is divided by city with the Vancouver section beginning on page 11 and the Victoria section on page 125. The Vancouver section offers nine chapters focusing on top attractions and activities. It also offers nine chapters dedicated to some of Vancouver's most exciting neighbourhoods.

The Victoria section of the guide includes general information, a brief history of the city, the top things to see and do and chapters on shopping and dining.

Following the section on Victoria, the guide covers some of the most popular excursions for visitors to the West Coast. Listings are carried at the end of the book. City and neighbourhood maps, as well as maps showing the locations of restaurants, hotels and attractions, appear at key points throughout the guide.

Like the other books in the Colourguide series, this is an independent publication. No payments or contributions have been solicited or accepted by the creators or publishers of this guide.

While every effort was made to ensure that the information in this book was up to date when it went to press, things do change over time. It is always wise to phone ahead to confirm that the information presented here is still current.

Brief biographies of the contributors follow.

KEVIN BARKER (Sunshine Coast) is a business writer and long-time resident of the Sunshine Coast.

MELANEY BLACK (Victoria Shopping) is a contributing writer for Victoria's *Monday Magazine*.

SHAWN BORDOFF (Entertainment) is an actor, scriptwriter and a TV producer who teaches for the Vancouver School Board.

CONSTANCE BRISSENDEN (editor; Exploring

VANCOUVER SKYLINE AT NIGHT

LIONS GATE BRIDGE

Vancouver; Whistler) is a Vancouver writer and editor with seven books and hundreds of magazine articles about Vancouver to her credit.

GAIL BUENTE (Vancouver's Top Attractions; Annual Events) has written for many magazines and publications, with a special emphasis on the arts and music.

CHUCK DAVIS (A Brief History of Vancouver) has shared his in-depth knowledge Vancouver history in many books and articles, including *Chuck Davis' Guide to Vancouver* and *Vancouver, An Illustrated Chronology*.

PATRICIA FRASER (Vancouver Shopping) is the coordinator for international programming, Fairchild Radio, and covers shopping for *Vancouver* magazine.

MARIAN GILMOUR (Kids' Stuff) is the manager of one of Vancouver's most beautiful historic buildings, Heritage Hall.

GARY HYNES (Victoria Dining) is a veteran food critic and publisher of *EAT* (Epicure and Travel).

LESLEY KENNY (Victoria's Top Attractions) is a researcher and writer who has organized tours for conference delegates and visiting business people.

ALMA LEE (Granville Island and False Creek) is the producer of the Vancouver International Writers Festival.

BOB MACKIN (Sports) is a sports reporter for the *North Shore News* and the author of *Baseball Trivia*.

GARY MCFARLANE (Commercial Drive) is a writer who lives and works in the Commercial Drive neighbourhood.

KELSEY MCLEOD (Kitsilano) is a Vancouver historian and member of the B.C. Historical Society.

MARG MEIKLE (Parks and Gardens) is the author of *Garden City: Vancouver*, as well as numerous other fact-based books and children's books.

JAMES OAKES (West End) is a veteran journalist and the former editor of a West End business newsletter.

CHRIS PETTY (University of British Columbia), a UBC graduate and historian, edits the *UBC Chronicle* alumni magazine.

JOANNE POON (Chinatown) has a degree in Chinese social history from UBC and works in Chinatown.

D. C. (DENNIS) REID (Exploring Victoria; A Brief History of Victoria) is a Victoria resident, published poet and historical novelist.

ANN ROSENBERG (Galleries), a retired art teacher, is now an independent curator and art critic.

LEANORE SALI (Gastown) is the director of the Gastown Business Improvement Society.

ANNE SMART (Gulf Islands) is the author of *All About Salt Spring Island*.

BARBARA TOWELL (Downtown Vancouver) has a BA in Art History and an MA in Archival Studies from the University of British Columbia.

ROCHELLE VAN HALM (North Shore) was born, raised and still lives on the North Shore; she is a veteran freelance writer.

KASEY WILSON (Vancouver Dining) is Vancouver's leading food writer and broadcaster; she is the author of the highly successful *Best of Vancouver*.

VANCOUVER

EXPLORING VANCOUVER

CONSTANCE BRISSENDEN

CANADA PLACE

It's official: Vancouver is the number one city in the world in which to live. According to a year 2000 survey by British human resources consultancy William M. Mercer, it shares the honour with the Swiss cities of Bern and Zurich, and Vienna, the capital of Austria. Not bad company, after all, for this city of approximately 2 million people. Thirty-nine factors measured the quality of life, from personal safety and transportation to the availability of public services. Other surveys by *Atlantic Monthly*, *The Economist*, *Maclean's* and *Condé Nast Traveler* confirm that Vancouver ranks high on the "best city" lists.

AN IDEAL CITY

Our secret is out. The world knows that Vancouver is a superb place for living and visiting. The weather is moderate as befits a coastal rain forest, the grass is always green and flowers bloom twelve months of the year. The North Shore mountains are a perfect complement to the Pacific Ocean, especially in winter when they are brushed with a fresh coat of snow. All in all, it's an ideal

STREET ARTIST

environment, which explains why Canadians flock here to live and to visit. In the past ten years, the Greater Vancouver area has grown by 400,000 people. The same is predicted for the next ten years.

Overall, the growth has been good for the city. Vancouver's attractions, services and infrastructure have grown up. What was once a small provincial town is now a cosmopolitan Pacific Rim player, with good

hotels, impressive restaurants and plenty to see and do at any time of the year. The mix of people here is unique, a blend of West meets East, with 30 percent of the population of Asian descent. Vancouver also has a high First Nations contingent. Their influence is evident in its galleries, museums, at annual events like powwows and even in stores, which often feature clothing and jewellery by native designers.

GROUSE MOUNTAIN SKYRIDE

While some residents complain about the traffic, getting around the city is easy for a visitor. Public transit is provided by SkyTrain, bus or SeaBus. With a day pass, you can visit the North Shore or explore as far away as historic Steveston fishing village and the Gulf of Georgia Cannery National Historic Site. For real efficiency, call TransLink's Customer Information number for routes and schedules. You don't even need a car to travel to Whistler. Transportation is available from Greyhound Canada or BC Rail. If you prefer driving, however, the roads in and around Vancouver are good, although rush hour can be slow.

VIEW FROM PROSPECT POINT (BELOW); CAPILANO SUSPENSION BRIDGE (BOTTOM)

FAVOURITE SPOTS TO EXPLORE

Ask any Vancouverite, and they'll enthuse about their favourite things to see and do in the city. For some, it's a walk along English Bay to Stanley Park. Depending on how ambitious you are, you may want to walk around the park's ten-kilometre seawall perimeter, passing under the Lions Gate Bridge and past Brockton Point with its array of totem poles. Or you may simply want to stop at a park bench and watch the world stroll, skate or bike by. Granville Island is completely different, with its busy market, multitude of small arts and craft shops and hustle and bustle. Yet here too you can find quiet spots and quiet moments. On a clear day, you may even see towering Mount Baker to the south in Washington State from your Granville Island viewpoint.

Across the water, on the North Shore, the pace of life slows down, with strolls along Ambleside Beach, or days spent hiking on Seymour Mountain. Rivers have carved deep canyons through lush forests. The canyons can be viewed at several spots, the best known of which is the Capilano Suspension Bridge.

To get to know the area quickly, try local tours by bus, train and boat. If you'd like to tour and explore at the same time, the Vancouver Trolley Company's "jump on, jump off" tour is ideal. Many types of tours are available, from the popular boat-train day trip aboard the *M.V. Britannia* and classic old Royal Hudson steam train to Squamish to boating experiences around Howe Sound. Note that some tours are not available year round.

Unique, informative and free walking tours are available in several of the city's neighbourhoods. If you're interested in the history of buildings, the Architectural Institute of British Columbia offers guided tours of downtown Vancouver in the summer months. Gastown and Chinatown also have free walking tours. For an overview of the city and the North Shore, visit The Lookout! atop Harbour Centre Tower. The revolving observation deck is 167 metres up via outside glass elevators.

For both Vancouver and Victoria, also included in this guide, you will find detailed information on climate, travel arrangements, currency, customs, accommodation, emergency care and other vital data in the Listings section at the end. In the "Top Attractions" sections, you will find in-depth descriptions of the main attractions of both cities. Please refer to the Listings for telephone numbers and other key information. Other chapters take readers through a variety of each city's fascinating neighbourhoods. Shopping and dining are also covered. For more on Victoria, see "Exploring Victoria."

The Vancouver Tourist InfoCentre is extremely helpful. The website, tourismvancouver.com, provides lots of great information. If you visit in person, the staff will make reservations for you at B.C. hotels. You can also book your hotel on line. For current information on entertainment, attractions and dining, check the Thursday editions of *The Province*, *Vancouver Sun* and free, weekly *Georgia Straight.*

VANCOUVER SKYLINE

A BRIEF HISTORY

CHUCK DAVIS

There are several accounts relating to Vancouver's origins, but a favourite involves the 1792 meeting between a Spanish exploration party and some of the local Salish people. (An earlier expedition, a 1791 visit by Don José Marie Narvaez, marked the first contact between Europeans and native people in this area.) It happens that 1792 was the same year Captain George Vancouver was exploring these waters. In fact, Vancouver met Dionisio Galiano, the leader of the Spanish expedition, here and the two men hit it off and became friends. Vancouver gave the name Spanish Banks to the area where that meeting occurred, and it bears that name more than 200 years later. Aside from Indian Arm, an arm of Burrard Inlet (today the city's harbour), Vancouver bestowed no native-inspired names, even though he had the Musqueam, the Squamish, the Kwantlen, the Tsawwassen and many other groups to choose from. Some of these groups were seasonal, coming down from the interior to the mouth of the Fraser when the salmon was running.

INUIT SCULPTURE IN STANLEY PARK

Simon Fraser made a very brief visit in 1808 before being chased back up the river by angry Musqueam men. Nearly sixty years were to pass before the white people returned ... this time to stay. What attracted them first were the area's magnificent trees. The forest industry then attracted other kinds of enterprise.

ORIGINS

September 30, 1867 marks the arrival in what is now Vancouver of John "Gassy Jack" Deighton. The Yorkshire-born Deighton, with a complexion, according to a chum, of "muddy purple," rowed into Burrard Inlet with his native wife, her mother, her cousin, a yellow dog, two chairs and a barrel of whiskey. A busy sawmill stood where

CAPTAIN GEORGE VANCOUVER

STATUE OF GASSY JACK IN *GASTOWN*

Gassy landed on the south shore of the inlet. A busier, bigger one existed on the North Shore. A kilometre or so to the west through the trees three fellows derisively nicknamed the "Three Greenhorns" (for paying the exorbitant price of $1 an acre for their land) were trying to make bricks from a vein of clay.

Gassy, retired from his career as a riverboat captain, jovially greeted the men who worked at the mill. He knew that the nearest drink for these thirsty fellows was a five-kilometre row east along the inlet to the North Road, then a long walk along a rude trail built by the Royal Engineers to New Westminster through the forest, the elk and the bears. A saloon near the mill on the South Shore was the ideal business opportunity. Gassy avowed that if the mill workers helped him build a bar, they could have all they could drink. The Globe Saloon was up within twenty-four hours.

The Globe is gone now, but it stood in the heart of what is now Vancouver's Gastown. The voluble Mr. Deighton, who well deserved his nickname because he never shut up, chose his location more wisely than he knew. The new country of Canada had been formed just two months earlier. British Columbia would soon join this Confederation, lured by the Canadian Pacific Railway's promise that it would link B.C. to Eastern markets. If they had known it would take fifteen years to arrive, they might not have agreed so readily. But in 1871, B.C. signed on, and now British Columbians were also Canadians. The population grew and Gassy Jack thrived. So did the Greenhorns. Their landholdings are today's apartment-crammed West End.

By the spring of 1886 there were enough people in Vancouver to form a city. The little ramshackle collection of tents and wooden shacks was incorporated on April 6. A little more than two months later, on June 13, the whole thing was destroyed by fire. A freak wind sprang up while some CPR workmen were burning brush, and in less than forty-five minutes the town disappeared. "Vancouver didn't burn," one of the survivors said, "it exploded." The heat was so intense that the bell at St. James Anglican Church melted to a puddle. You can see it today at the Vancouver Museum. The survivors began to build, more solidly this time, while the ashes were still smoking.

THE RAILWAY

The CPR's first train arrived on July 4, 1886 at Port Moody. Contrary to expectations, it didn't stop there: the railway extended the line to Coal Harbour, what is now part of the Vancouver waterfront. That enraged the speculators who had bought land at Port Moody based on the CPR's promise to put a terminal there. It turns out that

the water at the end of the inlet wasn't deep enough for the oceangoing ships that were part of the CPR's plans to establish links to China and other Far Eastern points.

Complaints were useless; the CPR was a hard-nosed firm, led by a single-minded, stocky, bearded bull of a man named William Van Horne, who ran his railway his way. Van Horne named Vancouver. It was originally named Granville, for the colonial secretary of the time, but Van Horne declared no one would ever know where "Granville" was. But "Vancouver," now that was a different matter. Everyone knew of Captain George Vancouver's famous Pacific Coast explorations. Van Horne had his way. He nearly always did.

William Van Horne was an American. Americans have played an important part in Vancouver's past: William Shaughnessy, a later CPR president and the man for whom the city's old-money neighbourhood is named, was an American. So was Benjamin Tingley Rogers, who built the huge B.C. Sugar Refinery company. L.D. Taylor, the man elected mayor of Vancouver eight times, more often than anyone, was from Michigan.

The first thing Vancouver's first city council did in 1886 was petition the federal government to lease it a 1,000-acre military reserve at the entrance to the harbour. The heavily forested reserve had been established as a potential defense point just in case the bumptious Americans tried to take over the area. That's how Vancouver got Stanley Park, one of the world's great city parks.

The railway, which had received thousands of acres of free land in return for coming into Vancouver, established a hotel named Hotel Vancouver some distance south of Gastown that, in effect, pulled the city's downtown around it. When Van Horne arrived in the city and saw the hotel, he confronted the architect: "So you're the damned fool who made it look like a hospital!" You see today the third Hotel Vancouver. This imposing, green-turreted landmark has hosted royal guests since 1939, beginning with King

SECOND HOTEL VANCOUVER

WILLIAM VAN HORNE

HOTEL VANCOUVER TODAY

George VI and Queen Elizabeth, now the Queen Mother.

One very tangible result of the Great Depression of the 1930s is still visible in Vancouver: the Lions Gate Bridge. This big, splendid and beautiful bridge opened in 1938, paid for and built by the Guinness Brewing Company of Ireland. The brewers had bought, at distress Depression prices of less than $19 an acre, a vast tract of land on the wooded slopes of the North Shore and began to sell the property. They built the bridge to encourage traffic, and buyers, to come on over. It worked. British Pacific Properties is still the most affluent neighborhood in Greater Vancouver. The residents in one of its postal zones have the highest per capita income in the country.

NEW GROWTH

After some years of relative quiet, Vancouver began to show signs of growth in the 1950s. A handsome office building erected on Burrard Street in 1955 by B.C. Electric was the first skyscraper built south of downtown. Much of what has been built since is distinctive, too. The city has given Canada some important architects, including Ron Thom, Bing Thom, Bruno Freschi, C. B. K. Van Norman and, preeminently, Arthur Erickson. Erickson's unique buildings dot the metropolitan area, and his provincial courthouse complex still draws admiring crowds in the city's downtown heart. His MacMillan Bloedel Building (no longer occupied by the giant forest company) is a striking and lofty landmark, noted for its immensely deep windows. Simon Fraser University, also his creation, in the suburb of Burnaby to the east, provided an apt setting for the hotbed of student revolt in the 1960s. Erickson's magnificent Museum of Anthropology on the University of British Columbia campus to the west is further evidence of the work of this globally famous architect.

Vancouver inherited a reputation as "Lotus Land" in the swinging 1960s and 1970s. More global attention was heaped on it in 1986 with the terrifically successful Expo 86, a world exposition that attracted more than 20 million paying visitors. The Expo lands were sold to Hong Kong financier Li Ka-Shing at a bargain-basement price and spawned a high-rise boom. In the past decade, Lotus Land has been superseded by the same frenetic energy that has infected

cities worldwide. Today the up-and-coming live in lofty "smart" high-rises, bristling with high-tech features. What remains are the breathtaking views of the city, the harbour and the looming Coast Mountains.

INFLUX OF NEWCOMERS

Suburban growth continues to this day, and so does the number of newcomers: over the last couple of decades, there has been a huge influx of Asian immigrants: Hong Kong Chinese (many of whom decided to leave Hong Kong in advance of the 1997 takeover by China), Vietnamese, Korean, Thai, Filipino, other East Asians and Indians. They've established neighbourhoods: suburban Richmond is one-third Chinese; suburban Surrey has attracted thousands of East Indian residents. By opening shops and restaurants and participating in the business, social and community lives of the region, these newcomers have added verve to the Lower Mainland, while sparking some grumbling among a minority of locals.

Besides the jolt to the economy the newcomers provide, Vancouver and its suburbs are thriving because of their fervent embrace of high technology. The slow decline of resource-based industries like forestry, mining and fishing is being counterbalanced (and more) by a sustained burst of growth in computer-related companies, multimedia houses, Internet website designers and related trades.

One trend that stopped happening in Vancouver in the 1990s was a decreasing share of the metropolitan population. The figures for 1995 show that the central city's population had increased by more than 107,000 since 1981. That's a 26 percent jump, and it's still climbing rapidly. "Our city," says Larry Beasley, a Vancouver city planner,"is emerging as an unbelievably unique place. We have tens of thousands of citizens who have elected to move into the city. Most of North America has an anti-urban philosophy. But here, people want to move into the downtown."

YALETOWN

TOP ATTRACTIONS

GAIL BUENTE

TOTEMS IN STANLEY PARK	There are many attractions in Vancouver that a visitor should not miss. Here are the top destinations and sites to see while you are in the city.

STANLEY PARK

Stanley Park is unquestionably Vancouver's number one attraction. The park is identified so closely with the city that it could almost be said that Stanley Park is Vancouver. Certainly, Vancouver would not be Vancouver without it. At twenty times the size of New York's Central Park, it is North America's third-largest urban park. Its location, almost entirely surrounded by salt water and adjacent to the city centre and the West End, makes Stanley Park unique. While paid parking is available, the best way to get to the park is by TransLink city bus, or on foot through the West End. A free shuttlebus (not a tour) operates inside the park on summer days.

STANLEY PARK'S MINIATURE TRAIN

In 1889, Governor General Lord Stanley dedicated Stanley Park "to the use and enjoyment of people of all colours, creeds and customs for all time." If His Lordship could see the park now, he'd be amazed at how prophetic his dedication was. With

an estimated 8 million visitors a year, this 405-hectare (1,000-acre) urban wilderness is treasured by all. At any time of the year, the trails and footpaths buzz with the sounds of dozens of languages, spoken by people of all ages, races and beliefs.

Back in Lord Stanley's day, a visit to the park was a dignified affair, culminating with a posed snapshot of the family inside the Hollow Tree. Today, people still visit the giant cleft tree located near Third Beach off Stanley Park Drive, but a day in the park now includes much more. Vancouver has grown and changed and so has the park. It has come to symbolize all the traits of this vibrant city: informality, naturalness, energy and diversity. But the century-plus since it became a park is only a brief moment in the life of this ageless patch of earth.

Stanley Park is full of geological hints of a past far older than the high-rise buildings around it. Siwash Rock, according to legend, is a Squamish Indian warrior turned to stone by the gods. In fact, it is an ancient deposit of lava. Fossils found in the park indicate that semitropical palms and sequoia trees once thrived here many millions of years ago. Where today visitors feed friendly squirrels, cougars and other wildlife thrived in the not-so-distant past. Remnants of Indian middens, ancient piles of sea shells and cultural debris, tell of thousands of years of native habitation when villagers hunted, fished and held potlatches on the peninsula. Today's Lumberman's Arch was once the site of the Squamish village of Whoi Whoi. Deadman's Island, now a military base and not publicly accessible, once provided a secluded funeral ground for these early peoples.

THE HOLLOW TREE (TOP AND MIDDLE); JOGGERS ON THE SEAWALL (BELOW)

Visitors to Stanley Park soon discover that there are really two distinct parks: an outer rim which is tamed, developed and well used, and a wilder inner heart, where the noise and hustle of the city seem light years away. The outer portion is circled by the ten-kilometre-long (six-mile) seawall. Started in 1917 and completed in 1980, the seawall surrounds all of the park's extensive recreational attractions:

*LOST LAGOON (TOP);
INLINE SKATERS ON
THE SEAWALL
(MIDDLE)*

Vancouver rowing and yacht clubs, the Vancouver Aquarium and Marine Science Centre, cricket and rugby fields, a petting farm and miniature railway for the kids, picnic areas, two swimming beaches and a children's water park, a cultured rose garden, a pitch-and-putt golf course, lawn bowling and tennis courts, Malkin Bowl (home to open-air Theatre Under the Stars musical theatre on summer evenings) and Lost Lagoon. Along the way, in-line skaters and cyclists glide by. Walkers can stop at any of a variety of concessions and restaurants: The Teahouse at Ferguson Point, Prospect Point Cafe, the Fish House Restaurant or the Stanley Park Pavilion. Among this array of amusements, all sorts of other activities take place spontaneously. On weekends, for example, budding as well as professional artists set up their easels and display their works at an impromptu gallery on the grass.

As the seawall winds around the rim of the park, it passes numerous structures of historic and cultural interest. A walk along the path will take you past the *Girl in a*

*THE TEAHOUSE AT
FERGUSON POINT*

PROSPECT POINT

Wetsuit sculpture, Brockton Point Lighthouse, the huge wooden Lumberman's Arch monument and Vancouver's unique acoustic landmark, the Nine-O'Clock Gun, at Hallelujah Point. Except for a brief stretch during the Second World War, the cannon has been fired at precisely nine p.m. since 1894. Originally, the gunshot helped mariners in setting their chronometers, but nowadays it continues simply out of affection for tradition. Nearby, sightseers and picture takers stop at the Brockton Point Totem Park to inspect a historic grouping of nineteenth-century original poles and replicas, by carvers of the Haida, Kwakwaka'wakw and Nuu-chah-nulth nations. A little farther along the seawall is another favourite with photographers, the lookout at Prospect Point. From here, the highest point in the park, you can survey all of Burrard Inlet and the North Shore.

Other crowd pleasers along the seawall are the sandy beaches. Second Beach is a city beach par excellence, sporting a saltwater swimming pool, children's playground, baseball diamonds and picnic areas. All summer, the air rings with laughter, radios and the thwack of baseball bats. On weekend nights, the sounds of ethnic folk dancing fill the air. The aroma of deep-fried fish and chips, a Stanley Park tradition, wafts across the grass. On warm afternoons, every log becomes a pillow for a sunbather.

Lost Lagoon is perhaps the most representative feature of the "outer park." Once a rough tidal basin off Coal Harbour, the lagoon was a favourite canoeing spot for poet Pauline Johnson, the daughter of a Mohawk chief, who named the lagoon for the way it disappeared at low tide. Today, pedestrians stroll along its banks or stop to feed swans and ducks in the shade of willow trees.

THIRD BEACH PLAY

The interior park, in contrast, is overgrown and wild. For the most part, it is densely forested, with a network of bike and foot paths crisscrossing beneath fir and cedar boughs. These trails follow the routes of the

VANCOUVER AQUARIUM MARINE SCIENCE CENTRE

skid roads used for logging many years ago. For a time, Deadman's Island was home to a sawmill. Beaver Lake, the inner park's freshwater counterpart to Lost Lagoon, is a natural-state pond, edged with cattails and teeming with frogs croaking from water lilies. You'll also find, without too much effort, that the boggy soil around the lake is teeming with skunk cabbage, a large, graceful plant with a pungent perfume that is, well, not to everyone's liking.

When venturing from the park's civilized exterior into its wilder interior, don't be led astray by the apparently easy-to-follow trailways. It's quite possible to get lost in the maze, and many first-time visitors have found themselves walking in circles before they discover the exit path. Walkers unfamiliar with the trails should take a map if they want to get back in time for dinner.

In many ways, Stanley Park's two sides reflect the contrasting attitudes about its future. Vancouverites fall generally into two camps. Half of them want to continue to develop the park "for the use and enjoyment of all people." Just as many would like to see it kept as natural and untouched as possible. The controversy is dynamic and healthy, and continues to remind Vancouver just how passionately involved it is with its very own urban wilderness.

VANCOUVER AQUARIUM MARINE SCIENCE CENTRE

Who can resist shark-feeding frenzy? Caimans on the prowl? A slithery anaconda dining on who knows what? Not the almost 1 million visitors to the Vancouver Aquarium Marine Science Centre in Stanley Park each year. Since 1956 when it opened, the aquarium has kept its visitors entertained with life-and-death dramas brought to life in 167 aquatic displays grouped in five public areas.

WITH A BELUGA

In the steamy jungle environment of the Amazon Rainforest gallery, two caimans, second cousins to the crocodile, set the tone. Every hour, "rainstorms" are created inside this space. Giant freshwater Amazon fishes that play a vital role in the survival of the rainforest, Scarlet Ibises and a pair of sloths add to the atmosphere.

Once a week at the Shark Penthouse in the Tropical Pacific Gallery, a research naturalist dives with the sharks, with dramatic effect. The waters literally thrash as the sharks gulp down their food. Overall, the gallery mimics a tropical reef at Indonesia's Bunaken National Marine Park, including black-tipped reef sharks, stone fish and rainbow-coloured tropical species.

Five beluga whales in the Arctic Canada presentation area can be viewed through an underwater gallery. It was a proud day when Qila, slightly smaller and greyer then the rest, was born at the aquarium on July 23, 1995. Older belugas, like mother Aurora, turn pure white in colour. Nearby, two sea otters keep company. The sea otters, like the belugas, are under constant study. Even the sea otters' feces provide scientific data on reproductive hormone and cortisol levels. The female, Nyac, is the oldest living female sea otter survivor of the Valdez Alaska oil spill of 1989.

FEEDING A BELUGA AT THE AQUARIUM (TOP); SEA OTTER (ABOVE)

In the Pacific Northwest area, local waters are the focus. Search in the watery habitats for playful sea otters, elusive wolf eels and giant Pacific octopi. Orcas, or killer whales as they are popularly known, and Pacific-sided dolphins are featured. Stellar sea lions, like the other residents here, are not only entertaining but are useful subjects for scientific observation.

Finally, in the new, $5.2-million Pacific Canada Pavilion, lingcod prey on herring as they would in the local Strait of Georgia. The exhibit features a 260-thousand-litre exhibit of thousands of fish in a believable simulation of a kelp forest.

As a privately operated, self-supporting, non-profit organization, the aquarium is dedicated to promoting conservation through display and interpretation, education, research and direct action. A typical temporary exhibit is the B.C. Salmon Story. Innovative and interactive, the exhibit is sponsored by Fisheries Renewal B.C. The "show" explores the ongoing relationship between the people of B.C. and its most famous fish, the salmon.

DISCOVERING MARINE LIFE AT THE AQUARIUM

The first public aquarium in Canada and now one of the five largest science facilities in North America, the Vancouver Aquarium is recognized for its displays and interpretation facilities. It was the first in Canada to incorporate professional naturalists on-site. In all, more than 9,000 invertebrates, 8,800 fishes, 66 reptiles, 41 birds and 22 mammals live here. In 1999 and 2000, the aquarium won Attractions Canada's national/international attraction award for British Columbia.

After the galleries, visitors can relax with a latte and sandwich in The UpStream Café, adjacent to the beluga whale habitat. At the colourful ClamShell Gift Shop, souvenirs come in many price ranges, from soapstone whale carvings to local postcards. Not surprisingly, anything with a killer whale image is an instant bestseller.

SCIENCE WORLD

SCIENCE WORLD/ALCAN
OMNIMAX THEATRE AT SCIENCE WORLD

Science World is housed in an Expo 86 legacy building. Originally the Expo Centre, it was affectionately called "the golf ball" during the 1986 world exposition. Three years later, the silver ball reopened as Science World, with Queen Elizabeth II on hand for the ceremonies. By day, the mirrorlike exterior reflects the waters of nearby False Creek. At night, the geodesic dome sparkles with 131 exterior lights.

Science World is now a hugely popular family attraction. More than 400,000 people visit each year to enjoy its permanent and evolving exhibits. A healthy 62,000 are students on school trips. Science World is designed as a hands-on experience for the hoards of energetic kids who visit daily. They run, scream, laugh and frolic. In other words, they love it here.

Adults and children come to Science World to be dazzled by science as entertainment. It certainly works. Hundreds of creative exhibits ensure that even science dropouts can find something intriguing and new. One exhibit makes your hair stand on end; another lets you blow square bubbles. In the main gallery's Matter and Forces area, physics is made simple (if that's possible) with ample demonstrations. Five additional galleries round out the offerings, featuring everything from Kids Space, an evolving environment for children three to six years of age, to Mine Games, focusing on the province's mining industry. If that doesn't grab you, check out Visual Illusions and play with optical tricks that leave you puzzling over what's real and what's not. In the Sara Stern Search Gallery, natural history is taught through hands-on "discovery boxes."

HANDS-ON STUDY AT SCIENCE WORLD

The Alcan OMNIMAX Theatre is found inside the centre's multi-million-dollar geodesic dome. Everything about the Alcan OMNIMAX Theatre is big and loud. The steeply raked, 500-seat theatre boasts one of the world's largest domed screens, capable of projecting an image nine times larger than a conventional movie. Sound pumps out of twenty-eight digital sound speakers backed by ten tons of equipment. The most comfortable viewing experience is near the top of the amphitheatre.

The fifty-minute documentaries vary in subjects from dolphins to the mysteries of Egypt to Olympic glories. The images are shot to make the most of the OMNIMAX technology. Don't be surprised if you duck when a flying dolphin appears to leap right out of the screen onto your lap. While most children enjoy the visual surround-and-sound combination, some may find the huge moving images overpowering. The theatre presents five shows each weekday, with an additional show at five p.m. on weekends and holidays. An additional fee is charged for Alcan OMNIMAX shows.

After taking in Science World, relax over snacks at the Bytes Cafeteria overlooking False Creek. Before you leave, drop by the Science World Gift Shop where you'll find some of the more amusing souvenirs of the city. Even plastic dinosaurs have a place. Among the better choices are science books for kids, including one that features "really gross experiments." Science experiment kits and ingenious toys are also sold here.

THE UBC MUSEUM OF ANTHROPOLOGY (MOA)

The University of British Columbia Museum of Anthropology's research collection of approximately 230,000 artifacts includes ethnographic and archeological materials from Europe, Africa, the Americas, Asia and the

MUSEUM OF ANTHROPOLOGY GREAT HALL

HOUSE POSTS CIRCA 1906 AT THE MOA

South Pacific. There is everything from ceramics to Asian textiles, but the high point of the museum is its collection of Kwakwaka'wakw, Nisga'a, Gitksan, Haida and Coast Salish art. Experts agree it is one of the finest collections of Northwest Coast First Nations art anywhere in the world.

In the Great Hall of the museum, sunlight streams in through 13.7m high picture windows. Immense totem poles, graceful cedar canoes and many other Westcoast First Nations artifacts appear as they might have in remote coastal villages. The spirits of ancient carvers seem to hover in the air above a cluster of visitors and their tour guide.

While the artifacts are given the careful treatment necessary for historic objects, they are also appreciated as works of art. The MOA feels like a gallery, displaying its artifacts elegantly and with as much natural light as possible. Only the most fragile items are kept encased in darkness, and even those are accessible to visitors through an innovative approach called "visible storage." By keeping the objects in glass-topped drawers, over 90 percent of the permanent collection is visible to the public. Most museums display about 2 to 5 percent of their collections.

The museum was a pioneer in both the visible storage system and the use of natural light, a concept that has since been incorporated into the design of the National Gallery in Ottawa. Both these innovations, now widely copied, were considered controversial back in 1976 when the museum opened its doors, leading to citations for both best design and worst design.

The architecture, evoking the plank houses of the Northwest Coast First Nations, was designed by Vancouver's Arthur Erickson. His challenge was unique: to create a building to house a group of already-existing artifacts. From its humble beginning in 1949, with a small collection of oceanic materials housed in the basement of UBC's Main Library, the holdings had grown over many years and the collection was well established. The new museum is magnificent, a building worthy of its subject matter and its majestic location overlooking Howe Sound. In the Visible Storage galleries, row upon row of Kwakwaka'wakw dance masks stare out in an eerie display of variations on a theme. Forty-three black raven heads with wild cedar-bark manes raise their red beaks defiantly, appearing to watch the passing crowds through steely white-rimmed eyes. Those masks see, and are

WOODEN FRONTLET AT THE MOA

seen by, more than 170,000 visitors yearly. In the Masterpiece Gallery, exquisitely carved jewellery and small sculptures of argillite, silver, gold and bone take the viewer back to an age when there was enough time for craftsmanship.

In the museum's central Rotunda, a skylight illuminates Bill Reid's sculpture *Raven and the First Men*, a highlight of the contemporary collection. The massive yellow cedar carving portrays Raven, the magical trickster, as he discovers the first humans in a clamshell and coaxes them out into the world. According to legend, the Haidas are descended from these shell people. The Museum of Anthropology's collection of Bill Reid art is the largest assemblage anywhere of works by this influential artist whose unique creations fused modern design with traditional Northwest Coastal native forms. An outdoor exhibit features two Haida houses designed by Bill Reid and Doug Cranmer and totem poles by some of the finest contemporary carvers of the coast.

BILL REID, *RAVEN AND THE FIRST MEN* (TOP); **BEAR SCULPTURE** (ABOVE)

Back in the Great Hall under the towering totems, the history of the coast's first people is recorded in red cedar. There are sturdy boxes made by steaming a single plank and used for everything from cooking to cradles to coffins for the dead. Bowls and feast dishes take the form of mythical beings like T'sonoqua, the wild woman of the woods. Carved canoes were used for fishing and whaling off the rugged British Columbia coast. The boxes, bowls and feast dishes conjure images of huge potlatches, traditional ceremonies essential to the survival of native coastal communities. At the potlatches, hereditary names and privileges were passed from generation to generation, and social status was publicly affirmed. Lavish feasts were served and gifts exchanged. From 1884 to 1951, the Canadian government banned the potlatch in an attempt to control and destroy a culture it did not understand or approve. The potlatch has re-emerged as a significant symbol of the contemporary resurgence in First Nations identity.

The MOA is truly a living museum, proud of its training programs and its record of hiring students who are its future conservators, anthropologists and archeologists. As the largest teaching museum in Canada, it has built a reputation for successfully integrating research with public access.

WOVEN BASKET PRE-1916

VANCOUVER ART GALLERY

The Vancouver Art Gallery houses British Columbia's largest collection of artworks, from classical museum pieces to the latest works of the avant-garde. Established in 1931, it moved into its present location, a neo-classical-style heritage building, in 1983. Formerly used as a provincial courthouse, the building

EMILY CARR, *UNTITLED*, AT THE VAG

was redesigned by renowned local architect Arthur Erickson to accommodate an additional 3,716 square meters of exhibition space. The internationally recognized gallery touches all the bases, with exciting touring exhibits alongside an outstanding permanent collection of close to 7,000 works.

In its mission statement, the Vancouver Art Gallery calls itself a place "to inspire and please through visual art," and that describes it well. Visit the four floors of exhibition space and you'll find numerous delightful surprises: one-person and group shows by established and emerging artists, exhibits arranged thematically and travelling exhibitions from other museums. You may see an exhibit of familiar paintings by Impressionist masters, or a show of vibrant new works by up-and-coming local artists.

Yet for many guests, the highlight of the gallery is the permanent collection of works by B.C. artist and writer Emily Carr. Now well known in Canada and internationally, for most of her life Carr was neglected by both the public and the art establishment. Though highly regarded by other painters, including members of Canada's influential Group of Seven, many regarded her solely as an eccentric Victoria boardinghouse keeper with a penchant for pet dogs and monkeys. Her treks in a dilapidated caravan took her into the province's remote corners in search of subject matter for her sensuously beautiful and spiritual paintings. This dowdy, down-to-earth, observant woman carted her paint box and canvases to isolated First Nations settlements. Her forays took her deep into the ancient forests to capture the essence of coastal British Columbia.

EMILY CARR, *A SKIDEGATE POLE*, AT THE VAG

When success finally did arrive, the modest artist was unprepared for it. Several major galleries began to acquire her work. When in 1937 the Vancouver Art Gallery purchased its first Carr painting, *Totem Poles, Kitseulka*, she wrote in her diary that "this sudden desire to obtain 'Emily Carrs'" made her afraid that the attention might "knock me into conceit." The Vancouver Art Gallery's Carr holdings, including 150 paintings and 100 works in other media, constitute the most important single

Carr collection. About fifty works, the core of the collection, were donated by the artist herself shortly before her death in 1945. Among them are some of her most famous works, including *Big Raven, Tree Trunk* and *Scorned as Timber, Beloved of the Sky.*

Tours and gallery talks add to the enjoyment of the Carr and other permanent exhibits at the Vancouver Art Gallery, and accompany many of the touring exhibitions. As well, demonstrations, lunch-hour concerts, hands-on interpretive centres, art-making studios and a wealth of other innovative programs make learning about art fun for everyone in the family. Finish your visit by browsing for quality posters, books and artist-made gifts in the Gallery Shop before making a relaxed stop at the licensed Gallery Café and patio.

EMILY CARR, *ZUNOQUA OF THE CAT VILLAGE,* AT THE VAG

VANCOUVER MUSEUM, H.R. MACMILLAN PACIFIC SPACE CENTRE, H.R. MACMILLAN PLANETARIUM, VANCOUVER MARITIME MUSEUM

Four Vancouver gems are found on the south shore of English Bay in Kitsilano near the Burrard Bridge. The Vancouver Museum, H.R. MacMillan Pacific Space Centre, H.R. MacMillan Planetarium and Vancouver Maritime Museum are all located in Vanier Park. En route to the park, you'll pass through several blocks of the "Kits Point" neighbourhood, with its lovely houses, just minutes from the beach.

Some say the Vancouver Museum resembles a First Nations woven hat; others liken it to a space ship. Outside the museum, George Norris's stainless steel sculpture, *The*

VANCOUVER SPACE CENTRE

Crab, is a longtime favourite for picture taking.

The museum got its start in the mid-1880s, when a group of Vancouver's founding citizens held a show of paintings and curios, including purchased Northwest Coast artifacts, in a rented space on Granville Street. A stuffed trumpeter swan was the collection's first donation. By 1905, the museum settled into the top floor of the Carnegie Library at Main and Hastings streets, now a community centre for the downtown eastside. The collection moved to its present site in 1968, becoming the largest administered and interpreted permanent collection of any Canadian civic museum. What you see as you wander through the many exhibits equals only 2 percent of the museum's entire holdings. The rest is stored in a football field-sized storage vault.

The museum's special mission, according to its curators, is to tell the story of Vancouver, and collect and interpret the objects that embody those stories. It's also a place where visitors can learn about the wider world through high-quality visiting exhibits on places such as Egypt, China and Japan.

All museums are time machines, and this one is no exception. The curators bring the past to life with seven permanent walk-through exhibits relating to the history of Vancouver. The first is a recreation of a fur-trading post. Step over the piles of fur as you move on to the below-the-decks steerage bunks of an immigrant ship. The room is dark, the ceiling low, and you can hear the creaking of the wooden ship against the wind, a nice touch provided on tape. Move ahead through Vancouver's lumbering days when its huge, valuable Douglas firs made it the envy of the world. Gastown, a riotous enclave of rabble-rousing

VANCOUVER MUSEUM MASKS (TOP AND MIDDLE); FOLK ART PIECE *THE PORCH* (BOTTOM)

men, is next, complete with saloon keeper Gassy Jack's famed trunk. It's said that when he came ashore, the trunk was all he had, yet within a day his saloon was built and opened. Walk on until the last exhibit, an Edwardian household, complete with parlour, bedroom and a detailed kitchen and pantry. The furniture, curtains, bed coverings, even the kitchen scrub board were all donated in the spirit of the trumpeter swan. One look at the pre-electric kitchen and you bless your dishwasher.

Vancouver's history is also highlighted with special temporary exhibits, such as City Lights, the history of neon. The museum recently renovated its temporary exhibits' gallery and added an orientation gallery to help visitors better understand Vancouver.

You can access the H. R. MacMillan Pacific Space Centre from the same foyer as the Vancouver Museum. Launched in October 1997, twenty-nine years after the venerable H.R. MacMillan Planetarium opened, the space centre features many styles of programming. Here's the place where the wonders of space come down to earth with innovative programs like the Cosmic Courtyard hands-on gallery. Visitors can discover the ups and downs of travelling the solar system, including the chance to touch a real moon rock or play state-of-the-art computer games.

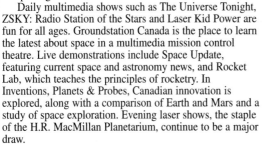

SPACE CENTRE'S COSMIC COURTYARD

Daily multimedia shows such as The Universe Tonight, ZSKY: Radio Station of the Stars and Laser Kid Power are fun for all ages. Groundstation Canada is the place to learn the latest about space in a multimedia mission control theatre. Live demonstrations include Space Update, featuring current space and astronomy news, and Rocket Lab, which teaches the principles of rocketry. In Inventions, Planets & Probes, Canadian innovation is explored, along with a comparison of Earth and Mars and a study of space exploration. Evening laser shows, the staple of the H.R. MacMillan Planetarium, continue to be a major draw.

Donated by one of the province's lumber barons in 1967 as a Canada centennial gift to the City of Vancouver, the planetarium is a city icon. These days, the famed multimedia shows are presented in the renovated Star Theatre. Its dome, Zeiss star projector and theatre interior have been fully upgraded and a large-format video, new

VANCOUVER PLANETARIUM

laser projection and other technological enhancements added. Sit back — well, lay back really — in the comfortable lounge chairs and view the night sky unfolding overhead.

VANCOUVER MARITIME MUSEUM

A short five-minute walk from the museum and planetarium, you'll find the Vancouver Maritime Museum at the foot of Cypress Street on the waterfront. Permanent exhibits as well as temporary feature exhibits bolster the Maritime Museum's most famous display, the RCMP schooner *St. Roch*, the first ship to cross the treacherous Northwest Passage in both directions, as well as the first ship to circumnavigate North America.

The Pacific Northwest's seagoing heritage dates back to the First Nations people who voyaged along the coast in sturdy seagoing canoes. European contact was made by Juan Perez of Spain in 1774. The Man the Oars and Map the Coast exhibit pays tribute to Captain George Vancouver, after whom the city is named, even though Vancouver was a latecomer who didn't arrive until 1792.

RCMP SCHOONER
St. Roch

Today's coastal waters are plied by tankers, fishing boats, pleasure craft and a host of other vessels. Fireboats,

another exhibit, goes back more than sixty years to honour these essential coastal work boats. Outside the museum, Heritage Harbour provides a closer look at heritage vessels of all types, including a small boat-building and repair workshop. Kids will also enjoy the Children's Maritime Discovery Centre with its full-scale replica tugboat wheelhouse and remote-controlled underwater robot, as well as the area known as Pirates!, complete with a treasure chest, pirate weapons and costumes and *Shark* the pirate ship.

Canada Place/CN IMAX Theatre at Canada Place

Built for Expo 86, Canada's 1986 world exposition, Canada Place was designed to give the stylish Sydney, Australia, Opera House a run for the money. With its five white, Teflon-coated "sails" echoing a nautical theme, the Canada Place complex may not entirely live up to its designer's goal, but it does stand out against the high-rise hotels of Vancouver's waterfront. Today Canada Place is a popular tourist destination, home to a cruise ship terminal, the CN IMAX Theatre, Vancouver Trade and Convention Centre and the World Trade Centre. The domed Pan Pacific Hotel is one of several major hotels in the area.

The complex resembles an immense ocean-going vessel, stretching three city blocks into Burrard Inlet. From the open-air promenade around Canada Place, you have one of the best views of busy Port Vancouver. Pleasure craft, working vessels, SeaBuses and seaplanes landing and taking off, make the promenade a great place to sit and have lunch.

Luxury cruise ships, en route to Alaska, dock at Canada Place, as well as the nearby Ballantyne Pier. More than 220 cruise ship stopovers are recorded every year in Vancouver. Between May and October, close to 1 million passengers depart Vancouver to enjoy the famed Vancouver-Alaska cruise, the third most popular cruise destination in the world.

Whether trekking at the top of Everest or walking in the CANADA PLACE

CAPILANO SUSPENSION BRIDGE

footsteps of dinosaurs, CN IMAX Theatre film presentations are designed to dazzle viewers with sound and images. IMAX technology is the largest film format in motion picture history, ten times that of conventional 35-mm film. The 440-seat, steeply pitched amphitheatre features a towering five-storey screen and six-channel IMAX Digital wraparound sound. Some shows even require the donning of IMAX 3D glasses for more intense "you are there" sensations. Open daily, for afternoon and evening features, shows at CN IMAX Theatre are approximately 40 minutes long.

CAPILANO SUSPENSION BRIDGE

What an adventure it must have been in the late nineteenth century when George Mackay's buddies, calling themselves the Capilano tramps, would trudge to the pioneering Scotsman's secluded cabin on the north shore of Burrard Inlet. Seventy metres (230 feet) above the Capilano River canyon, George had suspended a rickety rope-and-cedar bridge for what certainly must have been a petrifying crossing. Today, the Capilano Suspension Bridge is recognized by Attractions Canada as British Columbia's best outdoor attraction. Built of sturdy steel cables, the 140-metre-wide (450-foot) bridge is certainly safer and more accessible, but the lush forest property is no less breathtaking than it was in Mackay's time.

The bridge's swaying span attracts 800,000 visitors each year. It's the world's longest and highest suspension footbridge. Since 1899 when the original bridge was built, the attraction has been improved and enhanced by each of its six successive owners. The Story Centre traces the history of the bridge and the development of the city around it. An English country garden planted with rhododendrons and azaleas, the Living Forest interactive ecology display, a tranquil Nature Park and a gift shop all add to guests' enjoyment. An especially popular attraction is the Totem Park, a display of locally carved poles collected since the 1930s. In the nearby Big House, visitors can watch First Nations carvers at work and ask them about their techniques. Tours, displays and special activities are designed to give guests a glimpse into the historic and botanical roots of the area. As well, the full-service Bridge House restaurant and two casual eateries serve hungry visitors with fresh West Coast-style cuisine. The décor is turn-of-the-century (the nineteeth century, that is). The park is a twenty-minute drive from downtown Vancouver.

GROUSE MOUNTAIN

It takes a maximum of eight minutes for the Grouse Mountain Skyride to climb 1.6 km to 1,128 metres above sea level. That's the only disappointing part of the Grouse Mountain experience because on a clear day, the panoramic view of Vancouver, the Strait of Georgia and far-off Vancouver Island is unsurpassed. You simply want the ascent to last longer.

Grouse Mountain, part of the Coast Mountain range, was named after the blue grouse. Located at the top of North Vancouver's Capilano Road, the mountain was one of the first ski areas developed near Vancouver. Noted for being the smallest and closest of the local mountains, the first skier on Grouse is reputed to be a Swede, Rudolph Verne, in 1911. Today, hardy types still prefer to make their way to the top the old-fashioned way with a strenuous hike known as the Grouse Grind. The Grind is a badge of honour for many, including an eighty-five-year-old man who is said to make the climb twice a day.

The majority of visitors prefer the more sedate Skyride. Once at the top, try downhill skiing, snowboarding, snowshoeing, sleigh rides and a mountaintop ice-skating pond. Ski lessons and equipment rentals are available. For summer visitors, try hiking on your own or with a guide in the alpine meadows. Helicopter and mountain bike tours, logger sport shows and tandem paragliding with a certified instructor are available. Peak Chair rides to the summit at 1,366 metres are another summer activity.

If you're not the outdoorsy type, you can spend your time at the top enjoying the free Theatre in the Sky show. The cosy theatre features the high-definition video presentation, *Born to Fly,* as part of your Skyride pass.

A newer attraction on the top of Grouse is the First Nations-developed hiwus feasthouse. Members of the local Squamish Nation and Sechelt Band ensure the authenticity of this dining experience, enhanced with live dances and songs performed in traditional regalia. To get to the hiwus longhouse, a First Nations guide leads visitors through the

**GROUSE MOUNTAIN
(TOP, MIDDLE AND
BOTTOM)**

SKY RIDE AT GROUSE MOUNTAIN

Alpine forest to the shores of Blue Grouse Lake.

To make the most of the view, try fine dining in The Observatory (advance reservations allow you to ride the Skyride free). Also open daily are the Bar 98 Bistro, a casual dining area with a large outdoor rooftop patio, and Lupin's Cafe for fresh, self-service food. Panoramic views, the specialty of the house, are provided by all.

DR. SUN YAT-SEN CLASSICAL CHINESE GARDEN

In Vancouver's Chinatown, families in search of the freshest vegetables mingle with visitors exploring medicinal herb shops. Traffic inches alongside throngs of pedestrians crowding the sidewalks. In the midst of all this kinetic energy, it would be easy to miss the tranquil Dr. Sun Yat-Sen Garden tucked away in a quiet corner a few steps off Main Street. But you won't want to miss this peaceful "Refreshment for the Heart."

Enter the garden near the intersection of Pender and Carrall streets, through a whitewashed wall behind the Chinese Cultural Centre. As soon as you pass through the doorway marked Yi Yuan, or Garden of Ease, you'll find yourself relaxing and slowing your step as you enter another time and place.

Classical Chinese gardens are an ancient art form, perfected over the course of twenty centuries. The most famous of these are in the city of Suzhou in China's Chiang-Su province. These contemplative "scholar's gardens" have influenced garden design worldwide. In 1986, the Dr. Sun Yat-Sen Garden became the first full-scale classical Chinese Garden constructed outside China,

DR. SUN YAT-SEN GARDEN

and the first of these gardens to be built in nearly 500 years. Once inside, you could be in Suzhou, it is so authentic. In less than half an acre, this microcosmic world is cleverly laid out to maximize its intricacy and complexity. Framed by round moon gates and lacy latticework, glimpses of exquisite vistas emerge, disappear and reappear to create infinite visual space.

Built in Ming Dynasty style, the garden reflects nature through the four elements of rock, water, plants and architecture. Everything within its walls conforms to the Taoist principle of yin and yang. Shadow is always matched by light, smooth surfaces by rough, so that all elements remain in perfect equilibrium. A gnarled pine grows side-by-side with a delicate gingko.

The overall design of the garden echoes features of the renowned examples that inspired it, right down to the painstaking adherence to tradition with which it was crafted. More than fifty skilled Chinese artisans came to Vancouver to build the garden using centuries-old techniques, ancient tools and authentic building materials. The Yun Wei Ting gazebo, for example, perches atop a miniature mountain built of a unique rock found only on the bottom of Lake Tai in Suzhou. China shipped some 450 tons of the rare limestone for use in the garden. But the garden is also an original, incorporating local plants and innovations. Not a relic of the past, it comes alive with year-round events, commemorating special occasions from Chinese New Year to the autumn Harvest Moon Festival. On summer nights, the Enchanted Evening series of concerts features Asian music. When your visit to the Dr. Sun Yat-Sen Classical Chinese Garden comes to an end, you're sure to step back into the twenty-first century with nerves calmed, eyes delighted and heart refreshed.

Admission to the Dr. Sun Yat-Sen Classical Chinese Garden includes tea and a tour. The garden offers special family and group rates and rental for private events. The gift shop features Vancouver's largest selection of English-language books about Chinese culture.

DR. SUN YAT-SEN GARDEN

STATUE OF DR. SUN YAT-SEN

DINING

KASEY WILSON

SUN SUI WAH SEAFOOD

Vancouver's culinary reputation is built on fresh food and fresh flavours. The variety of dining experiences continues to grow each year, with some of the country's finest chefs devoted to creating food that is innovative, and in many cases, unique to the West Coast.

If there is a quintessential West Coast food, it is salmon. It comes in five varieties, including sockeye, pink, coho, spring and chum, and can be cooked in an unlimited number of ways. The original inhabitants, First Nations people both on the Pacific as well as the inland rivers, barbecued and baked it. Local restaurants sometimes feature traditional delicacies such as alder-grilled salmon, with First Nations-style panfried oolichans, toasted seaweed and bannock (an unleavened bread).

CREEK RESTAURANT & BREWERY

With some 30 percent of its population of Asian origin, it's not surprising that Oriental cooking is found everywhere in the city. No matter where you go within Vancouver or neighbouring suburbs — Burnaby, New Westminster, the North Shore or Richmond — you'll find the diversity of Asia represented in the kitchens. With a light touch, the chefs offer up a tasty mix of textures and colour, flavour and flair.

These days, dining in Vancouver encompasses all nationalities, whatever your fancy: French, Italian, Lebanese, Hungarian, Swiss, Persian, Portuguese and Spanish. No matter what the style, cooking on the coast is buoyed with top-quality ingredients, brought in from the

"I'll do it my way" farms and ranchers of the hinterlands.
The perfect complement to fine dining in Vancouver is late-
harvest and ice wines grown in the Okanagan Valley.
Almost as good are the handcrafted ales, beers and stouts
from local micro-breweries. And don't forget the coffee.
It's not just a pick-me-up but a way of life in the multitude
of coffee bars that dot the city's streets.

CHINESE

Chinatown is naturally, rightfully, the first place to go in
search of Chinese food.

Getting a table at the Floata Seafood Restaurant on
Keefer shouldn't be hard, even at the notoriously busy dim
sum hour. At 1,000 seats, it is immense. The ease and skill
evident in the service and cooking, however, belie its size.
A second Floata Seafood serves Richmond. Not far along
this same Chinatown street is Hon's Wun Tun House, an
institution revered for fast, cheap servings of Cantonese-
style rice and noodle dishes and vegetarian dim sum.

Just outside Chinatown, the Pink Pearl on Hastings is
crowded with discriminating Chinese families, especially
between eleven p.m. and two p.m. on weekends, when dim
sum is a tradition. Eating is easy here for visitors. Servers
urge you to make a choice from the wares displayed on
their carts. Coming for dinner instead? You could catch a
glimpse — and get an earful — of a Chinese wedding
banquet, usually a boisterous affair.

The Chinese food experience doesn't end at
Chinatown's border. Across the Oak Street Bridge to
Richmond, another Chinatown of sorts, newer and slicker,
is housed in several Asian-style malls of Richmond. The
Aberdeen Centre hosts the Top
Gun Seafood Restaurant.
Cantonese-style lobster, crab
and fish figure prominently on
the menu. Next to the Yaohan
Centre, the Radisson President
Hotel harbours the President
Chinese Seafood Restaurant,
distinguished by its creative
dim sum menu and masterful
repertoire of Cantonese dishes.
You might want to try the Asian
street food at bargain prices in
the food courts.

Between the new Asian
centre of Richmond and the
pioneering region of
Vancouver's Chinatown are
literally hundreds more Chinese
restaurants. The popularity of
humble Hon's, for instance, has
translated into additional
venues in downtown
Vancouver, Richmond, New
Westminster and Coquitlam.
Hon's has also spawned a
thriving trade in frozen

HON'S WUN TUN HOUSE

SWEET AND SOUR SOUP AT SPINNAKERS BREW PUB

potstickers, buns and dim sum, as well as wun tun noodles and chili oil. Every visiting food writer dines at Sun Sui Wah, designed by noted B.C. architect Bing Thom; owner Simon Chan designed the Cantonese-style menu of dim sum specialties. The absolute best is the live Alaska King crab, in a world where almost everyone else's is frozen. The Won More Szechuan Restaurant serves reasonably priced hot and sour soup, potstickers and other dishes, mainly spicy, in a crowded, upstairs space in West End Vancouver and bigger, slightly more expensive digs in Kitsilano. At the Shanghai Chinese Bistro, a skein of noodles makes its first appearance as a rope of dough, undergoes a fascinating ritual of twisting and stretching, and ends up as your plate of Tan Tan noodles with peanut sauce. Szechuan cuisine reappears in a slightly costlier incarnation at the Szechuan Chongqing Seafood Restaurant with locations in both Vancouver and Burnaby. Both restaurants showcase cooking from the Chongqing region and specialize in seafood.

The Dynasty brings Chinese fine dining to the downtown business district. Its serene atmosphere frequently breaks down in the face of giggles from its younger patrons. It's equally likely to be shattered by the adults, whose unsuppressed admiration for a perfect, glistening rock cod, whole and steamed with ginger and scallions, is often hearty and spontaneous. Look to the elegant Kirin Mandarin, also downtown, for specialties such as Shanghai smoked eel, Beijing duck and Szechuan hot and spicy scallops.

TOJO'S SUSHI BAR

JAPANESE

The popularity of teriyaki, teppan and especially sushi has taken Japanese food far from the small stretch of Powell Street named Japantown. At Tojo's, in central Fairview, the privileged and prudent few who reserved a place at the ten-seat sushi bar are treated to a show of Hidekazu Tojo's consummate skill with sushi. Tojo's edible masterpieces are the main draw for the knowing Japanese businessmen, filmmakers and celebrities that crowd the joint, but a wide range of non-sushi dishes round out the somewhat pricey menu.

The West End's Musashi Japanese Restaurant offers more sensibly priced sushi and sashimi. Its menu includes the usual soups, salads, tempura, teriyaki chicken and beef, rice and noodles, many assembled nicely into combination dinners. The same can be said of Taka Sushi, in Kitsilano, which also offers good quality at reasonable prices.

Gyoza King has a much narrower focus. While noodle dishes and inexpensive specials do appear on the menu, there's no sushi to be seen in this West End eatery. The place is crammed with young Japanese locals and tourists alike, who consume one plateful of plump meat, seafood or vegetable gyozas after another. And for ramen in all its forms — regular (pork), miso and soy — try Ezogiku Noodle Cafe, a short walk away, where little else, only a fried rice dish, a fried noodle dish, a curry and gyozas, are offered. A second Ezogiku is perfectly situated near the Vancouver Public Library.

SOUTH ASIAN

South Asian cooking has spread into diverse areas of Vancouver. Vij's Restaurant showcases artistic, B.C.-influenced Indian curries and other specials. Centrally located Sami's puts a similar twist on Indian cookery and offers modestly priced seafood poached in coconut nectar, and beef short ribs braised in cumin and ginger, among other dishes. Both places are modern, high-profile eateries. In contrast, the more mature Rubina Tandoori rests on a traffic-heavy street on Vancouver's East Side. The dowdy façade hides a contemporary heart and the deft hand of Krishna Jamal, matriarch and chef.

THAI AND OTHER ASIAN

Thai restaurants represent one more sector of the city's multi-faceted Asian community. Montri's Thai in Kitsilano is hot, in every sense of the word (but you can ask for milder). Often cited as the city's best Thai, Montri's presents authentically spiced dishes that make the scaled heat ratings — from one chili (mild) to five chilies (hottest) — required reading. Or try the Chili Club where the food is no less authentic, with scarce supplies flown in from Thailand. The modern room, almost under the Burrard Bridge, looks out onto False Creek and Granville Island.

The two Phnom Penhs are family-run places focusing

BORGO ANTICO

on Vietnamese and Cambodian food with some Chinese dishes. Suffer the plain, practical surroundings for the hot and sour soup, tender flash-fried squid tubes and the fresh-oyster omelet.

FRENCH AND ITALIAN/MEDITERRANEAN

For French dining, look to Le Crocodile. Located downtown, it offers roomy, luxurious surroundings with a patio, French wines and Alsace regional dishes that are well worth the expense. Owner/chef Michel Jacob's Alsatian onion tart has been hailed as the best in Vancouver. For a bistro experience, try Café de Paris in the West End. The warm dark woods, wine racks and lace curtains instantly bring to mind the Paris bistro. The menu includes moderately priced classics: duck confit, steak tartare and cassoulet; all are served with the pommes frites that have become legend in the city. A table d'hôte, as well as original contemporary French creations by chef André Bernier, are also available. Pastis also produces solid bistro fare. Look for an outstanding cheese plate and, in cooler weather, satisfying braises, cassoulets and roasts. The Smoking Dog Bar and Grill will sate a hunger for uncomplicated food — coq au vin, steak au poivre, duck à l'orange, salade niçoise. On a sunny afternoon, watch the Kitsilano crowd from the patio.

Italian, French and Spanish flavours meld at Cioppino's Mediterranean Grill, where chef and owner Guiseppe (Pino) Posteraro infuses his philosophy of "Cucina Naturale" into light, fresh dishes. In the same Yaletown area, Villa Del Lupo delivers a generous and contemporary menu of excellent pastas and favourites such as lamb shank osso buco.

Gastown's cobbled streets embrace a Tuscan villa, in the form of Borgo Antico. Enter via an iron-grated doorway into a spacious interior of stone walls, pillars and terra-cotta floors. Ask to sit among the more than 300 wines in the wine room. You can enjoy an equally impressive Tuscan menu from any seat in the house.

INSIDE BORGO ANTICO RESTAURANTE

Downtown, another bit of Italy resides in Il Giardino di Umberto, a seaside villa recreated on Hornby. The Tuscan menu emphasizes pasta and game. Traditional northern Italian cooking rules at the West End's Piccolo Mondo, where the soups are outstanding. And at Quattro on Fourth, the rooms are mosaic-tiled and mahogany, with a

Mediterranean feel. Quattro prepares some unusual Italian pastas; the combination plate provides a good overview.

PACIFIC NORTHWEST

The Pacific Northwest's original First Nations cuisine cannot be ignored. The Liliget Feast House occupies a stunning longhouse near the beach in the West End. There are wood walkways, pebbled floors, cedar plank tables and walls hung with contemporary native art. A feast or potlatch platter ensures a wide sampling; it includes bannock, baked sweet potato with hazelnuts, alder-grilled salmon, toasted seaweed with rice, steamed fern shoots and barbecued venison.

IL GIARDINO DI UMBERTO

Plentiful, readily available seafood is a characteristic of Pacific Northwest cuisine. At Rodney's Oyster House in Yaletown, oysters are the main attraction: a dozen or so varieties lie on ice, in long stainless steel beds, while customers line the oyster bar. Other fresh seafoods, chowders and slapjacks are also popular. Search out the Cannery, isolated among the Burrard Inlet wharves. The interior is lined with seafaring memorabilia, and fittingly, the Cannery always makes good on the seafood promises offered by the "daily fresh" sheet. The Beach House at Dundarave Pier, on the other side of the Burrard Inlet, is also especially strong on seafood and offers a good view of the West Vancouver waterfront.

The Beach Side Cafe in West Vancouver has deck dining to capitalize on views of Stanley Park and Kitsilano across the water. A strong wine list and simple, subtle food preparation characterize the restaurant. At the Raincity Grill, near English Bay, the menu changes according to whatever ingredients are fresh locally. Wine is available by the glass from an extensive, award-winning wine list. The West Coast theme is upheld by a trio of hotel restaurants as well. At 900 West, Dino Renaerts presents the best of B.C.'s bounty with preparations that emphasize simplicity and purity. Many of the wines on their much-lauded list can be had by the glass. The Five Sails at Canada Place presents a menu that also focuses on imaginative presentations such as pan-seared orange-crested sea bass with crispy basil garnish and citrus sauce. To top it off, diners enjoy a spectacular harbour view. Diva at the Met was recently named best regional restaurant by *Vancouver Magazine's* Critics' Poll. It optimizes an airy, natural space with multi-tiered seating, and out of its Waldorf-style open kitchen come both stylish, contemporary items — miso-glazed

STILTON CHEESECAKE AT DIVA

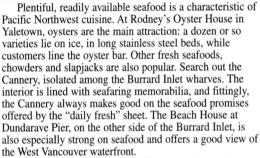

FISH HOUSE AT STANLEY PARK

halibut cheeks, for example — and traditional Japanese, Chinese and English breakfasts.

The Fish House at Stanley Park has an enviable location, surrounded by trees, tennis courts, a golf course and lawn bowling greens in one of the world's best urban parks. Even the aromatic cedar can't compete with the aroma and taste of Karen Barnaby's cooking. Flaming prawns are one of the Fish House's most popular dishes, and her Ahi Tuna Steak Diane with mashed potatoes has become a classic.

Bishop's location streetside in Kitsilano, away from the harbour and the beach, lets you fully appreciate master host John Bishop's superlative standards of service and cuisine. Should your attention stray to the modern Canadian works gracing the walls, the crème brûlée (which may be cappuccino, roasted pear, or sun-dried cherry) will easily recapture your interest. The Pear Tree in Burnaby lures Vancouver visitors and residents out to the suburbs with the promise of Scott Jaeger's reasonably priced and inventive menu, which might, for example, offer a braised lamb shank with seared scallops and roasted pear risotto.

In the midst of all the West Coast innovation, a bit of tradition stands firm. Patrons at the Teahouse Restaurant at Ferguson Point in Stanley Park won't allow traditional favourites such as the Teahouse's stuffed mushroom caps off the West Coast Continental menu. Seasons in the Park in Queen Elizabeth Park also has a conservative menu, Continental in style, focusing mostly on fish and poultry. The restaurant overlooks the quarry garden, the mountains and the Vancouver skyscape.

UPSCALE AND HOTEL DINING

At Lumière. talented chef Rob Feenie has found the perfect balance between classic French preparation and contemporary presentation. Feenie introduced tasting menus to the city; his vegetarian tasting menu is superb. C, located on the downtown perimeter, has extravagant caviars, a private wine cellar, a patio and a million-dollar marina view. C's chef creates distinct dishes that taste as intriguing as they sound: the Lapsang Souchou – cured gravlax from the taster box, and any of the items from their West Coast dim sum menu are good examples.

Some of the city's best restaurants are ensconced within downtown hotels including the Five Sails, 900 West and Diva

LILIGET FEAST HOUSE

at the Met (see Pacific Northwest). Fleuri may be tucked away at Sutton Place, yet is widely known for its Chocoholic Bar, afternoon teas, Sunday brunch, seafood buffet and ever-changing, always excellent, menu. Chartwell inside the Four Seasons Hotel is a classic choice for Vancouverites and their visitors. The dining room's rich wood panelling and fireplace are as conducive to successful dealing as they are to soothing dining, and chef Douglas Anderson's superb menu is one of the best in town. The Bacchus Restaurant in the small, exclusive Wedgewood Hotel is a beautifully and discreetly lit room that unfailingly delivers fine food.

SPECIALTY

The Hart House in Burnaby is remembered as much for its Tudor-style, heritage-home setting as it is for its service and food. The cooking ranges from daring dishes, like roasted Arctic wild caribou, to more traditional English roast prime rib. The desserts have a traditional streak as well: steamed bread pudding topped with chocolate cherry caramel custard, blueberry crisp, rum-raisin butter tart.

Vegetarians and non-vegetarians seek out Habibi's for bargain-priced dishes of perfectly prepared traditional Lebanese home cooking, including falafels and vegetarian dishes. Hon's (see Asian) has a dedicated vegetarian cooking facility at its downtown Robson location and can fashion vegetarian versions of dim sum and almost any dish you can think of, even vegetarian goose (actually bean curd skin rolls filled with dried Chinese mushrooms). Planet Veg, close to Kitsilano Beach and Vanier Park, cooks up East Indian, Mexican and Mediterranean vegetarian fast foods. Takeout is available if a lineup forms, which happens fairly frequently.

Tapas are served at Bin 941 downtown, a warm, close room, where the tasting bowls are generously filled, and don't cost much. A similar concept operates

TEXAS FLANK STEAK AT BIN 941

**THE CREEK
RESTAURANT &
BREWERY**

at Bin 942. The room is larger, but has much the same atmosphere and offers repeats of many of the menu items.

For many families, Earl's, which has several Vancouver locations, is the restaurant of choice. The service is fast; the food is fresh and healthy. It's also licensed, and many of the locations have patios. For even faster service, look for White Spot Triple O's for fries, milkshakes and Vancouver's favourite burgers with the legendary Triple O sauce. Diane Clement's Tomato Fresh Food Cafe distinguishes itself from other diners with healthy, colourful comfort food such as BLTs, turkey sandwiches, tomato and pesto sandwiches and vegetarian chile. Around the corner, Tomato to Go makes the same food available for takeout. The very hip Subeez with its thirty-speaker sound system fits in well with its Yaletown neighbours. Don't miss the killer fries with garlic mayo, sun-dried tomato turkey burger or any of the vegetarian dishes.

As the name promises, The Creek Restaurant and Brewery and Bar on Granville Island fuses a casual restaurant with a micro-brewery and bar/lounge. The large open kitchen is versatile, alternating between pub grub and gourmet fare. The lounge offers a full bar of spirits and a range of lagers and ales from their highly regarded on-site brewery. However, some say the best beer in town flows from the custom-designed taps at Steamworks, an extraordinary Yaletown brew pub with a wide-ranging brunch, lunch and dinner menu.

Visit Notte's Bon Ton Pastry and Confectionary, a downtown institution since the 1930s for tea and traditional French pastries after shopping. The Diplomat Cake is a tempting concoction made up of three layers of puff pastry, sponge cake, butter cream and rum. For really good bread, stop in at Terra Breads at the Granville Island Public Market to try something from the seemingly endless fresh-

**NOTTE'S BON TON
PASTRY &
CONFECTIONARY**

baked selection: foccaccia, olive breads, grape and walnut bread, currant and millet loaves. Ecco Il Pane's two locations (in Kitsilano and near the Cambie Bridge) also hold a wondrous selection, with specialty breads like dark chocolate and sour cherry and pannetone.

SHOPPING

PATRICIA FRASER

Stand at the corner of Granville and Georgia streets and you'll find yourself at the centre of Vancouver life. Look up, and see the sky-scraping towers of commerce. Below the streets, SkyTrain light rail transit whisks travellers to the suburbs. Georgia Street travels west to Stanley Park and the ocean. Look north along Granville and see the North Shore mountains — this is the heart of this cosmopolitan city. It's also the starting point for some serious shopping. No matter which direction you take, you'll find major malls (Pacific Centre) or mini-malls (Sinclair Centre), shopping promenades (Robson Street) or boutiques specializing in antiques or locally designed fashion (Gastown).

GEORGIA AND GRANVILLE

On the northeast corner of Georgia and Granville streets is the Hudson's Bay Company, known as "the Bay," established in 1824 as a network of fur-trading posts. With the recent demise of Eaton's, it's now Canada's sole national department store, and a handy stop for everything from scarves to soup plates. The other corners once housed Eaton's and Duthie Books, city institutions now departed, although Duthie's still has a store on 4th Avenue.

Head downstairs through the Bay to the underground Pacific Centre Mall. Running north from Georgia Street,

DESIGNER SHOPS ON ROBSON

CANADIAN CRAFT MUSEUM

49

this large and comfortable mall holds chains such as the very posh Canadian store, Holt Renfrew, as well as The Gap, Baby Gap, Club Monaco, Banana Republic, The Museum Store, Fairweather, Eddie Bauer and Jacob. It also provides easy access to the SkyTrain beneath the Bay.

Back above ground, walk west along Georgia and you'll pass the Vancouver Art Gallery, with a gallery shop well stocked with quality arts and crafts, books and games. Kitty corner from the art gallery is the Canadian Craft Museum, a trustworthy source for local artists' jewellery, scarves, glass and pottery. Keep going west until you come to Burrard Street. You could go underground again to the Royal Centre and Bentall Centre malls, or turn south for a block and head up to Robson Street.

DESIGNER SHOPS ON ROBSON (TOP); HILL'S INDIAN CRAFTS IN GASTOWN (MIDDLE)

ROBSON STREET

WATER STREET

Once a quiet ethnic street known as Robsonstrasse for its European-style delis and coffee shops, Robson is now blocks of youth-oriented chains such as The Gap, Banana Republic and Mexx, interspersed with a special blend of coffee shops. Visitors love to take home bags of Roots casual togs. (Their street-chic caps are great!) Walk west along Robson to Denman Street and you're in the depths of the West End. The shopping area is more residential with flower stores and framers, fish-and-chip shops and beachwear (being minutes from English Bay).

GASTOWN

Built after the Great Fire of 1886, this former warehouse area is chock-a-block with tourist shops and restaurants in refurbished heritage buildings along the waterfront. The former Canadian Pacific Railway station is now the terminus for SkyTrain and connecting station for the SeaBus to the North Shore. Take the

SeaBus for a fifteen-minute waterborne jaunt across Vancouver harbour for a visit to Lonsdale Quay Market on the North Shore. You can buy lunch and hand-crafted souvenirs at the same time at the quay, which is located right at the SeaBus dock.

GRANVILLE ISLAND

Granville Island on the south side of False Creek is a former industrial peninsula reclaimed by the city and reborn as a shopping and arts centre. The Kids Only Market, housed in original warehouses, is home to over twenty different shops for children. The huge Granville Island Market is a collection of vendors of gourmet food items, fresh produce and hand-crafted jewellery and gifts. In the Net Loft, another large building packed to the gunwales with boutiques, find Edie's Hats (a Vancouver fashion landmark), Nancy Lord's handwoven clothes and accessories, El Greco Jewellery and a multiplicity of artists' studio shops, galleries and gift stores.

KIDS ONLY MARKET ON GRANVILLE ISLAND

ANTIQUES AND COLLECTIBLES

Vancouver loves antiques. Shops and galleries are concentrated in three areas: West Tenth Avenue by the University of British Columbia (Canada West Antiques Co., Folkart Interiors, Forest Hills); South Granville Street between 7th and 14th avenues (William Robert, Hampshire Antiques, Carmen Boré, Farmhouse Collections); and Main Street between 12th and 29th (Second Time Around, Deeler's, Ages Ago, Blue Heron, Baker's Dozen).

BOOKSTORES

If you've seen the movie *You've Got Mail*, you know all about the battle of the bookstores, between the mega stores and the little corner shops. The big guys are represented by the three Chapters (downtown, South Granville and Metrotown), each with its own Starbucks coffee shop, children's story times and comprehensive database of books in print. The little guys include the Granville Book Company downtown, Duthie Books on 4th Avenue, the new age Banyen Books on West Broadway and gay lit Little Sister's Bookstore in the West End. Children's books are found at Kidsbooks on West Broadway and in North Vancouver, with a helpful and knowledgeable staff.

CANADIAN CLOTHING DESIGNERS

Western style starts here: First Nations fashion maven Dorothy Grant in the Sinclair Centre uses her Haida

KIDSBOOKS ON WEST BROADWAY

background as inspiration for clothing based on "button blanket" design. Zonda Nellis on South Granville has developed a worldwide following for her subtly coloured, elegant hand-loomed designer wear. Canadian RozeMerie Cuevas has created the cooly classical Jacqueline Conoir Line for Esmode Boutique on South Granville. Nancy Lord produces handwoven fashions and accessories from her loom on Granville Island, while in swank Kerrisdale, Margareta Design offers clothing that is conservative and classic. A-Wear is the house label for a team of local designers at Leone in Sinclair Centre. For hard-wearing, attractive sportswear, visit Tilley Endurables Adventure Clothing on South Granville.

CHILDREN'S STORES

Clothing for the well-dressed tot can be found at Bobbit's for Kids! on West 4th, Bratz on South Granville, Isola Bella in Kerrisdale and Please Mum on West Broadway. As for toys and games, sure we have Toys R Us (on West Broadway and in every single suburb in North America) but for more individual attention, you can check out Kaboodles on West 10th and The Toybox on West Broadway. As well, the Kids Only Market on Granville Island is a collection of more than twenty shops, including one devoted to kites.

THE TOYBOX ON WEST BROADWAY

CHINA AND CRYSTAL

Apart from the Bay, which has everything, you can find what your heart desires at Atkinson's at West Sixth and Granville. The whole store sparkles. Chintz and Company in Yaletown boasts "entertaining tablewares." W. H. Puddifoot & Co. is a favourite in Kerrisdale.

DESIGNER BOUTIQUES

Not only will you find favourite labels, but petites will be pleasantly surprised at the selection. Nearly one-third of Vancouver's population is of Asian heritage and sizes are appropriately geared to the market. Most shops are temptingly close to major downtown hotels. You'll find international design labels at Chanel on Burrard; Leone, Escada Plaza Escada and Gianni Versace Boutique at Sinclair Centre; Enda B, Edward Chapman's Ladies Shop, Bacci's and Boboli on South Granville; Boutique

Zolé, Romeo Gigli and Instante on Hornby; and E.A. Lee for Men and Women on Howe.

FIRST NATIONS ARTS AND JEWELLERY

Vancouver offers a fine selection of artistic, authentic First Nations art and jewellery. In Gastown, Hill's Native Art on Water Street (formerly Hill's Indian Crafts) stocks carved jewellery and chunky, indestructible wool Cowichan sweaters. The Inuit Gallery, also on Water, is a respected gallery for collectors of quality Inuit and First Nations carvings and prints. Marion Scott Gallery on Howe has Inuit sculptures. Leona Lattimer on West 2nd Avenue near Granville Island offers masks, jewellery, prints and drums. The Eagle Spirit Gallery on Maritime Mews on Granville Island also carries Haida-carved argillite. The Museum of Anthropology at the University of British Columbia has a good selection of jewellery, books, prints and sculpture, including soapstone, a traditional local material.

FINE ART GALLERIES

South Granville between the bridge and 16th Avenue offers a good selection of art galleries, many featuring local artists, some world-renowned. In just a short stroll, you can find Uno Langmann Limited, Graham Sayell Gallery, Simon Patrich Galleries, Baux-Xi Gallery, Harrison Gallery, Heffel Gallery and Ramsay John Gallery, among others. Downtown, see Art Beattus on Nelson Street and Buschlen-Mowatt Fine Arts on West Georgia.

MEXX ON ROBSON
(TOP); DR. VIGARI
GALLERY (MIDDLE)

GIFT SHOPS

You will find well-designed objects from pottery to jewellery at the Vancouver Craft Museum Gift Shop on Georgia, Circle Craft on Granville Island and the Vancouver Art Gallery, on Robson between Hornby and Howe. For bookworms, there is the Vancouver Public Library, on Robson at Hamilton. And for birthday/ wedding/ anniversary gifts for every budget and occasion, try Chachkas on Robson, Lightheart and Co. on Howe, Moulé on West Fourth and Park Royal Mall in West Vancouver and The Museum Company in Park Royal.

HILL'S INDIAN
CRAFTS IN GASTOWN

JEWELLERY

In Vancouver, as in every other major Canadian city, the Grand Dame of jewellery stores is Birks, now presiding at the corner of Hastings and Granville. Toni Cavelti, a major local designer noted for combining precious stones in

BIRKS AT HASTINGS AND GRANVILLE

MACK'S LEATHER ON GRANVILLE

startling presentations, is now distributed exclusively through Birks. Other long-respected jewellers are Georg Jensen and Tiffany in Holt Renfrew, both in the Pacific Centre. Other sparkling stars are Karl Stittgen for gold and precious metals in clean, modern lines and the internationally recognized Martha Sturdy for jewellery and home fashion accessories in unexpected fabrications and organic forms (both on South Granville).

LEATHER

Those who are, as they say, "into" leather will find a wonderful selection of readymade and custom apparel at Mack's Leather's Inc. on Granville Street. But more prosaic choices may be made at Castle Milano in the Sinclair Centre, Danier in the Pacific Centre and on Robson, Neto on East 4th Avenue and Marquis of London on Beatty Street.

MALLS

Downtown, the shopping malls are underground and include Pacific Centre Mall (the largest), Royal Centre, Vancouver Centre and Bentall Centre. Elsewhere in Vancouver, you can shop indoors at Oakridge, City Square (across from Vancouver City Hall on Cambie Street) and Arbutus Village Square. Burnaby boasts Metrotown, with its own SkyTrain station and Lougheed Mall. West Vancouver has the enormous Park Royal (North Shore) straddling Marine Drive. Surrey Centre and Guildford Mall are located in nearby Surrey. And in Richmond, you'll find Aberdeen Centre, North America's first mall dedicated to the Chinese market, as well as Richmond Centre, Yaohan and Lansdowne, built on a long-departed race track.

MUSIC

Vancouver has some of the best CD prices in the world, and it's all due to A & B Sound's downtown and other locations. They keep the prices down, but they have plenty of competition.

Sam the Record Man is right beside them on Seymour Street, and HMV and the Virgin Megastore are nearby on Robson. For those hard-to-find eclectic recordings, try Black Swan on West Broadway, D & G Collectors on East Hastings, Highlife Records on Commercial and the Magic Flute and Zulu Records on West 4th Avenue.

MEN'S CLOTHING
Pour monsieur, Boboli on South Granville; Harry Rosen, Boys' Co and Holt Renfrew in the Pacific Centre; E. A. Lee on Howe; Mark James on West Broadway; S. Lampman in Kerrisdale; and Chevalier Creations on Seymour for custom-mades. For a sportier look, try Eddie Bauer in the Pacific Centre, Roots on Robson and Tilley Endurables Adventure Clothing on South Granville.

BOBOLI ON SOUTH GRANVILLE

SECONDHAND CLOTHING
Of course, there's always Value Village at several locations about town, but if you're interested in high-quality, high-end labels, smart shoppers flock to The Comeback in North Vancouver, Kisa's of Kerrisdale and Turnabout Collections on South Granville and West Broadway. For consignments for children's clothes, footwear and furniture, it's MacGillycuddy's for Little People in Kerrisdale.

SHOE STORES
Save your shoe leather for a walk along Robson Street, where you'll find Salvatore Ferragamo, Simard & Voyer Shoes and Stephane de Raucourt. Over at Robson and Granville, John Fluevog creates perfectly outré styles, strictly for those willing to put their funkiest foot forward (the store also carries a wide range of Doc Martens).

JOHN FLUEVOG SHOES

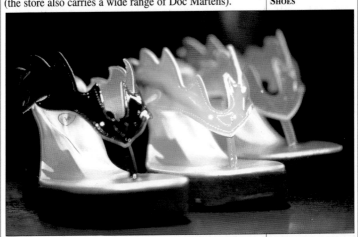

ENTERTAINMENT

SHAWN BORDOFF

Vancouver is well known for entertainment, offering everything from big-name performers to talented amateurs in small theatre venues. If you enjoy music ranging from folk to classical, live theatre or dance, you'll find events happening every night of the year. The after-hours scene is also lively, with clubs offering something for all ages and persuasions. Most performing arts shows sell tickets in advance. Ticketmaster has the monopoly in this area, with a telephone line dedicated to arts events.

LITTLE VOICE AT
VANCOUVER
PLAYHOUSE

LIVE THEATRE

The Vancouver Playhouse (part of the Queen Elizabeth Theatre complex) is one of the best regional theatres in Canada. Plays presented here employ the top actors, directors, designers and craftspeople from across Canada. The theatre has been home to the Vancouver Playhouse Theatre Company since 1962, a company that often premieres award-winning Canadian plays. A terrific example of this is *The Overcoat* conceived by Morris Panych and Wendy Gorling, a unique play without words that tells the moving story of a man whose life is transformed when he finds a colourful coat.

In the 1930s, the Stanley Theatre on Granville Street near Broadway was the place for vaudeville. It later became an excellent movie theatre but eventually closed in the heyday of multiplex madness. In 1997, the Arts Club Theatre completed lengthy and difficult renovations to transform the dilapidated but distinguished cinema into a first-class professional theatre. Today it's a delightful 650-seat venue with a charming interior, home to many of Vancouver's most

entertaining productions, including many smaller musicals. The plays are just as good at the Arts Club's 450-seat mainstage theatre on Granville Island. A string of hits, including homegrown and international plays, contribute to the Arts Club's longevity. Having run the Arts Club since it opened in 1972, artistic director Bill Millerd is the most respected, and probably most decorated, theatre practitioner in the country.

If you thought that Granville Island was just for shopping, you'll be surprised at how many live theatres coexist here. Across the walkway from the Arts Club's mainstage theatre is its Revue Theatre. This cabaret-style venue hosts the Vancouver Theatresports League, offering comic improvisation fine-tuned to a science. If you haven't seen a live improv show, catch one of the regular early-evening performances. Vancouver Theatresports is suitable for the entire family. The Waterfront Theatre is another Granville Island venue, noted for performances of new Canadian plays.

For some adult comedy improvisation on the edge, the Urban Well Restaurant and Lounge hosts hilarious shows every Monday night. And if merely watching an improv is not enough and you want to get involved in a show, consider some interactive theatre. Since 1995, people have been raving about Tony and Tina's Wedding, dinner theatre with a twist. You start off at a "church wedding" at St. Andrew Wesley's Church in the West End and end up flirting at the "dinner reception" a few blocks away. The audience member initially too embarrassed to respond to the actors usually ends up being the star of the show. For an alternate opportunity to get involved, drop by Doll & Penny's Cafe on a Friday evening. Crowds at this entertaining drag show often spill into the street.

OF MICE AND MEN AT VANCOUVER PLAYHOUSE

Constructed in a former fire hall, the Firehall Arts Centre on East Cordova is just two blocks from Vancouver's troubled Main and Hastings corner. Devoted to new plays, performance art and dance, the Firehall has a loyal audience. In addition to its professional theatres,

SWING AT STANLEY THEATRE

FIREHALL ARTS CENTRE

Vancouver has several good community theatres. Presentation House in North Vancouver is as good as most professional venues. Metro Theatre in South Vancouver's Marpole area has mastered the art of dry British comedy. At the Jewish Community Centre's Norman Rothstein Theatre, a state-of-the-art auditorium seats 318 people in luxury.

If you're looking for a New York-style Broadway production at Vancouver prices, the Queen Elizabeth Theatre is the place to go. Throughout the year, large musicals with elaborate sets and all the trimmings stop by to dazzle Vancouver audiences at the "QE." The City of Vancouver built the Queen Elizabeth Theatre in 1959 — by West Coast standards, that makes it a historical monument. Nevertheless, the building is perfect for Broadway shows. The stage is seventy-feet wide with a proscenium arch; the seats are plush and the décor is elegant.

MUSIC

Vancouver has a strong musical history. The Vancouver Symphony Orchestra (VSO) has existed since 1919, and now performs more than 130 concerts annually. Over the years, the VSO has welcomed many outstanding artists, among them Sir Yehudi Menuhin, Maureen Forrester, Isaac Stern, Dame Janet Baker, Yo-Yo Ma and even Bobby McFerrin. You'll usually find the symphony at the historic Orpheum Theatre built in 1927. The Orpheum, like the Stanley Theatre, opened as a vaudeville house. At the time, it was one of the largest and most impressive theatres on the West Coast. Later, it dwindled into a movie house. In 1977, after five years of extravagant renovations, the City of Vancouver reopened the Orpheum as home to the Vancouver Symphony Orchestra. It still impresses with its classic ambiance of old-time elegance.

MAESTRO TOVEY CONDUCTING THE VSO (MIDDLE); ORPHEUM THEATRE (BOTTOM)

Like the symphony, Vancouver Opera grew out of historic roots, with the first opera performances in the city in the late 1880s. The

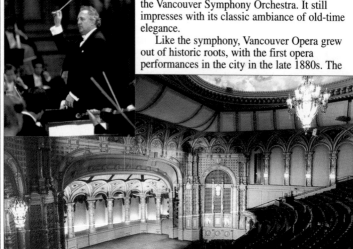

VANCOUVER OPERA'S
DIE FLEDERMAUS

Vancouver Opera company was launched in 1960, with a performance of Bizet's *Carmen*. Today Vancouver Opera is one of the largest performing arts organizations in B.C., with a strong commitment to the development of Canadian talent. While the opera hires principle singers of international fame, preference is given to Canadians. The company also employs its own orchestra and chorus made up of local musicians and singers. There is plenty for the traditional opera fan, from *Don Giovanni* to *Madama Butterfly*. All performances are at the Queen Elizabeth Theatre.

One of Vancouver's newest musical venues is the Chan Centre for the Performing Arts at the University of British Columbia. This 1,400-seat facility was designed to have optimum acoustics. The UBC Opera Society performs here a few times a year, as does the Vancouver Symphony Orchestra. If you want to hear something really special, look for the Vancouver Cantata Singers performing at the Chan Centre. This forty-voice award-winning choir is recognized as one of Canada's foremost ensembles.

One of the most enjoyable places for an informal concert is the Commodore Ballroom on Granville Street downtown. Once a fancy black-tie room, the Commodore gradually deteriorated into little more than a beer hall. For years, the main attraction remained its bouncy, horsehair-sprung floor. The floor eventually gave out from years of hard dancing. In the mid-1990s, the club closed, was renovated and reopened. Although the floor was repaired, there is still a bit of bounce left in for fun. Check in advance to see who's playing because the Commodore is very eclectic. Artists have included Anthrax, the Powder Blues, Kim Mitchell, and even Dal Richards and his Big Band Orchestra.

BEN HEPPNER IN
PETER GRIMES

The best place to see jazz is the Purple Onion in Gastown. Relax to some swing or more mellow sounds in its intimate lounge. There's also a large dance room that caters to a younger crowd on weekends. For rocking blues, the Yale (near the Granville Bridge on the downtown side) boogies on in one of the oldest buildings in Western Canada. When the Yale was built in 1889, it was a place for miners and loggers to get a drink. They still serve beer, but it's now one of the best blues bars in the world. Dress casually and enjoy.

DANCE

For modern dance, the Vancouver East Cultural Centre on Venables is B.C.'s most diverse performance space. "The

BALLET BC'S *IN THE COURSE OF SLEEPING*

Cultch" opened on October 15, 1973 with a two-week run of the locally based Anna Wyman Dance Theatre. Today the Cultch offers a marvellous array of unique dance performances and performing arts. Beware of the balcony though. It's terrific to look at but not a good place to sit. Sight lines are best from front row centre on the lower level. You may want to keep an eye out for Kokoro Dance, an innovative troupe that performs here and at various other venues throughout the city. Dance Arts Vancouver also presents several festivals, the most popular being the annual KISS Project. This mid-winter event began in 1994 and has developed a real following. The KISS Project can be seen at Performance Works on Granville Island.

For classical and modern dance, Ballet British Columbia has built an international reputation for artistic excellence. The company first performed on April 11, 1986 and was quickly recognized for its combination of talent and creativity. You can see the ballet at the Queen Elizabeth Theatre.

CLUBS

For star watchers, the bar of choice is the Gérard Lounge. Located on the first floor of the Sutton Place Hotel, Gérard's is one of Vancouver's trendiest lounges. It is also exquisitely furnished, luxurious, and the bar prices reflect the surroundings. It's not uncommon to spot some of Hollywood's most memorable faces here. Vancouver is known for its politeness, so please be discreet. If you're more intent on meeting someone available, attractive and of the opposite sex, Richard's on Richards is the place to go. The crowds at this big dance club tend to be in their late twenties and early thirties. On the weekend, the music leans towards hip-hop and house.

BABALU PARTY-GOERS

A few blocks from Richard's, you'll find one of the country's most sophisticated night clubs. BaBalu's is the place to be seen. The club features live swing and Latin musical acts.

In Vancouver, the downtown clubs with the least amount of attitude are the gay clubs. The Odyssey, geared toward alternative dance music, has always been a popular club with a loyal gay crowd. If you're looking to meet a gay man while you're in town, your best bet is Numbers. It's the gay equivalent to Richard's on Richards. Vancouver also has a cool lesbian bar called the Lotus. A newer club, The Lava Lounge offers conga music one night, a Latin dance party the next.

The biggest problem with Vancouver clubs are the lineups. Any place worth going to usually has a lineup after nine p.m. Smoking is also not permitted inside public buildings, so be prepared to smoke outside.

GALLERIES

ANN ROSENBERG

In 1961, the New Design Gallery, founded by Abraham Rogatnick and Alvin Balkind, was the most important commercial gallery in town. By the mid-1960s, the influential Bau-Xi was operating in its first premises across from the old Vancouver School of Art on Hamilton Street. The Douglas Gallery on Davie, owned by Douglas Christmas, became another outlet for the city's most adventurous artists. The Fine Arts Gallery at UBC, and the fine arts department's Festival of Contemporary Arts, were crucibles for vanguard artists and events. Downtown, the now-defunct Intermedia was the venue for performance art and multimedia experimentation.

These few art spaces fuelled the explosion of galleries over the last twenty years. Today there is harmony and interchange among the various components of the gallery scene, which is remarkable for its quality and variety.

SOUTH GRANVILLE

Known by art lovers as "The Row," the South Granville area around Granville and Broadway is Vancouver's most impressive enclave of galleries. There is something here for every taste ranging from the Art Emporium's early modern works to the avant-garde photographs of Ian Wallace at Catriona Jeffries Gallery.

Granville is a busy thoroughfare not renowned for its architecture but well placed in one of the more affluent neighbourhoods of Vancouver's West Side. Most of the venues promote established and emerging Canadians. Some also deal important figures in Canadian art history. The Bau-Xi Gallery, for example, retains works by printmaker Alistair Bell and the titan of Canadian art, Jack Shadbolt. The Equinox Gallery is the home of Gathie Falk, a

BUSCHLEN MOWATT GALLERY

DIANE FARRIS GALLERY

prominent Vancouver painter and ceramist, as well as the great senior landscape painter Gordon Smith. The Heffel Gallery specializes in the famed Group of Seven as well as B.C. Binning and E.J. Hughes.

John Ramsay and the Atelier Gallery feature attractive works on a smaller scale. The Simon Patrich Gallery is distinguished by its Latin American connections. The Monte Clark Gallery is committed to contemporary photography and upcoming art stars.

There are also several important galleries on 6th and 7th avenues near The Row. Chief of which is the Diane Farris Gallery whose stable includes younger artists like Atilla Richard Lukacs, Chris Woods and Janieta Eyre.

GRANVILLE ISLAND

Just a few minutes' walk away is Granville Island, where art is featured in dozens of open studios and shops.

Circle Craft Co-op, the largest outlet, sells works by BC artists. Here you will find everything from candle holders to one-of-a-kind knitted wares. At Crafthouse, art by some of the region's fine artisans is on display including pieces of extraordinary furniture. And across the street at the Gallery of B.C. Ceramics, clay refreshes one's notion about useable wares.

Two ateliers for fine art limited-edition prints are in close proximity: Malaspina Printmakers Gallery and Dundarave Print Workshop. Crowd-pleasing, hot glass-blowing displays are held most afternoons at the New Small and Sterling Studio Glass. Just off-island, the Andrighetti Glass Gallery has a similar showing space for its member artists.

BUSCHLEN MOWATT GALLERY (MIDDLE); CHARLES H. SCOTT GALLERY (BOTTOM)

Granville Island is the home of the famed Emily Carr Institute of Art & Design. Here you discover exhibitions of student works in the Concourse Gallery and an exciting program of exhibitions in the Charles H. Scott Gallery.

DOWNTOWN

Catch a bus to Granville and Georgia and you are in the heart of Vancouver's business district. Given the smell of money, it's not surprising that a number of galleries are located here. The Buschlen Mowatt Gallery on West Georgia sells leading-edge contemporary art and also works by international luminaries Helen Frankenthaler, Chaki and Chadwick. A cathedral-like structure houses the Canadian Craft Museum, providing an elegant showcase for craft artists. An entrance fee is charged. Art Beatus, specializes in international and Chinese artists. The Contemporary Art Gallery, like its non-commercial ally, the Morris and Helen Belkin Gallery at UBC, offers a rich program of exhibits of vanguard Canadian art and works from other countries.

ALTERNATIVE GALLERIES

Outside of Quebec, British Columbia has the largest number of galleries in the not-for-profit category. These venues feature installations and interactive work, including video and performance art. Since 1972, Western Front has played host to national and international artists in many genres. The nearby grunt Gallery also specializes in performance art, with special interest in gender issues and First Nations art. Artspeak in Gastown features phototext installations and interactive video. The Helen Pitt Gallery and the Or Gallery are two others in the downtown core that emphasize emerging artists and their thought-provoking creations.

FIRST NATIONS GALLERIES

Another impressive subplot in Vancouver's gallery scene is the number of outlets for works by First Nations artists. On Granville Island, the Eagle Spirit Gallery sells Northwest Coast masks, button blankets and bentwood boxes. On South Granville's "Row," the Douglas Reynolds Gallery offers art by Northwest Coast established and emerging artists as well as silver and gold carved jewellery. Nearby, the Leona Lattimer Gallery shows a similar range of work and specializes in limited-edition prints. Downtown, the Appleton Gallery features Haida, Kwakwaka'wakw and Coast Salish masks, paddles, talking sticks and wall plaques. Coastal People's Fine Arts offers a mélange of Northwest Coast, Inuit and Plains art. The Marion Scott Gallery is exclusively devoted to Inuit art, particularly that produced by artists with a traditional lifestyle. The Inuit and Spirit Wrestler galleries stage museum-quality exhibits of aboriginal work. Like the Marion Scott, these shows are finely curated and exquisitely presented. Nearby in Gastown, Images for a Canadian Heritage extends the purview to include wildlife art.

SPIRIT WRESTLER ART AND STOREFRONT

PARKS AND GARDENS

MARG MEIKLE

VANDUSEN GARDENS
(TOP AND BOTTOM)

It will come as no surprise to visitors that gardening is currently the number one outdoor leisure activity in Vancouver. It has always been in the top five — and it shows. The combination of a mild climate, plenty of precipitation and very diverse immigration to this area makes for a wide variety of gardening styles. From the abundant crops of the Chinese vegetable gardens around Chinatown to the amazing tomatoes and grapes of the Italian community around Commercial Drive, from the seemingly out of place palm trees on Beach Drive in the West End to the lush perennial borders in many neighbourhoods, there is much to enjoy around here. To say nothing of the fact that Vancouver is one of the few cities in the world blessed with two botanical gardens. VanDusen Botanical Garden and the UBC Botanical Garden are both superb living research libraries.

UBC BOTANICAL GARDEN AND UBC GARDENS

The University of British Columbia Botanical Garden sits on the ocean edge of the campus, overlooking the Strait of Georgia. Open to the public for wandering, breathing in that fresh sea air and the gorgeous scents, this seventy-acre theme garden is also used for teaching and research. The various gardens include: Alpine Garden, Asian Garden, Winter Garden, B.C. Native Garden, Physick Garden (herbs), Food Garden and Perennial Borders. The 25-hectare David C. Lam Asian Garden has a huge variety of woody Asian plants, maples, clematis plants, roses, rhododendrons, azaleas, magnolias and rare Oriental plants. In addition to the huge array of outdoor experiences

available, the Shop-in-the-Garden offers an enormous variety of gardening books and a particularly great nursery, including plants developed through the UBC plant introduction program and unusual plants propagated by members of the Friends of the Garden.

Of special interest at UBC is the classical Japanese Nitobe Memorial Garden designed with a very West Coast view, by Japanese landscape architect Kannosouke Mori. He used many native trees and shrubs, training and pruning them in the Japanese fashion. Within this two-and-a-half-acre garden are many more: the Tea Garden with a Tea House, the Nightingale Fence, the Tenth Bridge, several water crossings and a stroll garden.

VANDUSEN GARDENS IN FULL BLOOM (TOP AND MIDDLE)

VANDUSEN BOTANICAL GARDEN

This fifty-five-acre garden is on the edge of Shaughnessy, a well-heeled, older and established section of Vancouver. But remarkably, the lush VanDusen Garden was only built on the former Shaughnessy Golf Course in the early 1970s. At any time of the year you can find plants, trees and shrubs in bloom. This garden also contains many theme gardens, including the Asian Garden, Children's Garden, Fragrance Garden, Meditation Garden, Mediterranean Garden, Rose Garden, and a Sino-Himalayan Garden. There's also a maze, a rhododendron walk, a Canadian

MAZE AT VANDUSEN

Heritage garden and a fern dell. There are many popular special annual events including the Festival of Lights at Christmas, the VanDusen Plant sale in April, the VanDusen Flower and Garden Show in June and various other club shows and sales throughout the spring and summer. There is a lovely gift shop, a fledgling plant shop and a very civilized restaurant called Shaughnessy's.

QUEEN ELIZABETH PARK AND BLOEDEL CONSERVATORY

The park is called Little Mountain, which is the highest point in Vancouver and offers a terrific view of the city and the North Shore mountains. June is a particularly showy month for Queen E. Park as the locals call it because the roses are in full bloom. But any time is worth a wander through the Quarry Garden at the peak of the mountain. It was created in the 1960s and there are similarities to Butchart Gardens near Victoria, which was created sixty years earlier, also in a quarry.

INSIDE THE DOME AT
QE PARK (MIDDLE
AND BOTTOM)

There is public art of note throughout Queen Elizabeth Park. The Henry Moore sculpture, *Knife Edge-Two Piece*,

is close to the Bloedel Conservatory. The conservatory is a huge dome that holds a large variety of tropical, desert and exotic plants as well as over 100 tropical birds. It is a particularly great destination on a rainy day, for inside this very warm and dry dome there is a magnificent variety of trees that creates a jungle of palms, banana trees and orchids.

DR. SUN YAT-SEN CLASSICAL CHINESE GARDEN

DR. SUN YAT-SEN CLASSICAL CHINESE GARDEN

The Dr. Sun Yat-Sen Classical Chinese Garden is the first authentic full-scale Classical Chinese garden built outside China. In a harmonious and peaceful environment behind a wall in the middle of Chinatown, you will find tranquil ponds, natural rock sculptures, courtyards and an interesting variety of plants. The garden reflects the Taoist philosophy of yin and yang. Every stone, pine and magnolia flower in the garden has been placed purposefully and carries a symbolic meaning. The Garden offers guided tours, which provide interesting perspectives on Chinese culture, life during the Ming dynasty, architecture and plants. A popular program offered at the Garden is the Enchanted Evening series. Every Friday night from July through September, visitors sip a cup of complimentary tea, enjoy a one-hour Chinese music program and then stroll through the garden. This is an especially nice place to go on a rainy day, as the walkways are covered and the tips of the eave tiles are designed to let the drops fall from them in a particularly gentle way.

VANDUSEN ROSE (MIDDLE); GARDEN WALK (BOTTOM)

**RELAXING IN
VANDUSEN GARDENS**

STANLEY PARK'S GARDEN DELIGHTS

The 1,000-acre heavily wooded Stanley Park has many attractions, including a variety of gardens. Of special interest in June and July is the Rose Garden, which features hundreds of roses divided in beds by colour. Also noteworthy, particularly in April and May, is the Ted and Mary Grieg Rhododendron Garden containing camellias, magnolias, maples, rhododendrons and azaleas. The park boasts many trails throughout the forested area. (See Stanley Park map, page 6.)

CENTURY GARDENS AT DEER LAKE PARK

If you like rhododendrons, Burnaby's official flower, this is the place to see a lot of them. Located on the grounds of the Burnaby Art Gallery, this three-plus acre garden was created in 1967 for Canada's Centennial. The garden overlooks Deer Lake and also has a good collection of roses and azaleas.

PARK & TILFORD GARDENS

Created in 1968 by a privately owned distillery, these gardens have been preserved despite rezoning and changes in the area. The owners and merchants of the nearby Park & Tilford Shopping Centre now fund the gardens, which consist of separate theme gardens or outdoor rooms devoted to roses, herbs, rhododendrons and West Coast native plants as well as the White Garden (perennials), Asia Garden, Townhouse Garden, Yellow Garden, annual display gardens, hanging baskets, a Victorian greenhouse and a Florentine pergola covered in vines.

The gardens display plants suitable for the West Coast climate and are developed with organic methods and integrated pest management. Park & Tilford works with Capilano College's horticultural students and staff to create a unique hands-on experience.

Vancouver has more flowering trees for the area than any other city in Canada. Trees have been the life blood of our economy and define this place. Vancouverites are truly passionate about their trees. As well as the tree collections in the public gardens listed here, consider visiting the Riverview Lands Davidson Arboretum. This collection of about 1,800 trees on the 244 acres of the Riverview Hospital grounds contains more than 150 varieties. It was one of the first arboreta in Canada, created around 1905. In the Shaughnessy area is a round park in the middle of "The Crescent," one of the most prestigious addresses in town. This park has a collection of unusual trees, some of which are more than 100 years old. See if you can spot the Japanese Snowbell, Winged Euonymus, Pyramidal Blue Lawson Cypress or Eddie's White Wonder Dogwood, the latter developed right here in Vancouver. For a complete map, a listing, and much more on trees, see Gerald Straley's *Trees of Vancouver*.

SPORTS AND ACTIVITIES

BOB MACKIN

In which North American city can you start the day on the golf course, go in-line skating at midday, hit the ski slopes or marina before sunset, then unwind at a professional hockey or basketball game? If you answered Vancouver, you're right. The city is a four-season destination for those who enjoy the sporting life as an observer, participant or both.

DRAGON BOAT RACING

BASEBALL

Vancouver tried hard to get a Major League Baseball franchise in the 1980s, a main reason B.C. Place Stadium was built. At the end of the 1990s, the city lost its Triple-A team, the Canadians, when a new owner moved it to Sacramento, California. The C's broke a lot of hearts when they won the Pacific Coast League championship in their final home game and, a week later, won a North American championship.

A new minor league team, also named the Canadians, begins play in the summer of 2000 in the Single-A Northwest League. These C's will play at Nat Bailey Stadium, the same ballpark as their predecessors. The old-style stadium with few modern amenities was built in 1951 in the shadow of Little Mountain and was originally called Capilano Stadium. It was renamed in 1978 for the late founder of White Spot Restaurants and owner of the Vancouver Mounties, a team that played there in the 1950s and 1960s. The Single-A Canadians' season runs from June until Labour Day. Tickets will be priced under $10.

BC LIONS

BASKETBALL

The Canucks share GM Place with the Vancouver Grizzlies, the National Basketball Association's twenty-ninth and youngest franchise. They began play in 1995, the same year as the Toronto Raptors, but were granted entry after their Eastern rivals.

Vancouver fans quickly warmed to the team, patiently watching it struggle through expansion infancy. GM Place from October to April is no different from any other NBA arena, where fans are dazzled at intermission and time-outs by dancers, fireworks, loud music and Grizz, the Grizzlies' mascot. Tickets are $13 to $275.

FOOTBALL

The BC Lions are the only major sports tenant at the 60,000-seat BC Place Stadium. The Canadian Football League franchise, founded in 1954, moved in 1983 from the outdoor Empire Stadium in East Vancouver to the downtown dome. Since then, the Lions' fortunes have fluctuated. It's always a struggle to bring the crowds indoors in summer, partly because the air-supported dome wasn't built with air conditioning. Action always intensifies after Labour Day when the CFL's eight teams begin to jockey for playoff berths. (CFL games are played on larger fields than traditional American football with three downs, instead of four.) The most exciting moment in the Lions' history took place here in 1994. With no time left on the clock, veteran kicker Lui Passaglia kicked the winning field goal to win the Grey Cup. The season runs from June to November. Tickets range from $15 to $60.

HOCKEY

Vancouver has a rich hockey history. Its Millionaires played at the long-gone Denman Arena near Stanley Park and won the Stanley Cup in 1915. The National Hockey League's Vancouver Canucks haven't been so lucky. Founded in 1970, they lost in the Stanley Cup finals in both 1982 and 1994. In 1994, the playoffs went seven games until the New York Rangers came out on top. The team is rebuilding in the post-Pavel Bure era, but isn't yet ready to challenge for the cup a third time. The Canucks moved from their original rink, the Pacific Coliseum, in 1995 to the $160-million General Motors Place in downtown. It's next door to B.C. Place Stadium and nestled between the Georgia and Dunsmuir viaducts. The Stadium SkyTrain station is across the street and False Creek and Chinatown are both a short walk away. Ticket prices at GM Place range from $27 to $100.

Beginning in fall 2001, hockey returns to the Pacific Coliseum in the form of a new franchise in the Western Hockey League, a major junior circuit throughout Western Canada and the U.S. Pacific Northwest. The team, co-founded by hockey legend Gordie Howe, will offer a glimpse of future NHL stars at a modest price; tickets will cost around $12 each.

HORSERACING

Vancouver punters have the option of watching thoroughbreds or standardbreds race live, or watching satellite feeds of either from racetracks around Canada, the U.S., Australia and Hong Kong. Hastings Park Racecourse on the Pacific National Exhibition grounds has perhaps the most scenic view of any track anywhere, with Burrard Inlet and the North Shore mountains in the distance. Thoroughbred racing runs April through November with ample nearby paid parking and plenty of covered and indoor seating. Races from other tracks are simulcast year round.

Surrey's Fraser Downs is located on the Cloverdale Fairgrounds forty-five kilometres from Vancouver. It offers harness racing from October to April.

OTHER SPECTATOR SPORTS

Vancouver hosts two major professional golf tournaments every year. The Telus Open is an early June stop on the

HASTINGS PARK RACECOURSE

MOLSON INDY

coast-to-coast Canadian Tour. The country's best up-and-coming amateurs and veteran pros compete annually at the Mayfair Lakes Golf and Country Club in Richmond. This is a popular course on converted farmland beneath the flight path to Vancouver International Airport.

On Labour Day weekend, the PGA Tour stops at Northview Golf and Country Club in Surrey for the Air Canada Championship. The tournament has seen some wonderful performances, but is still trying hard to attract superstars like Tiger Woods.

On the same weekend, the streets at the east end of False Creek roar with the sound of ChampCar engines when the Championship Auto Racing Teams tour comes to town for the Molson Indy Vancouver. It's the biggest annual outdoor sporting event in Western Canada and was first run in 1990.

The False Creek waters near Science World host competing dragon boat teams in the latter half of June. The sport, similar to canoe racing, was imported from Hong Kong and remains a legacy of the 1986 world exposition, Expo 86. The Dragon Boat Festival is a weekend-long celebration of the city's ethnic diversity.

From May to September, the Vancouver Eighty-Sixers play soccer in the A League with teams from around North America. The venue is Swangard Stadium in Burnaby's picturesque Central Park. The team was the perennial powerhouse of the former Canadian Soccer League. The challenges are greater in the A-League circuit, which is graded just below Major League Soccer, the U.S. first division. Unlike Vancouver's other major sports teams, this one is stocked almost entirely with locals who rose through the ranks of amateur soccer. Tickets are $7 to $18.

DRAGON BOAT RACERS

RECREATIONAL SPORTS

There's no shortage of water in Vancouver for canoeing, kayaking or windsurfing. The waters of Deep Cove and Howe Sound are ideal for these activities, but nearby False Creek, Kitsilano and Ambleside (in West Vancouver) are also viable options. Watch out for commercial vessels. Windsurfing's best local venue is English Bay, where rental equipment and lessons are available. Experts head to the blustery north end of Howe Sound in Squamish for some of North America's finest conditions.

Cycling around Vancouver is the best and fastest way of seeing the natural and manmade sights. Not all of Vancouver's streets and bridges are bicycle-friendly, though officials in the city and its suburbs have slowly moved to construct special routes dedicated to cyclists.

Favourite routes include the Richmond dike system on Lulu Island, passing through the quaint fishing village of Steveston. Another popular bicycle route is the False Creek to Point Grey waterfront path. The Pacific Spirit Regional Park near the University of British Columbia is one of North America's largest urban parks with a wealth of trails for all abilities. But the undisputed champ for popularity and accessibility is the Stanley Park seawall. Don't forget your helmet: it's the law to wear it on the roads.

CYCLING AT WHISTLER (TOP) AND ON THE SEA WALL (MIDDLE)

Some people wouldn't take a walk in the park without a club, balls and a tee. Luckily, there are many places to do that in Vancouver. The area boasts a variety of public, private and semiprivate golf courses. For the novice, there are pitch-and-putt courses at Stanley Park and Queen Elizabeth Park. University Golf Club, Langara and Fraserview are among the nearest to downtown.

Richmond's Mayfair Lakes offers plenty of water hazards on what was once a farm. En route to Whistler, the Furry Creek course spills down a mountainside, providing unique challenges and an unbeatable view of Howe Sound. Continuing onward, the Whistler area now has five courses, designed by the likes of Jack Nicklaus, Arnold Palmer and Robert Trent Jones Junior.

GOLFING AT WHISTLER

Grouse Mountain, Cypress Bowl and Mount Seymour all offer top-quality downhill and cross-country skiing and snowboarding. Grouse offers the ultimate wintertime experience

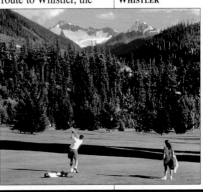

with sleigh rides and outdoor ice skating. Cypress and Seymour are similarly popular with those who use toboggans and inner tubes. Grouse is the most accessible, with direct public transit service and a breathtaking aerial tram ride from its parking lot.

Hiking is another popular activity on the West Coast. You don't have to go far, either, to get away from the hustle and bustle of city life. In Vancouver, visit UBC's Pacific Spirit Regional Park and Stanley Park. In nearby Richmond, the dike system is flat and close to the Gulf of Georgia and the Fraser River. On the North Shore, Seymour and Cypress provincial parks offer a multitude of trails. Lighthouse Park in West Vancouver is another option, but the most challenging is the Grouse Grind, a 2.7-km hike up Grouse Mountain. Depending on the avalanche risk, it's open from April through October. Why take the tram when you can beat the trail? When climbing or hiking in any of B.C.'s mountains, always be prepared with the proper equipment and clothing. Even on the sunniest days, the weather can be unpredictable.

If you'd rather have wheels on your two feet than two wheels and a seat, try in-line skating. Helmets, gloves, knee and elbow pads are highly recommended. The Stanley Park seawall isn't just for bikes. In fact, in-line skaters outnumber cyclists some summer days. For a more serene skate, try the wooded wonders of North Vancouver's Lower Seymour Conservation Reserve, until recently known as the Seymour Demonstration Forest.

Vancouver is known for its abundance of rain. But in the mountains on the North Shore, where it's higher and colder, winter sports enthusiasts will find a variety of recreation options.

There's no better place to relax or work up a sweat during the summertime than one of Vancouver's many sandy beaches. Kitsilano and English Bay are the most popular, which means space is at a premium on the best days. You might want to try Second or Third Beach at Stanley Park, or venture westward toward UBC to Jericho or Spanish Banks. If you can do without clothes, the nude Wreck Beach at the end of Point Grey is always an option. Another good bet is Ambleside, over the Lions Gate Bridge in West Vancouver. All are good for swimming, but the best outdoor swimming is available at the 137-metre-long Kitsilano Pool, open mid-May to mid-September.

KIDS' STUFF

MARIAN GILMOUR

PLAYLAND RIDE

CAPILANO
SUSPENSION BRIDGE

In Vancouver you don't have to be big to have fun. Adults
and kids can choose from a variety of interactive cultural
activities or sample second-to-none outdoor experiences.
Many of the best things in Vancouver are free. Almost
every green space offers opportunities for play and the
city's multicultural makeup lends excitement to just about
every aspect of the city.

If it should happen to be raining, head for indoor
venues such as Science World, the H.R.
MacMillan Pacific Space Centre or the
Vancouver Aquarium. The films shown at the
CN IMAX Theatre at Canada Place and the
Alcan OMNIMAX Theatre at Science World
offer cinematic opportunities to climb Mt.
Everest, swim with whales, run with wolves
and generally experience pure adrenaline. The
size and intensity of these productions may be a
bit overwhelming for younger children. Check
with venue staff before taking the whole family.

Many of the attractions mentioned
throughout this guide make special provisions
for young children. It is always wise to call
ahead to find out what is going on the day you
visit. Phone for hours, admission prices and
travel directions.

OUTDOOR ATTRACTIONS

Hold on to your kids for a spectacular walk
across the swaying wood and cable footbridge
of the Capilano Suspension Bridge. This
popular North Shore attraction spans the

Capilano River Canyon and hangs sixty-nine metres (230 feet) over the raging river waters. Towering evergreens, tall totem poles, Living Forest and Story Centre exhibits and rushing mountain waters make this a quintessential West Coast experience. Also on the North Shore, Lynn Canyon Park hosts an ecology centre, great hiking and another swinging footbridge, which is seventy-three metres (240 feet) above the rapids of Lynn Creek.

From June to September, Harbour Cruises offers a well-paced train and boat excursion that kids will find thrilling. The Royal Hudson, a vintage steam locomotive, chugs its way up the coast to Squamish through truly spectacular mountain and coastal scenery. After a two-hour train trip, you'll have enough time for a picnic or restaurant lunch and a walk through Squamish before your return trip on the boat, *MV Britannia*. The return boat ride through the water provides an equally magnificent view. Call for reservations since this is a popular attraction.

TOTEMS ON THE NORTH SHORE (TOP); THE ROYAL HUDSON (MIDDLE)

LYNN CANYON ECOLOGY CENTRE

The VanDusen Botanical Garden is home to an Elizabethan Hedge Maze that kids will love to get lost in. The hedge is about five feet high and you'll enjoy going in with your younger children. (There are wooden steps throughout so short people can climb up and discover they are not really lost.) Over 6,500 diverse plants flourish in this twenty-two-hectare (fifty-five acre) garden. Young folks and old will find many living things to admire.

The best urban walk in the forest can be found at Pacific Spirit Regional Park, which surrounds the University of British Columbia. It's a good place to experience a typical coastal forest with cedar and fir trees. Expect to share the fifty kilometres (thirty-one miles) of trails with joggers, dog walkers, cyclists and horseback riders. Trail maps are available at the Park Centre on West 16th Avenue just west of Blanca Street.

Stanley Park offers numerous attractions spread throughout its 1,000 acres. Kids of all ages will want to ride the miniature train that travels almost a mile through forest and by lake. The Children's Farm Yard features barnyard animals and is always a hit with the younger set. Lower Brockton Oval features a display of totem poles that represent various B.C. First Nations.

Another great place for children to experience birds and animals is the Greater Vancouver Zoo in Aldergrove. Its parklike, forty-eight hectares (120 acres) are home to 126 species of animals, including tigers, wolves, zebras, rhinoceroses, bears, elephants and camels. The zoo is forty-eight

PLAYLAND'S RIDES AT NIGHT (TOP); GREAT HORNED OWL (MIDDLE); MAPLEWOOD FARM (BOTTOM)

kilometres (29.8 mi) east of Vancouver and is open year round. The George C. Reifel Bird Sanctuary located on Westham Island at the south arm of the Fraser River provides an outing that goes well with a bag of seeds. Feed the birds or climb the four-storey wooden observation tower to get the big picture. Most paths are wheelchair accessible and there are picnic tables. North Vancouver's Maplewood Farm is a two-hectare (five-acre) petting farm of barnyard animals including rabbits, goats, cows, horses, donkeys, sheep and lots of ducks, geese and chickens. Little kids will love the big white bunnies and residents of the goat pen. The farm features seasonal special events and weekend pony rides in summer months.

Playland, open from April to the end of August, offers thirty-five outdoor rides ranging from the traditional wooden roller coaster and ferris wheel to the Ring of Fire and the Rainbow. There are also games and attractions and, of course, cotton candy and foot-long hot dogs. Playland is located on the PNE grounds on East Hastings Street. Call for times and days.

WATER PLAY

Depending on the time of the year, Vancouver's eleven sandy ocean beaches offer fine swimming. The water rises to approximately sixty-five degrees, perfect for a hot summer day. Lying in tidal pools, digging holes or building sandcastles and driftwood structures can be a lot of fun. Lifeguards are on duty from Victoria Day through Labour Day at Second Beach and Third Beach in Stanley Park, English Bay, Sunset Beach, Kits Beach, Jericho Beach,

THIRD BEACH

Locarno Beach and Spanish Banks.

Kitsilano Pool is a huge outdoor heated pool and its graduated slope makes it excellent for small children. It's open from Victoria Day to mid-September. Second Beach Pool in the heart of Stanley Park, is another favourite outdoor destination. After exhausting the pleasures of the pool's three small water slides, take a stroll to the nearby sandy beach or check out the ever-popular children's playground that boasts a real fire engine.

Truly fabulous indoor pools include the Vancouver Aquatic Centre, Burnaby's Eileen Dailly pool, New Westminster's Canada Games Pool and Surrey's Newton Wave Pool.

A swim in a clean, relatively warm mountain lake can be yours after a short trip to Sasamat Lake north of Ioco. There is no lifeguard at Sasamat, but it's the kind of place where older kids can spend the whole afternoon floating on inner tubes or air mattresses. Weekdays are definitely the preferred time to go to this popular local spot.

The Granville Island Water Park and Adventure playground offers water cannons (ground-level spouts that gush water), a safe waterslide and shallow wading areas. The park is supervised in season and parents can sit on the grass and enjoy the excitement. The Stanley Park Water Park, just north of Lumberman's Arch, offers much of the same action but also has equipment suitable for children with physical disabilities.

SECOND BEACH FROLICS

Splashdown Park is located just before the Tsawwassen ferry terminal and offers a mile of twisting waterslides. There are also hot tubs, patios to picnic on, small slides for little kids, a toddlers' pool, video arcade and mini-golf.

CHILDREN'S CULTURE

Vancouver's premiere event for kids is the Vancouver International Children's Festival. Ocean front Vanier Park becomes a festival village for this seven-day event, which begins the last

WRITERS FESTIVAL

Monday in May. Outstanding international and topnotch local talent present fine-quality performing arts. After almost a quarter of a century, the festival still aims to create lifelong lovers of arts and culture. The purchase of show tickets includes admission to the festival site. Check out the box office at the festival gates for often-available rush tickets. Otherwise, a small fee allows you on site to enjoy the roving entertainers, face painters and the multicultural community stage.

Spring break (mid-March) brings the Theatre Festival for Young Audiences to life. Five different companies offer performances at the Waterfront Theatre on Granville Island and Burnaby's Shadbolt Centre for the Arts. Year round, the Vancouver East Cultural Centre, a delightful heritage performance space in the heart of the East Side, presents a Saturday afternoon Kids Series. Exciting musical or dramatic performances are offered about once a month.

The Centre's Youth Program offers those between the ages of fourteen and nineteen the chance to see almost any performance for a $2 admission. This is a true bargain since nearly all performances at the centre are outstanding. For a good laugh, take in the Vancouver International Comedy Festival, which runs the last ten days of July at Granville Island. Outrageous and hilarious free street entertainment is presented every hour from noon to five p.m. Some ticketed events are suitable for families.

For longer stays with children, Arts Umbrella on Granville Island offers a wide range of exciting classes for young folk. Several classes offer year-end public performances at the end of May into early June. Dancers (modern, tap and ballet) as well as actors, animators and filmmakers showcase their work at public venues.

On the third Sunday of each month the Vancouver Art Gallery offers SuperSunday, an opportunity for families with school-aged children to experience art in a new way. An annual visual arts show by budding artists is also mounted at the Buschlen-Mowatt Gallery at the end of May.

Young readers take a place of honour at the Vancouver International Writers (& Readers) Festival. Held in mid-October at various Granville Island locations, the festival

dedicates three days to children's events. Twelve months of the year, head for the lower level of the Vancouver Central Library at Library Square. The area is devoted to children. Kids can spend hours cruising the picture books, but there are also computers available and a great selection of children's reference works, foreign language books and videos. Displays of children's art are often featured. If you're buying books, Vancouver Kidsbooks treat kids as serious readers. They offers the best of children's literature, and from time to time have readings, book launches and book signings with favourite authors. The knowledgeable staff and the outstanding collection of books make this a delightful place to shop and browse.

HISTORY AND LIVING CULTURE

BC SPORTS HALL OF FAME

The Cedar Cottage/Trout Lake Pow Wow held at Trout Lake Community Centre on Mother's Day weekend offers a glimpse into the rich cultural traditions of Canada's First Nations people. This event features intertribal dancing and drumming, hoop dancing, a princess pageant and arts and crafts displays.

FIRST NATIONS DANCING

Take a walk into the past at the Burnaby Village Museum & Carousel in Burnaby. More than thirty authentically restored buildings and a costumed staff recreate a 1920s village. There are hands-on activities for children

and seasonal special events at Christmas and throughout the year. There is also a beautifully restored C.W. Parker Carousel, circa 1912. Open seven days a week from late April to September and in December. The Fort Langley National Historic Park marks the site of a reconstructed Hudson's Bay Company post. Open year round, children can see and sample life as it was in the last century.

The B.C. Sports Hall of Fame, located at Gate A in B.C. Place Stadium, is more than a collection of medals, trophies, personal mementoes and photographs. Touch-screen computers help explore the lives of top athletes. High-energy kids can get a workout in the Participation Gallery, climbing a rock wall, testing their pitching arm or sprinting against the clock.

ANNUAL EVENTS

GAIL BUENTE

Vancouver is known as a city of hale-and-hearty outdoor types who spend their leisure time communing with nature. What isn't so well known is that these rugged individualists are also fiercely loyal to their festivals and cultural events. Whether it be Canadianized versions of age-old celebrations of its many ethnic groups, or brand-new locally created traditions, Vancouverites treasure their annual festivals.

JAZZ FEST IN DAVID LAM PARK; SNOWSHOEING AT WHISTLER RESORT

WINTER

During the holiday season, you will see the locals coming out for two festive traditions: a musical sail around Burrard Inlet and False Creek on the Christmas Carol Ships and then, on New Year's Day, the notorious annual Polar Bear Swim at English Bay Beach, proving that Vancouver is indeed the tropics of Canada. In the past few years, a third outdoor winter tradition, the Annual Winter Eagle Festival in the Squamish-Brackendale area, has become immensely popular. An eagle count is taken just after New Year. In 2000, the grand total was 2,607 eagles spotted. During the month of January, guided walks, concerts, a photo contest and an eagle art show round out the main event.

Instead of celebrating winter, many Vancouverites spend the cold months looking ahead to summer. In the dead of February they hide out at B.C. Place Stadium, daydreaming at the Annual Boat Show, and soon after at the Home and Garden Show.

PAINTED DRAGON PROWS

SPRING

Springtime starts in April with a gathering of wine enthusiasts at the Annual International Wine Festival. Held at the Vancouver Convention and Exhibition Centre as a fundraiser for the Vancouver Playhouse, it's a lavish week-long wine and culinary event.

In May, the festivals really begin to blossom. For lovers of old-time down-home music, the month-long Granville Island Bluegrass Festival offers a variety of free outdoor concerts every weekend throughout the month, winding up with two full days of events on the final weekend. Also in May, the Vancouver International Marathon, Canada's largest marathon, attracts thousands of runners from across North America and around the world.

Kids have a festival all their own in late May, though it's just as much fun for older folk. Featuring dance, theatre, music, puppets and clowns, the Vancouver International Children's Festival is unquestionably one of the high points of the spring season.

In June, False Creek fills up with dragon-prowed boats for the annual Alcan Dragon Boat Festival. As legend has it, dragon boats began 2,000 years ago in Chou Dynasty China. These days, dragon boat races are a spectacle of rare beauty. Each brightly painted twelve-metre boat is powered by a team of twenty, all paddling in unison to the beat of a drum. The Vancouver race is the largest dragon boat festival in North America, and one of the best in the world.

JAZZ CONCERT IN VANCOUVER'S GASTOWN

SUMMER

Summer in Vancouver is a non-stop festival. Leading off the season from the end of June into July is the du Maurier International Jazz Festival. It promises something for every jazz lover, and it's not false advertising. With nearly 400 performances in forty clubs and halls, plus dozens of free outdoor concerts, the offerings range from hot to cool, from familiar standards to wild innovations. Truly international in scope, the Jazz Festival embraces Brazilian samba, African soukous, European free

jazz, Asian fusion and North American blues, to name a few.

Throughout the summer months, a professional Shakespeare festival known as Bard on the Beach takes over Vanier Park in Kitsilano. Productions are staged in a backless tent, so the audience can enjoy the play, the sailboats gliding past the cityscape and the glow of sunset on the distant mountains. It's a truly magical backdrop to the performances. Tickets often sell out for this popular series, so make a reservation to ensure a seat.

Mid-July is the "folkal" point of the summer for about 25,000 diehard fans at the Vancouver International Folk Music Festival. Crowds have gathered at Jericho Beach Park annually for more than twenty years to listen to hundreds of artists sing and play. The following weekend, folkies who want something smaller and more intimate head out to the Mission Folk Festival in the Fraser Valley.

July also brings the Vancouver International Comedy Festival, the Symphony of Fire Fireworks Festival and the Illuminares Lantern Festival, a community-based paper lantern festival that now attracts a crowd of thousands while retaining its magical neighbourhood feel. Out of town, the Harrison Festival of the Arts focuses on international Afro-Latin cultures in the spa town of Harrison Hot Springs.

The new festival on the block, Festival Vancouver, may be an upstart on the summer schedule, but the individuals and groups composing the organization are all pros with decades of experience. For two weeks from late July to mid-August, a remarkable array of opera, early music, jazz

BARD ON THE BEACH

LOVE'S LABOUR LOST AT **BARD ON THE BEACH**

MOLSON INDY RACE and world music concerts feature topnotch touring artists from around the world at venues throughout the city.

The fun continues into August, when on the first weekend, lovers of speed and fanfare will be found on the banks of False Creek for the annual Molson Indy race. The following weekend, all eyes are on the sky at the Abbotsford International Airshow, held in Abbotsford, B.C., about an hour's drive from Vancouver.

The final fling of summer is the Pacific National Exhibition (PNE), held during the final two weeks of August. Take the kids to visit the petting farm, ride the roller coaster and chow down on corn dogs and candy floss. Be sure not to miss the Demolition Derby. It's good, old-fashioned fun.

FALL

Summer officially ends with the close of the PNE on Labour Day weekend, but there's no need to slow down quite yet. Visitors can still look forward to a weekend of camping out at the Chilliwack Bluegrass Festival. Or come inside and immerse yourself in one of the fall performance festivals. The Vancouver Fringe Festival, for two weeks in September, is a theatre event for those who enjoy a gamble.

Combining established and emerging performing companies, the productions are wildly varied. You're always sure to find at least one unexpected gem in the lineup.

Hot on the heels of the Fringe is the Vancouver International Film Festival, one of the finest film festivals on the continent. The VIFF has a reputation for innovative yet accessible programming, with an emphasis on films from Pacific Rim countries.

Taking place on Granville Island in mid-October, the Vancouver International Writers (& Readers) Festival is a week of readings, roundtable discussions and talks by the most exciting writers from around the world and around the corner. There's nothing dry about this festival of books; the atmosphere is always relaxed and festive. Some of the most popular annual events are Authors À La Carte, a brunch with visiting authors; the Poetry Bash; and the Literary Cabaret, each a feast of words, music, food and drink. Some of the readings are planned with young people in mind. One program of activities, *Le Salon*, is entirely in French.

VANCOUVER
NEIGHBOURHOODS

DOWNTOWN

BARBARA TOWELL

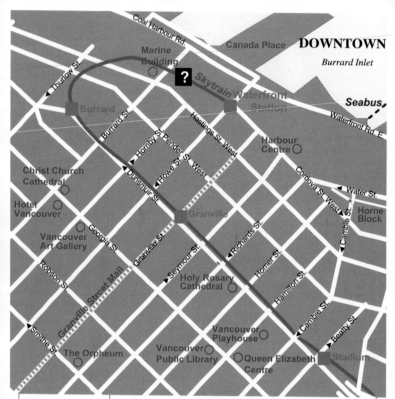

Vancouver is a relatively new city. In 1884, William Van Horne, the influential general manager of the Canadian Pacific Railway, visited what was then the logging village of Granville. He made two recommendations: that the tiny village of approximately 100 buildings become the terminus of the first cross-Canada railway, and that it be renamed Vancouver. In spite of the Great Fire of June 13, 1886, which totally destroyed the new city, a boom was on. By 1889, more than 10,000 people lived here. The Greater Vancouver area today numbers more than 2 million people.

Throughout its brief history, Vancouverites have fought hard to preserve the city's heritage buildings. Downtown Vancouver is proof of some success. A walk in the area reveals a satisfying mix of old and new. Old here means buildings from the late nineteeth century and early twentieth century. New is as recent as the Vancouver Public Library's central branch, which opened in 1995.

Vancouver's history can be traced through the

architecture of its downtown core, which encompasses W. Georgia Street to the south, Burrard Street to the west, Cordova Street on the waterfront to the north (look for the mountains) and Cambie Street to the east. It's fair to say that politics, business and faith shaped the city. The result is an eclectic mix of buildings, starting from the château-like Hotel Vancouver at Georgia and Burrard and ending with the Roman coliseum-like public library further east on Georgia Street. Although the number of permanent residents in the area is miniscule compared to the West End, Gastown or Yaletown on False Creek, downtown Vancouver does not empty out at night. Because of the many hotels, restaurants and entertainment venues in the area, the streets of the inner core remain fairly busy until midnight.

HOTEL VANCOUVER

First came the Canadian Pacific Railway (CPR), then came progress. Our walk begins at the corner of Georgia and Burrard where, in 1928, construction began on the Hotel Vancouver. This grand hotel, designed by the CPR in the impressive style of its Château Lake Louise and Banff Springs Hotel, would convince travellers that Vancouver was not a damp parochial backwater but a glistening modern metropolis. The next year, the stock market crashed and construction came to a standstill. For nearly a decade, the hotel's unfinished steel skeleton stood as a reminder of grim economic times. Only the impending royal visit of King George VI in 1939 brought about its hasty completion.

In the intervening period between start and completion, tastes changed. Ideas of tradition gave way to faith in the modern. As a result, the lower arcade, lobby and VIP suites were finished in an Art Deco style rather than the original classical approach. When Hilton took over management in the 1960s,

ROBSON AT THURLOW (TOP); NEON RAINBOW RAMADA (MIDDLE)

HOTEL VANCOUVER

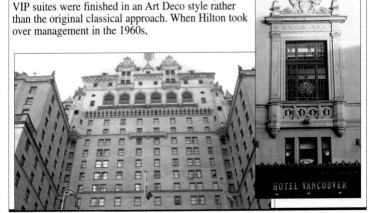

HOTEL VANCOUVER

DAVIE VILLAGE

much of the interior was redecorated yet again. Modernization now meant returning the lobby to a more classical form. The most impressive features of the hotel, however, remain its steep green copper roof and its sly, slightly impish gargoyles.

CHRIST CHURCH CATHEDRAL

Across the street from the Hotel Vancouver is the lovely and vibrant Christ Church Cathedral (690 Burrard), seat of the New Westminster Anglican Diocese. Designed by C.O. Wickenden, churches in this Gothic-revival style thrived in Canada in the nineteenth century, with each denomination mounting its own modifications (compare the Catholic Holy Rosary Cathedral noted later). The austere lines and interior atmosphere of Christ Church speak of its ties to Britain. Christ Church was built to serve the growing population of the city's West End, but initial funds were sparse. The inaugural service on October 6, 1889, was held in a granite basement, the only finished part of the building. In the aptly named "Root House," fifty-two parishioners were warmed by a coal-fire boiler. To raise money, parishioners purchased stock in the church's construction company. Within six years, the sandstone structure was complete, with additions in 1909 and 1940. The interior boasts an impressive ceiling with beams of Douglas fir. Of the church's twenty-nine stained-glass windows, three are by William Morris. They were acquired in 1984 on permanent loan from the Vancouver Museum and can be seen on the north-facing wall on the west side. The first organ was installed in 1895, employing an organ blower at the rate of five dollars a month. The pipes of the second organ can be seen in the church, though they are no longer functional. Be sure to check out the regular musical events taking place here. Information is available at the church or on their website at www.cathedral.vancouver.bc.ca.

CHRIST CHURCH CATHEDRAL

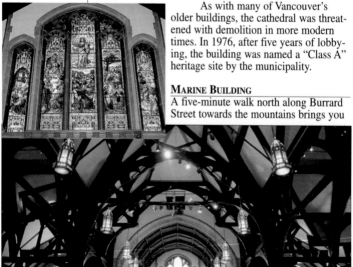

As with many of Vancouver's older buildings, the cathedral was threatened with demolition in more modern times. In 1976, after five years of lobbying, the building was named a "Class A" heritage site by the municipality.

MARINE BUILDING

A five-minute walk north along Burrard Street towards the mountains brings you to the spectacular Marine Building (355 Burrard). Erected in the Art Deco style, its construction cost its Toronto-based developers $2.5 million in 1929. By 1930, the developers were broke and offered the building to the city for 1 million dollars. When legislators refused to pay, Britain's Guinness family spotted a bargain and stepped in, purchasing it for much less. The same fiscally astute family built the Lions Gate Bridge in 1938, and ran it as a toll bridge until it was sold to the B.C. government in 1963.

The Marine Building's architects, McCarter and Nairne, suggested a design reminiscent of a "great crag rising from the sea, clinging with sea flora and fauna, tinted in sea-green, touched with gold." Indeed, no other Vancouver building is more finely finished. No visit to the Marine Building would be complete without a venture inside, through its extraordinary front door with its bronze grills and Art Deco zigzags. The lobby's walls include terra-cotta friezes depicting the history of transportation and the colonial discovery of the Pacific Coast. The building was restored in 1989.

MARINE BUILDING

WATERFRONT STATION

Crossing over to W. Cordova, proceed past Canada Place with its five white "sails" to Waterfront Station, built by the Canadian Pacific Railway (601 W. Cordova) in 1914. The present edifice was preceded by two earlier ones, a timber structure in 1887 (where the first passenger train arrived on May 23, 1887) and a château-style station in 1898-99. Waterfront Station was the only building in Vancouver designed by the firm of Barott, Blackader and Webster. In the words of architectural historian Harold Kalman, their creation is the most "self-consciously pompous building type [made] in the early part of the century." It is indeed a grand terminus with its expansive column façade and pilastered waiting room. It now serves as an entrance to both SkyTrain and SeaBus public transit systems.

Shops fill the former waiting room, but the public aspect of the site has eroded, as there are no longer public washrooms and seating is scant. Paintings on the upper walls depict Canadian landscapes en route to the West. The building was restored in 1976-77.

MARINE BUILDING INTERIOR

SINCLAIR CENTRE

Crossing Cordova, you can enter the Sinclair Centre from its rear entrance or head a block up the hill to its main entrance at 757 W. Hastings. The building was completed by the department of public works in 1910 to house the post office and other federal offices. In 1939, an extension was added at 325 Granville Street. The two "faces" of the Sinclair Centre reflect very distinct economic periods.

The original building was executed in

RENOVATING THE
SINCLAIR CENTRE

an Edwardian Baroque style that married architectural influences from both the French and English. Built for $600,000, its rusticated granite basement continues up to smooth columns reaching past the second and third floors. The fourth floor includes dormer windows. The entire structure is finished off with an impressive clock tower. The granite exterior hides an early example of a fireproof steel frame.

King George VI was kept busy on his royal visit to Vancouver in 1939. He not only opened the Hotel Vancouver but also the extension to the post office. The addition could not be more contrary to the design and intent of the original building. The first building was erected during Vancouver's construction and land speculation boom. As a result, it is highly ornate, expressing optimism in the future wealth of the country. The extension, on the other hand, was finished at the tail end of the Depression. Its exterior walls are bereft of decoration except a minimal application of pilasters used to harmonize with its predecessor. Interestingly, it was the original building, not the extension, that was occupied in 1935 by 750 unemployed men, as it more aptly captured the spirit of federal power. Their demands for relief led to a violent backlash from police and a number of the protesters were hospitalized.

The Sinclair Centre is now a shopping mall, retaining many of its original architectural and decorative highlights.

HARBOUR CENTRE AREA

Exit the Sinclair Centre on Hastings Street and walk east to Simon Fraser University's Harbour Centre Campus (515 W. Hastings). There is usually a small but interesting art show in its impressive modern lobby. The Harbour Centre Tower is home to the Lookout!, a visitor attraction. Not notable architecturally, the tower does offer one of the finest views in the city.

A block away, at 342 Richards Street, the Century House is worth a peek. Designed by J.S.D. Taylor and completed in 1912, it is noteworthy not because of its classical style (there are other, finer examples to be found), but for the detail which is best described as magic realism. The building is crowned with a pair of winged beavers. Its construction belongs to Canada's most self-consciously imperial period, a time when beavers represented the wealth of the colony. One can only wonder how contemporaries

VIEW FROM THE
HARBOUR CENTRE
TOWER

viewed these particularly whimsical little creatures that are part beaver and part bird. The best view is from across the street.

Continuing south along Richards to Pender Street, note the neon waterfall of the former Niagara Hotel, now Ramada Inn (435 W. Pender). Fifty years ago,

Vancouver was ablaze with neon, winning it the title of the neon capital of North America. It's hard to imagine a landscape where the Ramada Inn's sign could be considered modest, but in neon's heyday there was one neon sign for every eighteen residents. Suburban expansion in the 1960s linked neon with urban decay. Modernization of the downtown core proved to be the demise of neon in Vancouver. The Vancouver Museum now houses a sampling of Vancouver's neon history.

HOLY ROSARY CATHEDRAL

Back on Richards, you can't miss the Holy Rosary Cathedral (646 Richards). At the turn of the last century, when most of Vancouver's buildings were no higher than three stories, the cathedral must have cast an impressive shadow. Built in 1900 during a period of considerable church debt, some parishioners questioned the sense of the monumental Gothic-revival structure. The building was dubbed McGuckin's Folly after the priest whose efforts made construction possible.

Built of Gabriola Island sandstone with granite foundations, the church's asymmetrical towers are its most prominent visual features. The cathedral bells are of particular auditory interest. In the east tower, eight bells are tuned to a full octave, producing up to 5,000 different sequences. Inside the cathedral, granite-encased marble columns support an arched ceiling. Among the many stained-glass windows are eight depicting biblical scenes. Visitors are welcome.

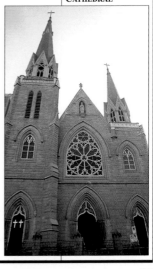

LIBRARY SQUARE

Continue south a few more blocks to Georgia Street, then head east to Library Square, the home of the Vancouver Public Library's central branch (350 W. Georgia). Described as a rectangle within an ellipse, the controversial design by Moshe Safdie & Associates with Downs/Archambault and Partners resembles a Roman coliseum. Opened in 1995, the nine-storey-high structure houses the library, an adjoining office tower and retail shops on the lower level concourse. Library Square includes two outdoor plazas, which often host special events. The concourse, with its six-storey-high view of the internal workings of the library, is a great place to catch your breath over an excellent cup of coffee, slice of pizza or ice cream cone. Sit, sip and do some serious people watching.

WEST END

JAMES OAKES

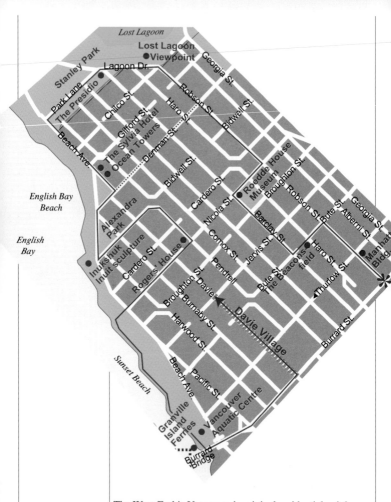

The West End is Vancouver's original residential neighbourhood, occupying the western half of the city's downtown peninsula. Once home to blue bloods living in stately
mansions by gardens and quiet streets, the area
has evolved into a remarkably diverse community — home
to single parents, upwardly mobile singles, gays and les-
bians, foreign students, recent immigrants, senior citizens,
low-income transients, condo owners and wealthy retirees.
The West End, in short, is a success story of urban livabili-
ty that is the envy of cities across North America.

BOUNDARIES

The West End is the most densely populated square kilometre in Canada. Zoning maps show Georgia and Burrard as the northern and eastern boundaries, while Stanley Park and English Bay create the western and southern extremes. Laid out on a simple grid pattern, the main streets of the West End running east/west are Beach, Davie, Robson and Georgia. The main north/south streets are Denman, Thurlow and Burrard. Included within the West End's boundaries are the three distinct shopping areas along Robson, Davie and Denman streets. The city's familiar electric trolley buses run frequently in a loop along these same streets. SkyTrain's Burrard Station is close to the northeast corner of the West End, with easy access to Robson's glitzy fashion scene.

DENMAN STREET

A WEST END WALKABOUT

Probably the best place to start your West End tour is right in the thick of things, heading west on Robson Street from Burrard or Thurlow. Contemporary, hip and self-consciously cosmopolitan, Robson has become the city's premiere shopping street, the mecca of Vancouver's young and fashionable. Just step into the stream and join the throng of shoppers, tourists, Asian students and local West Enders as they jostle for space on the crowded sidewalks. The corner of Robson and Thurlow is renowned for its two (count 'em) Starbucks coffee shops located kitty-corner from each other. One is located in the elegant Manhattan Building, the West End's earliest apartment block, completed in 1908.

Continue west along Robson for another block, then turn left on Bute Street, and suddenly you're venturing into the heart of residential West End. At the top of a short rise is a leafy parkette complete with fountain, benches and flower beds. Standing graciously on one side of the plaza is The Beaconsfield, a stately if somewhat run-down stone and brick structure. This is one of the West End's remaining early apartment buildings.

ROBSON STREET

ROEDDE HOUSE MUSEUM

Three blocks farther on (take a right at Barclay and proceed down the hill to Broughton), you'll come to the Roedde House Museum (1415 Barclay), another architectural treasure of the West End. Roedde House stands among a collection of restored, turn-of-the-century wood-frame houses in Barclay Heritage Square. Carefully restored with period furnishings and décor, the museum is a journey back in time to the height of Victorian and Edwardian elegance.

After soaking in the atmosphere of the public gardens, head back out to Robson Street and continue west down the hill towards Stanley Park. Although the lower end of Robson is being gentrified with upscale shops and condominiums, there is a friendly atmosphere of an urban village with buskers performing outside the local government liquor store, green grocers, pizza shops, video rental outlets and a 1960s-style Safeway grocery store.

On the far side of Denman Street, in the exclusive area known to locals and realtors as "West of Denman," Robson becomes strictly residential for its final two blocks until it merges with Lagoon Drive. Here, on a slope overlooking Lost Lagoon, visitors are greeted with one of the best city views, a 180° panorama of Stanley Park, Coal Harbour and the North Shore mountains.

Admire the view while walking south along Lagoon Drive, but when you reach Nelson Street take a moment and look upwards at the row of high-rises bordering the park. Standing among the conventional 1960s and 1970s towers, is the post-modernist Presidio, designed by Vancouver architect Richard Henriques who in turn was inspired by Austrian architect Adolf Loos' Villa Karma near Montreaux, Switzerland. Many of the Presidio's multi-million dollar suites were purchased in the early 1990s by offshore buyers who reportedly enjoy their residences for only a few weeks every year. Once you've come back to earth, follow the pedestrian path running along the edge of the park until you come to Beach Avenue and the shores of English Bay.

THE SEASIDE

Swimmers began flocking to English Bay when the West End was first developed in the 1890s. By the turn of the twentieth century, summertime crowds travelled to the popular bathing beach on the newly opened Robson and Denman streetcar line.

Today, the Brighton-style pier has long since disappeared, but the holiday-resort atmosphere along the beach is as strong as ever. At the first sign of a sunny day, the area is invaded by sunbathers, beach lovers, dog walkers and windsurfers.

The ivy-clad Sylvia Hotel on Beach Avenue,

overlooking English Bay, still offers visitors perhaps the best accommodation location-wise for the money. It was built in 1911 as the Sylvia Court Apartments before the Depression forced the owner to rent it out as a seamen's hostel. After the war, it moved upscale and branched out into the liquor business, opening the city's first cocktail bar in July 1954, thus allowing Vancouverites to enjoy a civilized cocktail at long last. You can still admire the view of the bay over a cocktail in what remains one of Vancouver's best bars.

Next door to the Sylvia, at 1835 Morton Avenue, stands the Ocean Towers, a jazzily shaped apartment building dating from 1957. Across the street, at the intersection of Denman and Davie, a cluster of imported palm trees completes the exotic "British California" ambiance. Take a brief side trip along Denman Street, which offers beachwear, bicycle rentals, cappuccinos, a fresh juice bar and an amazing variety of international cuisine. Pedestrians like to think they rule the street and traffic moves by at a crawl.

THE SYLVIA HOTEL

Don't forget that English Bay is also an evening destination. Locals and visitors come out to walk along the seawall promenade, listen to musicians and pause to watch the sunset beyond the anchored freighters and the mountains of Vancouver Island. During the annual Symphony of Fire spectacle in August, upwards of 300,000 people gather around the bay to watch the spectacular international fireworks competitions.

INUIT SCULPTURE (BELOW); ALEXANDRIA PARK BANDSTAND (BOTTOM)

At the eastern most end of the English Bay beach, you'll find an Inuit sculpture by Alvin Kanak. Commissioned by the Northwest Territories for Expo 86, the large granite blocks represent a human figure with welcoming, outstretched arms and is based on the signposts that guide hunters in the North.

From here, cross Beach Avenue at the pedestrian light to the lovely Alexandria Park, named after the consort of King Edward VII. It boasts a pretty wooden bandstand constructed in 1914 for outdoor concerts, as well as a

95

marble fountain adorned with a brass plaque honouring the city's beloved Seraphim "Joe" Fortes. Generations of children learned to swim from this Barbadian immigrant, who acted as lifeguard and special constable at English Bay until his death in 1922.

From the northeast corner of the park, walk north on Bidwell to Davie Street, turn left, and head up the hill until you come to the impressive Roger's House at 1531 Davie. One of the last survivors of the West End's age of opulence, this elegant mansion-turned-restaurant was designed by Samuel Maclure, one of the most prolific architects of well-heeled Vancouver society, for local sugar magnate Benjamin Tingley Rogers.

To continue exploring the West End's southern flank, return to the seashore via Nicola Street and then stroll toward the Burrard Street Bridge until you arrive at Sunset Beach. This marks the end of the English Bay Seawall and the entrance to False Creek. At the foot of Thurlow Street stands the Vancouver Aquatic Centre, which houses a fifty-metre pool, a children's pool and a diving tank, among other indoor recreation facilities. Behind the Aquatic Centre you'll find the West End landing of Granville Island Ferries. The little passenger ferries run regularly from dawn until dusk, serving English Bay, Vanier Park in Kitsilano Point and Granville Island.

THE TWENTY-FOUR-HOUR VILLAGE

IN DAVIE VILLAGE

It's a bit of a hike to reach our final destination — Davie Village — located up on the West End's central plateau. First, follow the pedestrian path across from the entrance to the Vancouver Aquatic Centre that leads to the north end of the Burrard Bridge. From here, walk north along Burrard Street for three blocks until you come to a pair of gas stations at the corner of Davie.

Here's where you'll find the locals going about their daily routines: picking up the dry-cleaning, dropping into the tanning salon, checking for e-mail at the Internet cafe, buying groceries at the twenty-four-hour supermarket, getting a prescription filled at the mega-drugstore or having a meal at one of the many reasonably priced restaurants along the street.

And just in case you hadn't noticed the profusion of rainbow freedom flags along the street, Davie Village is also the traditional core of Vancouver's thriving gay community, with clubs and services located close by. The Gay and Lesbian Centre on Bute Street is a hub of activity, housing a drop-in centre, lounge and library. By night, Davie supports a lively social scene. Gay bars like Numbers and Celebrities are always packed. When the club goers finally spill into the street, local all-night eateries are open to receive them. For midnight snacks, try Hamburger Mary's, Fresco Inn and Doll & Penny's. The latter, with a red, 1950s Cadillac mounted above the front door, is an attraction in itself.

GASTOWN

LEANORE SALI

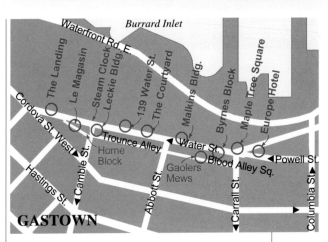

Stand in Maple Tree Square looking west along Water Street. The red-brick streets of Gastown are bustling with people. Local residents stop to chat with their neighbours, international students rush to their classes, business people dodge the throngs to make their luncheon appointments and visitors from around the world wander through the shops and restaurants, stopping en route to pose for photographs by Gastown's world-famous steam clock. In Gastown, residents and tourists have learned to enjoy life in the streets in much the same way Europeans do.

The handsome façades of the brick buildings reveal a mix of antique stores, boutiques and street-level galleries that contain a broad selection of Canadian First Nations art. In restaurants housed in former warehouses, diners are

WATER STREET AT NIGHT

STREET ARTIST

offered a variety of cuisine and price ranges. The nightlife is lively with a selection of nightclubs, cabarets and pubs that cater to every age group.

Although Gastown still remains a favourite location for architectural firms, design companies, music promoters and advertising agencies, it is also beginning to attract the interest of the high-tech industry.

GASTOWN'S HISTORIC PAST

The original name of the small settlement around which Vancouver grew was unofficially known as Gastown. The first settler was Captain John "Gassy Jack" Deighton, a Yorkshire man who'd been a sailor, prospector, steamboat pilot and saloon keeper. Gassy Jack arrived at Burrard Inlet in the fall of 1867, opened his Globe saloon and prospered. Almost immediately others came to join him.

By the 1870s, Gastown was a multicultural community of saloons, hotels and grocery stores catering to mill workers, lumbermen, ships' crews and whalers. During the next decade, the community underwent a growth spurt following the announcement that it would be the site of the Canadian Pacific Railway terminus. By 1886, it had 1,000 buildings and 3,000 residents. On April 6 of that year, it was officially re-named Vancouver.

Shortly after, on June 13, 1886, a brush-clearing fire blazed out of control and burned the town to the ground. While destroying the old town, the Great Fire spurred the biggest building boom in West Coast history. The area prospered until Vancouver's economic boom collapsed in 1914. From the 1930s to the 1950s, Gastown, once the heart of Vancouver, became a virtual backwater.

Gastown remained in decline until the early 1960s when a few enterprising merchants and property owners, recognizing the architectural heritage underneath the grime of the old buildings, began to put some money into restoring them. City Hall joined in the cause. New street lamps were installed, streets and sidewalks were bricked, and the meandering courtyards and mews were left intact. In 1971, the Province of British Columbia designated Gastown a historic district.

STEAM CLOCK

GASTOWN TOUR

Start your tour at Gassy Jack's statue in Maple Tree Square. Facing east, you'll see the Europe Hotel built in 1908 by Angelo Calori. A flatiron-shaped building, built to fit the triangular-shaped lot, the Europe was the earliest reinforced concrete structure in Canada and the first fireproof hotel in Western Canada.

The building directly behind Gassy Jack's statue is the Byrnes Block (2-8 Water Street). Built in 1886 by George Byrnes, a former sheriff of the Caribou during the gold rush days, this was one of the first brick buildings in Vancouver. It once housed the Alhambra Hotel, one of the city's fancier establishments at the time.

Take the entrance off Carrall Street to the central courtyard known as Gaolers Mews. This is where the town's first jail and home of Gastown's first constable were located. Vancouver's first city council meeting was held here. The site later housed the city's first post office and later the city's first fire hall. The building was renovated in 1974 to create the interior courtyard and office and retail complex.

Exit onto Water Street. As you stroll west along Water, take the time to browse through the many galleries and shops along the way. Many galleries specialize in West Coast and Inuit art, offering the largest selection in Western Canada and representing internationally renowned First Nations artists.

On the north side of the street you'll see a large building housing the Old Spaghetti Factory Restaurant (55 Water). It was built in 1907 as the warehouse and headquarters for Malkins, one of B.C.'s main food wholesalers. Continue along Water Street crossing to the north side at the corner of Water and Abbott. As you continue your stroll west along Water, notice the Courtyard, built in 1974 and designed to blend in with its older neighbours. Just west of the Courtyard is 139 Water Street, built in 1898 as the first warehouse for Malkin's wholesale grocery business. Renovated in 1996 into apartments, this building is an excellent example of Gastown living today.

At the corner of Water and Cambie is Gastown's famous steam clock. Although built in 1977, the movements of the steam clock are based on an 1875 design. A continuous supply of steam feeds the clockworks from the steam vent beneath the street.

Cross over to the south side of the street. The red-brick

EUROPE HOTEL

GAOLERS MEWS

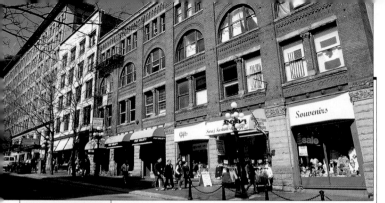

building on the corner housing a contemporary furniture store is known as the Leckie Building. It was built in 1910 by the Leckie family as a shoe and boot factory. Renovated in 1990 for office and retail use, the Leckie Building is an example of the timber construction used in early Gastown buildings.

Stroll south on Cambie to Cordova Street. Turn right at the corner and meander west along Cordova. The buildings along this strip of Cordova Street once housed merchants outfitting gold seekers headed for the Klondike. Today, the area specializes in antique stores and boutiques offering clothes by Vancouver fashion designers. The building on the northwest corner of Cambie and Cordova was built in 1888. It was known as the Masonic Temple as it housed the Masonic Grand Lodge. Next door is the Horne Block, built by land investor and city politician J.W. Horne. Designed by Nathaniel Stonestreet Hoffar, the city's first important architect, the Horne Block was the mid-1880s most exquisite venture into the Victorian Italianate style of architecture.

At the entrance to the alley off Cordova is the Le Magasin building. Check out the face ornaments on the fibreglass frieze. These face ornaments are life masks of notable entrepreneurs from Gastown's 1960s revival and the individuals responsible for the revitalization of the area during the 1970s. Take the back entrance of Le Magasin and walk through the building to exit onto Water Street. On both sides of street you will see the best examples of 1890s architecture still standing in the city.

Cross over and continue west along Water Street until you get to The Landing (375 Water). This converted warehouse, built by the Kelly Douglas grocery company in 1905 from profits made from outfitting Klondike gold seekers, reflects the general history of wholesaling in

WATER STREET (ABOVE); THE HORNE BLOCK (MIDDLE)

THE HORNE BLOCK

Gastown. The building was renovated in 1988 as a retail and office complex. Enter the building and walk over to the large window overlooking the harbour. From here you get a spectacular view of Vancouver's port and railway system.

CHINATOWN

JOANNE POON

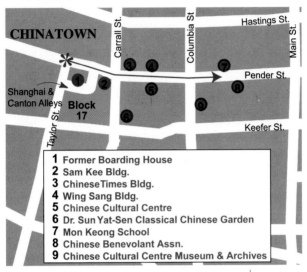

1 Former Boarding House
2 Sam Kee Bldg.
3 ChineseTimes Bldg.
4 Wing Sang Bldg.
5 Chinese Cultural Centre
6 Dr. Sun Yat-Sen Classical Chinese Garden
7 Mon Keong School
8 Chinese Benevolent Assn.
9 Chinese Cultural Centre Museum & Archives

Vancouver's Chinatown is the second-largest in North America, a bustling community encompassing Chinatown proper as well as neighbouring Strathcona. Back in the early 1880s, the then-swampy Chinatown land was on the edge of False Creek. Geographically, Chinatown stretches from Gore Avenue east to Carrall Street, and west on Pender and Keefer streets. This historic area began to grow in the late nineteenth century after the completion of the Canadian Pacific Railway. Many Chinese railway workers stayed in Canada, moving to the "Saltwater City" for jobs. The majority lived in Chinatown. A predominantly male society, the workers contracted for seasonal jobs in canneries and lumber mills. They lived alone, far from their families in China, unable to bring them to Canada because of the repressive head tax and a closed-door immigration policy introduced in 1885. Chinese entrepreneurs like merchant Chang Toy and Canadian Pacific Railway Chinese agent Yip Sang were precursors of Chinatown's commercial development.

CHINATOWN TOUR

The epicentre of historical Chinatown is the intersection of Carrall and East Pender streets. Stand on the corner and look around. The southwestern block of the intersection was known as Block 17. It was here, at 87 East Pender, that a seven-storey boarding house complex once stood. Built by a group of Chinese merchants, the complex included stores on the ground floor and residential quarters on the

SHOPPING ON PENDER NEAR GORE

upper floors. The majority of the residents were the Chinese "married bachelors" who came to Canada alone. After the anti-Asian riot in 1907, when 2,000 members of Vancouver's Asiatic Exclusion League stormed Chinatown and Japantown, an iron gate was erected at the building's main entrance to protect its residents from attack. At night, the gate was locked for security purposes. More recently, the building housed SUCCESS, the city's major agency for community and immigrant services (now relocated to new headquarters).

Shanghai and Canton alleys also ran off Block 17. They were once busy with stores, restaurants, barbershops and Chinese opera theatres. When Dr. Sun Yat-Sen visited Vancouver in 1910, he drew an audience of 1,000 to one of the theatres. Both alleys were demolished in the 1940s when non-Chinese industries began to move into the area. Look for the street plaques commemorating their history.

DR. SUN YAT-SEN (BELOW); SAM KEE BUILDING (BOTTOM)

The Guinness Book of Records calls Block 17's Sam Kee Building (8 West Pender) the narrowest building in the world. The Sam Kee Building belonged to a wealthy Chinese merchant, Chang Toy. When he bought the land in 1903, it was a standard-sized lot. In 1912, the government decided to widen Pender Street and expropriated twenty-four feet from the front of the lot, leaving only six feet on which to construct a building. Which is what Chang Toy did to spite the officials. Although narrow, the 1913 building included a bathhouse in the basement for the use of the married bachelors living upstairs. As there were no bathroom facilities in the building, the residents had to pay to use the bathhouse. The building is now owned by Jack Chow Insurance.

Across the street (116 East Pender) stands a building that belonged to the Chinese Freemansons (Cheekongtaong). It was the office of the *Chinese Times*, one of the first locally printed Chinese newspapers. When Dr. Sun Yat-Sen visited Vancouver to raise funds for the 1911 Revolution in China, he stayed here.

To show their support, the Freemansons mortgaged the building for the cause of the revolution.

The location of the Chinese Cultural Centre (50 East Pender) and Dr. Sun Yat-Sen Classical Chinese Garden (578 Carrall) was the site for Vancouver's Jubilee Celebration in 1936. For the festivities, the entire area was lit up and decorated with a Chinese arch and pagoda. In 1980, the Chinese Cultural Centre was built. The colourful China Gate marking the entrance of the centre was originally displayed at Expo 86. Near the China Gate are two bronze inscriptions. One commemorates the industry and sacrifices of Chinese railroad workers. The other honours the efforts of Chinese-Canadian Second World War veterans to gain voting rights for Chinese people living in Canada, a goal accomplished in B.C. in 1947.

CHINA GATE (TOP); STORE INTERIOR (MIDDLE)

Stop in at the Chinese Cultural Centre Museum and Archives (555 Columbia) to view exhibitions on Chinese arts and the history of Chinese-Canadians.

Across from the Chinese Cultural Centre stands the Wing Sang Building. Constructed in 1889, it is both the oldest building and the first brick building in Chinatown. It was built by Yip Sang, a successful Chinese merchant with four wives and twenty-three children. The entire family lived here and Yip ran his import-export business, the Wing Sang Company, on the ground floor. If you look up, you'll note the inscription "1889" on the original building. As the family and the business grew, Yip Sang expanded with a bay-windowed addition and a six-storey building on the back. He linked the front and back buildings with a staircase on the third floor. One of the interesting architectural features is the door on the second floor facing Pender Street. Since the swamps of False Creek still extended to the area, the door was used for loading and unloading goods.

CHINESE CULTURAL CENTRE MUSEUM AND ARCHIVES

STORES AND ASSOCIATIONS
Walking towards Gore on Pender, you enter another section of Chinatown. Here, you might be

ON PENDER NEAR GORE (TOP AND MIDDLE)

MON KEONG SCHOOL (BOTTOM)

attracted at first by the different storefronts, including herbal outlets, jewellers, restaurants and arts and crafts companies. When you look up, you'll be amazed to see the historic buildings around you. All share similar features: a slender shape, decorated with Western-style pillars and Chinese-style recessed balconies. Balconies like these were common to the buildings in South China. The pillars and the pediments supporting them were heavily influenced by Western architecture. This combination of Chinese and Western styles is a characteristic of Chinatown architecture.

Many of these buildings are now the offices of Chinese associations. They are surname associations, for example the Lee, Wong and Chin associations. Others were formed with people from the same village in China. All played a significant role in the life of early Chinese immigrants. Associations offered help and financial aid to members in need, and places to gather socially and share news from home. Today, members still visit their associations to play mahjong, meet friends, practice Cantonese opera and celebrate Chinese festivals.

The Chinese Benevolent Association (108 East Pender Street) was formed at the turn of the century and the building erected in 1901. After the Second World War, the Chinese Benevolent Association, together with other associations and individuals in the community, successfully lobbied for the vote and the repeal of the Chinese Exclusion Act of July 1, 1923, which had effectively suspended Chinese immigration to Canada.

In this section of Chinatown also stand the Wong Association and the Mon Keong School (123A East Pender). The Wong Association is one of the largest surname associations in the community. The association founded the Mon Keong School in 1925, mainly for the children of the Wong clan. Children attended Chinese-language class after their regular public school classes, one of the ways that Chinese parents ensured language proficiency for their children. The school is still in operation. There are many more historic buildings to visit in Chinatown. More can be learned about them by taking one of the popular walking tours offered by the Chinese Cultural Centre.

COMMERCIAL DRIVE

GARY MCFARLANE

"The Drive" isn't the only drive in Vancouver, but everyone knows it means Commercial Drive, a remarkably diverse assemblage of shops, cafes, parks and community and cultural centres. Like much of Vancouver, the area was densely wooded late into the nineteenth century. The Salish Indians once hunted elk here and its long-gone forests fed the historic Hastings lumber mill. The first homes were built in the working-class suburb of Grandview in the early years of the twentieth century. If you walk randomly through the streets east of The Drive, you can easily re-imagine Vancouver as it was in 1910. Grant Street, Lakewood, Rose, Salsbury and Napier, among others, retain many of these beautiful and eccentric buildings.

ITALIAN NEIGHBOURHOOD

Following the two world wars, waves of Italian immigrants settled in the area. Although the influence is now waning, The Drive is still the place where you can shop for prosciutto, sausages, great rounds of cheese and biscotti at the numerous bakeries, delis and produce markets. During soccer season, sitting in Caffé Roma Sports Bar (1510 Commercial) is an overwhelming sensation not unlike Milan at rush hour. Soak in the atmosphere at Calabria Bar (1815 Commercial) where you dine in the shadow of classic Italian sculpture.

   The many restaurants on The Drive are great places to

eat and hang out, without compromising your wallet. Go with the special of the day, as you would in Italy. Lombardo's, in the Il Mercato shopping mall (1641 Commercial), is famous for its pizza. Other favourites are Spumante's Cafe (1736 Commercial) and La Rocca (1565 Commercial). For lunch, Tony's Deli (1046 Commercial) has great panini. For perhaps the best fresh pasta in the city, check out The First Ravioli Store (1900 Commercial). Off The Drive, at 1033 Venables, is the La Casa Gelato, renowned for 138 fancifully flavoured ice creams.

CAFFÉ ROMA (TOP); FIRST RAVIOLI STORE (MIDDLE)

COFFEE AND CULTURE

Social life on The Drive centres on tiny cafes and eateries. Vicious Cycle Laundro & Leisurama (2062 Commercial) is a cafe and coin laundry. Nearby is Clove (2054 Commercial), an Indian bistro and trendy CD shop. Reincarnated beatniks lounge at Bukowski's (1447 Commercial). La Quena (1111 Commercial) serves the politically correct. Harry's Off Commercial (1716 Charles) is a gay hang-out and Circling Dawn (1045 Commercial) is organically inclined. Havana Restaurant (1212 Commercial) features an art gallery, dance lessons and Cuban cigars on the menu. This being Vancouver and not Havana, they cannot be smoked on site.

Eccentric specialty shops abound. Worth browsing are the Magpie Magazine Gallery (1319 Commercial) and Beckwoman's (1314 Commercial), a be-beaded and be-incensed curiosity shop. Vancouver artisans fill Dr. Vigari Gallery (1312 Commercial) and Cosmopolis (1009 Commercial).

DR. VIGARI GALLERY

Local cultural meccas include the Vancouver East Cultural Centre, also known as The Cultch (1895 Venables), located in a former Methodist church. One street

over, WISE Hall (1882 Adanac) headlines folk acts. Live music is an evening staple at the jazz-with-your-tapas Latin Quarter (1305 Commercial). The funky Waazubee Cafe (1622 Commercial) has turntabling DJs on many evenings, and Café Deux Soleils (2096 Commercial) has rootsier rock or folk fare.

GRANVILLE ISLAND AND FALSE CREEK

ALMA LEE

Granville Is Ferry
False Creek
Downtown Vancouver
99
English Bay
Aquabus Ferry
Granville Island Public Market
Duranleau St.
Granville Bridge
Creekhouse Gallery
Arts Club Theatre
GRANVILLE ISLAND
Railspur Alley
Johnston St.
Emily Carr Institute of Art & Design
Promenade
Sea Village
Anderson St.
Kids Only Market
Cartwright St.
Entrance under bridge
Old Bridge St.
Arts Umbrella
Granville Island Hotel
False Creek

Before Granville Island was built, there were two sandbars at this location used as a fish enclosure by First Nations people before European contact. As Vancouver grew, the sandbars' proximity to False Creek made them the ideal site for industry. After many failed attempts to reclaim the sandbars, the newly formed Vancouver Harbour Commission gave the go-ahead in 1915 for them to be turned into an island. Until just after the Second World War, the area was choked with sawmills and factories manufacturing everything from barrels to boilers and from chains to

PUBLIC MARKET MERCHANT

107

GRANVILLE ISLAND FERRY

cement. By the 1950s, the area was a toxic wasteland. Something had to be done. In 1972, a group of young architects and urban planners known as "The Barefoot Gang" brainstormed the redevelopment of Granville Island. Their vision, scoffed at by many, created the unique environment it is today.

A UNIQUE URBAN TRANSFORMATION

Although the grimy industries are gone, Granville Island remains a place where people work. These are merchants from all walks of life and cultural backgrounds. The butcher, the baker, the candlestick maker would be an apt rhyme to describe the island. In the Granville Island Public Market, it's fun to get to know the folks who are so incredibly knowledgeable about their products, whether it's fresh fruit from the Okanagan, exotic fish from the Southern Hemisphere or fine cheeses from around the world. One of my favourite places is the bakery and French specialty foods store La Baguette et L'Echalote which appeals to my thinking that I must have been French in another life.

You can get to the island by Aquabus ferry or False Creek Ferry, TransLink bus (the #19 bus from Granville and Broadway), on foot, by bike or in-line skates. Getting your car onto the island and parking it can be a chore, although paid covered parking is fairly copious. If you prefer a little exercise, park off-island in the day lot at Lamey's Mill Road and The Castings and walk west along the False Creek seawall for the flavour of the terraced residences and their lovely gardens. The view of the city and the mountains from here is spectacular. The walkway takes you north onto the island at the False Creek Community Centre, close to the children's water park. This free water park is a good choice if you have younger children. Sit and rest while you watch them play in safety. Check out the Kids Only Market next door to the Crystal Arc. In the adjacent pond, look for turtles basking on

IN THE PUBLIC MARKET

stones in the summer. Across the street is the Granville Island Brewing Company where you can stop and sample their product.

Pick up a map at the Information Centre (1398 Cartwright Street), to help you circumnavigate the island. If you get lost, don't worry — you just might stumble onto a little-known treasure. After I'd worked on the island for six or seven years, I walked into Dig This, a gardening shop, and exited by the back door to find two or three hitherto unknown great little shops and a tiny cafe. One special off-the-beaten-track spot is the mound at the far east end of the island, a great place to take in the tranquil view of boats moored on False Creek, to say nothing of the view of Mount Baker on a clear day.

MARKET HONEY (TOP) AND FOOD COUNTER (MIDDLE)

A TOUR OF THE ISLAND

To make a circle of Granville Island, head east on Cartwright Street. You'll pass Arts Umbrella, a facility for young aspiring artists, dancers and musicians. At the end of Cartwright is the Granville Island Hotel, a boutique hotel with an excellent patio restaurant, brew pub and many charter boats moored close by. Walking west on Johnston Street, Sea Village on the north side is an eclectic mix of float homes with impressive container gardens on the decks. Continue along to the Emily Carr Institute of Art & Design. Drop in and see what's on at The Charles Scott Gallery. As you stroll on, you can't miss Ocean Cement, one of the last industrial tenants located here. You'll remember that the industrial nature of Granville Island still exists when you dodge cement trucks or pass a shop that makes nails. Notice that many of the islands' buildings are constructed from corrugated metal, retaining the industrial look. Check for names of the original companies on the roofs and sides of some of the buildings. Next to Ocean Cement, the Creekhouse Gallery is home to a mix of shops, galleries and offices.

As you walk past the Arts Club Theatre, you'll come to the star of the Island, the Granville Island Public Market. From the vivid bouquets of flowers outside to the locally grown, fresh fruit and vegetables inside, it's a feast for the eyes and taste buds. Best advice: nibble your way through the market; there are often free samples.

Leaving temptation behind, check out The Net Loft across from the Public Market. In the past, fishers repaired

ART IN THE PUBLIC MARKET

their nets here; today, it's yet another surprise of little shops. On the water nearby, you'll find Vancouver's love affair with the water continues with boat builders, boat repairers, chandlers, boat charter rentals, kayak rentals, fishing boats and live-on moorages. You'll pass the Maritime and Fishing Museum, an interesting spot for anglers and collectors of historical seafaring trivia.

I often forget just how many choices we have on Granville Island. Every day, visitors travel around the world with the music of the buskers, whether they are flute players from the Andes or a piper from Scotland. Young student musicians play for money in the market, their instrument cases open for donations. Stand-up comics and magicians entice you to stop, take a break and laugh at their antics. The arts come to life as you watch artisans at work at Blackstone, David Clifford's hand press (1249 Cartwright); at Paper Ya, purveyor of handmade paper, in the Net Loft; and in the Diane Sanderson weaving studio (#15-1551 Johnston). Festivals are an ongoing attraction, including Spring Rites New Play Festival in May, the comedy festival and jazz festival in June, folk music Festival in July, wooden boat festival in August and the Vancouver International Writers (& Readers) Festival in October. In December, the Christmas Carol Ships form a convoy to dazzle onlookers along False Creek with a myriad of sparkling lights. As a visitor, you might even plan a special visit to enjoy one of these annual events.

Granville Island is justifiably famous. And famous people come here to visit. You never know whom you'll see, from award-winning Canadian author Margaret Atwood to Hollywood star Arnold Schwarzenegger. You

BLACKSTONE HAND PRESS

can do practically anything on Granville Island — exchange money, buy books, learn how to scuba dive or to

kayak, even live there. Anything to do with the outdoor West Coast style is pretty much available here. Granville Island is the kind of place that invites you to explore again and again.

KITSILANO

KELSEY MCLEOD

Kitsilano, often simply called Kits, is one of Vancouver's oldest neighbourhoods. Stretching along the waterfront from the Burrard Bridge to Alma Road, extending south to 16th Avenue, Kitsilano presents amazing diversity in every aspect. It is home to two museums, a space centre and the coast guard. Its many parks include Kitsilano Beach, Vanier and Hadden.

Kitsilano harbours Canada's highest rate of well-off young singles, laying claim to the boast that as a neighbourhood, its citizens are better educated than the average. In 1992, a local newspaper looked at Statistics Canada research on Kitsilano and responded, "You've got a degree of intellectual arrogance here. Some of them don't even have a T.V. set."

WATERFRONT PANORAMA

From downtown, take the MacDonald #22 bus and get off on Cornwall Ave. at Cypress Street, the first stop after the Burrard Bridge. Across the street, note the Henry Hudson Elementary School (1551 Cypress) standing foursquare, its brick-hued walls and white-trimmed windows drawing attention. Henry Hudson school, aptly named for a seventeenth-century English navigator, is one of Vancouver's oldest educational institutions. Early in the last century, a favoured pastime for its pupils was catching frogs in the then-swampy surrounding area.

Head north down Cypress towards Kitsilano Beach and the mountains. You'll reach a towering 30.5-metre-high totem pole in Hadden Park, a replica of one given to Queen Elizabeth II in 1958 to commemorate B.C.'s Centennial. Carved by famed Kwakiutl carvers Mungo Martin, Henry Hunt and David Martin, the totem is a fitting reminder that

HASTINGS MILL STORE MUSEUM

Burrard Inlet

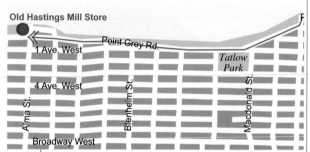

KITSILANO

this area was originally a Squamish Indian village called Sun'ahk. The name Kitsilano itself is derived from that of Chief Khahtsalanough of Sun'ahk and his descendants. The park is named after millionaire property developer and philanthropist Harvey Hadden, who bequeathed half a million dollars to Vancouver parks before his death in 1931.

Retrace your steps two blocks to Whyte Avenue and turn left. Walk to Chestnut Street, and cross over to the Vancouver Museum. Pause a moment to view its Haida hat-shaped roof and the huge crab-shaped fountain. Continue on past the H.R. MacMillan Planetarium and Vancouver Observatory. Around the corner you'll see the Vancouver City Archives, looking like an underground bunker. At the foot of the street is the coast guard station. Above, you just might see a bald eagle in the air or sitting in the tall trees.

TOTEM POLE IN HADDON PARK

Now turn left along the shore. The land here is fill, dumped during the construction of Pacific Centre mall in downtown Vancouver. If you're lucky, you'll see a coast guard ship heading in or out. Or you might see a tug with a scow loaded with sand and gravel, chugging into False Creek. Ahead is the Kits Beach area. The bathhouse rests on the spot where eccentric and belligerent pioneer Samuel "Gritty" Greer built Kitsilano Point's first dwelling.

Unfortunately, Gritty's homestead interfered with the provincial government's grant to the Canadian Pacific Railway of 6,000 acres between Burrard Inlet and the Fraser River. In 1884, the CPR began legal proceedings to prove that his claim was worthless. In 1890, the railway was given permission to evict him. When the sheriff arrived to do his duty, Gritty fired buckshot into both the sheriff and deputy. He was convicted of common assault; the CPR gained possession and extended their tracks to the foot of Balsam Street.

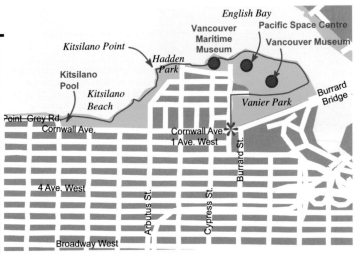

KITSILANO SHOWBOAT

Nearby is the 137 metre-long Kitsilano Pool, an outdoor summer classic. The Kitsilano Showboat, an institution since 1936, is located above the pool. The Showboat amphitheatre showcases amateur performers free of charge during the summer months, giving tiny dancers in tutus a chance to strut their stuff. Leaving Kits Park, it's a pleasant winding stroll to the foot of MacDonald Street. Cornwall Street becomes Point Grey Road at one of the curves.

OCEAN VIEW

Tatlow Park slumbers on your left at MacDonald Street, complete with rounded bridge and the remnants of what was once a salmon-spawning stream. Beside it is an apartment complex built on the site of Killarney, a palatial estate that was once the gathering place for the city's early elite. Mrs. Jessie Hall, its hostess, was the daughter of Gritty Greer. She was the first child of European descent born in the Cariboo and spent her youth netting smelt along nearby Kitsilano beach. She married James Z. Hall, who had his own string of firsts as Vancouver's first notary public and first volunteer soldier. They built Killarney in 1908, complete with a fireplace with inlaid shamrocks. Rest here awhile or in one of the parkettes overlooking the outer harbour where international ships lay at anchor, bows

TATLOW PARK

113

BRIDGE IN TATLOW PARK

to the wind.

This area was once home to summer cottages. People rowed across English Bay before the bridges provided access. Most of these cottages have been torn down, but one at the foot of Alma Road across from the Hastings Mill Store Museum is little changed. The Hastings Mill Store Museum was originally built around 1865 at the Hastings Mill sawmill on Burrard Inlet. It was moved here in 1930 to be maintained by the Native Daughters of British Columbia. Inside, a collection of First Nations artifacts and items from pioneer days are well worth a visit.

INLAND

Kits has an amazing variety of housing. You will notice only a few high-rises in the Kits Beach area. (A by-law prevents more.) If you're interested in real architecture, wander the neighbourhood streets and avenues. Streets run north and south, avenues run east and west. Many of the original stately homes survive, complete with their peaked roofs and front verandahs where pioneers sat on summer evenings. MacDonald, between Cornwall and 7th Avenue, is a good area for these.

Shopping? In the 1960s, 4th Avenue was infamous as a haven for youthful hippies. Today, the avenue is all about shopping, from Burrard to Balsam. A few blocks up, there's more shopping along Broadway to Alma. Browse the jewellery stores, ethnic importers, clothing boutiques, thrift stores, bookstores (including Kidsbooks, one of the city's best children's bookstores). When you need a break, choose from dozens of Kitsilano restaurants, cafes and coffee shops.

The foot of Alma Street is a fitting end to your Kitsilano stroll. Sink your tired bones into one of the benches facing the salt chuck overlooking the Jericho Yacht Club anchorage. Gaze towards West Vancouver. The white pinnacle of Point Atkinson lighthouse catches the eye, its light flashing rhythmically. Just off Point Atkinson is Manson's Deep, the traditional place for sea burials for Vancouver's mariners.

ALMA STREET SHOPPING

UBC

Chris Petty

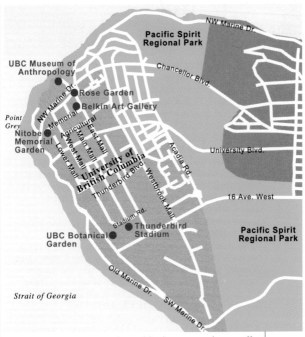

The University of British Columbia, in essence, is a small city. On any given day in the academic year, 40,000 or more students, faculty, staff and visitors arrive on campus to work, study and enjoy the ambiance of Canada's third-largest university. Perched out on the end of Point Grey, UBC boasts one of the prettiest campuses in the country. With its forest setting and spectacular views across the Strait of Georgia and Howe Sound, visitors can often be heard to mutter, "How the heck do they get any work done around here?"

Like a city, it has all the amenities: concert halls, restaurants (from greasy spoons to fine dining), theatres, sports facilities, bars and shops. As a university, it has the vitality that goes along with a population skewed towards the younger end of the scale.

UBC is a walker's paradise. Gardens, wide boulevards, outside eateries, stunning architecture, gorgeous viewpoints and quiet, off-the-beaten-path spots for rest and reflection draw visitors throughout the year.

HISTORY

UBC was originally an affiliate of McGill University, but it became a degree-granting institution on its own in 1915.

MAIN LIBRARY

Originally housed in old warehouses and church basements around 12th and Cambie, plans were developed to move UBC to Point Grey, but the First World War stopped construction. "The Great Trek" in 1922, in which students, faculty and alumni marched in demonstration from downtown to Point Grey, was the culmination of a noisy campaign to get the government of the day to resume building the campus. It worked. The Great Trek, and the sense of intrepid adventure shown by the marchers, has become a working metaphor at UBC, and is celebrated at every opportunity. The Point Grey campus opened in 1925.

Those first buildings remain some of the most remarkable on campus and are quite wonderful examples of neo-Gothic architecture. Main Library, just off Main Mall, features superb stone masonry, stained-glass windows and brass fittings. Look for the two little stone monkeys on the front wall. Each holds a book, one saying "Funda," and the other "Evolut," reflecting the Scopes Monkey Trial controversy that raged at the time. These, like most other buildings on campus, are open during daytime hours and are fun to wander through.

A TOUR OF UBC

The university offers free walking tours daily from May to August, starting at the Student Union Building, which include orientation to the main campus amenities and academic facilities. You can also pre-book group tours. But the best place to start your own tour is at the Rose Garden. Drive on campus via Chancellor Boulevard (an extension of 4th Avenue), until you get to the Rose Garden parkade. You can park here all day for a few dollars. Take the elevator up from the parkade and look north towards the mountains. You're on the Flagpole Plaza above the actual

ROSE GARDEN

Rose Garden. The view from the Rose Garden — Howe

Sound and the North Shore mountains fading off into the distance — stretches before you like a travel poster. The garden itself is spectacular and in bloom from early spring until well into fall.

As you're contemplating the great view, remember that the world-class UBC Museum of Anthropology is just across the road and to the left. The museum, along with the Nitobe Memorial Garden and UBC. Botanical Garden, should not be missed on a trip to UBC The museum has one of the top First Nations art collections in the world, and the Arthur Erickson–designed building is a wonder on its own.

MAIN MALL

Main Mall stretches the length of the university from the Flagpole Plaza to Thunderbird Stadium. Short side trips from the Mall bring you to virtually all the university's features. The Chan Centre is nearby (that big, round building that looks like a giant industrial widget), as is the Belkin Art Gallery, Frederic Wood Theatre and the UBC School of Music. The Chan Centre auditorium, which seats 1,400, is said to have the best acoustics in town. In addition to ticketed performances, free recitals by local and international performers, as well as practices by the UBC School of Music, are often held here. For tickets, free tours and free events, check with the box office. The Belkin Gallery just across the way shows travelling art exhibits as well as the university collection. It is open daily. Check, too, the program at the Fredric Wood Theatre, home to UBC's theatre program.

Continue along Main Mall to the huge library plaza and the Koerner Library. Brand new and state-of-the-art, it is called the "green jewel" of the campus by the architect. Locals think it's either beautiful or horrifying, but all agree the Koerner stands out. Take the elevator up to the top and look east to the Main Library and the Coast Mountains in the distance.

SITES OF INTEREST

UBC has many great buildings. One of the most interesting

C.K. CHOI BUILDING

is the C.K. Choi building west of the Koerner Library on West Mall. It's the most environmentally tuned building on campus and is built out of recycled materials from the Old Armouries (demolished a few years ago). It's also probably the only new building in Vancouver that has chemical toilets. South on West Mall is another UBC wonder, the First Nations Longhouse. Built to house First Nations programs, it also serves as a gathering place for First Nations students. Enter and note the huge sculpted log poles and other pieces of First Nations art. Outside, follow the cool sounds of a waterfall to one of the most relaxing (and little-known) hideaways on campus.

From the Longhouse walk east on Agricultural Road, past Main Library to East Mall and the Student Union Building. That building and the nearby Aquatic Centre (indoor and outdoor pools), War Memorial Gym and Student Recreation Centre, make up the most active non-academic area of the campus. UBC has the largest intramural sports program in Canada. A visit to any of the latter three buildings shows why. The facilities are first rate.

The UBC Bookstore, the largest university bookstore in Canada, is located across the bus loop from SUB. It has a huge selection of academic books, a well-stocked fiction and magazine section, as well as gifts, clothing, computers, art supplies and electronics.

FOREST SCIENCES BUILDING

Back on Main Mall heading south is the dome of the Astronomical Observatory, just beside the UBC Geophysical Observatory (which monitors earthquake activity) and the Geological Museum. All these facilities are open to the public.

Farther along Main Mall you might wonder what's up with the ten-ton, four-sided chunk of concrete with large "E"s (for Engineering) carved into each side, sitting in the middle of the road. Its colour will depend upon which arts faculty has vandalized it most recently. Unless it's red, of course, which means the engineers have repainted it. Every fall, the Engineers' undergrad society holds a day-long toga party on campus, and every fall some arts department shows its contempt by painting the "E." All in good fun, of course.

Perhaps the most interesting building at UBC appears just before Main Mall descends into parking lots and athletic fields. The lobby and study areas of the Forest Sciences building are nothing short of a post-modern forest glen. Huge, first-growth (recycled) beams spread up to the roof three storeys above.

NORTH SHORE

ROCHELLE VAN HALM

AMBLESIDE PARK

A century ago, city dwellers escaped to the mountains of the North Shore for holidays. Outdoor recreation is still the reason North and West Vancouver are so popular, but now the North Shore is a residential area as well. Ski in the morning, play tennis or sail in the afternoon, head home to discover black bears in the backyard and still catch a live show at night. North Shore residents lament travel over the Lions Gate Bridge but rush-hour delays and community debates over improving the crossing don't deter many from living here. You can tour the North Shore in a day by car or bus but you'll want to return to explore.

WEST VANCOUVER

After crossing the Lions Gate Bridge, the first exit takes you into West Vancouver, one of Canada's richest communities, evidenced by the visible presence of luxury import cars on the roads. Like its residents, the municipality takes pride in its appearance. Every year, it plants 30,000 spring flowering bulbs, tends 180 hanging flower baskets and creates major floral displays. Follow Marine Drive between the two sides of Park Royal Shopping Centre, home for fashion mavens. Next comes Ambleside Park, boasting beaches, a playground, skateboard park, duck pond, Par 3 golf course and an off-leash dog park. The West Vancouver Sea Walk begins along the shoreline, one of the community's best-used facilities. Dogs are relegated to their own path on the other side of the fence, between 18th and 24th streets. Seals bob in the distance, salmon leap, summer cruise ships pass nightly and savage winter storms toss logs high onto the shore. The steam-driven Royal Hudson runs parallel to the Sea Walk on its scenic rail trip to Squamish and back.

At the foot of 14th Street, the fishing pier at Ambleside

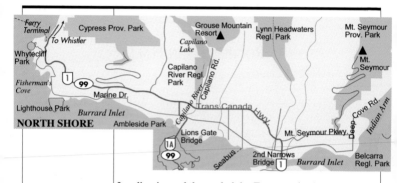

North Shore

FERRY BUILDING GALLERY

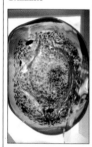

Landing is used day and night. Ferry service began here in 1909 and ended in 1947. The terminal, built in 1913, was renovated into the well-visited Ferry Building Gallery for community art exhibits. History lives at the West Vancouver Museum and Archives, housed in an old ballast-stone house built in 1940 by Gertrude Lawson, daughter of John Lawson, known as the father of West Vancouver.

Back to Marine Drive, where Ambleside is fashion central, including a hairstylist just for kids. West Vancouver's Memorial Library has the highest per capita circulation of any library in Canada. Across Marine Drive is Memorial Park, where large rhododendrons bloom each spring. Follow the path over the bridge to the playground by the stream, where the historic Village Walk begins.

In the 2,400-block of Marine Drive, the village of Dundarave blooms with hanging baskets and a summer flower boulevard. The shops include an old-style hardware store full of whatever you might need. Delany's is the latest coffee bar in town, and Capers is the choice for an organic lunch. In late summer, the annual country-and-western hoedown fills the street with square dancing.

Another pier at the foot of 25th Street marks the end of the Sea Walk, with new playgrounds, an interesting sculpture of a girl on a turtle, a sandy beach for swimming and excellent hamburgers from the concession stand. The Beach House at Dundarave Pier offers more upscale dining in a building from 1912. The restaurant has a patio so that diners can enjoy stunning sunsets with their meals. Marine

AMBLESIDE PARK

Drive meanders scenically westward, past grand estates with multimillion-dollar cliffhanging homes and a few original seaside cottages from the 1920s and '30s. In the 3,700-block of Marine Drive, the once treacherous Suicide Bend allows room to pull over for a photo of the sea. Explore local beaches with their own natural attractions at West Bay (public access off Radcliffe Avenue), Sandy Cove (at Rose Crescent) and Stearman (off Ross Crescent).

SEYMOUR MOUNTAIN LOOKOUT (TOP); MEMORIAL PARK (BELOW); SEA WALK (BOTTOM)

Environment Canada's Pacific Research fisheries station (4,200-block Marine Drive) is on the site of the Great Northern Cannery, built in 1891 and operated until 1967. Outside the Cypress Park Market (4,360 Marine Drive) historic photos show the neighbourhood of years ago. Watch for Piccadilly Road South, and take a left turn into lower Caulfeild, the English-style village designed by Francis Caulfeild in the 1920s. The neighbourhood celebrates on the village green in front of St. Francis-in-the-Wood Anglican Church, a favourite for weddings.

Returning to Marine Drive turn left at Eagle Harbour Road to visit a small beach and marina nestled in the harbour, where Eagle Island

ST.-FRANCIS-IN-THE-WOOD ANGLICAN CHURCH	residents use a cable ferry to haul themselves and their groceries home, a stone's throw from the mainland.

From Marine Drive, turn left onto Cranley Drive for Seaview Walk. The path leads from Nelson Creek to the old rail bed, overlooking hundreds of boats moored in Fisherman's Cove and leading to the overflow parking lot of the Gleneagles Golf Course. The municipally owned 18-hole course and clubhouse provide ocean views from the greens and a great spot for coffee. Retrace your steps and continue west on Marine Drive, snaking up the rocky hillside. |

NORTH VANCOUVER

Follow the signs to Highway 1 East/Highway 99 South, known locally as the Upper Levels Highway, for a quick trip east with views of English Bay, Burrard Inlet and Vancouver. When the skies are clear, you can see as far as Vancouver Island and Mount Baker. Take Exit 22 and follow Mount Seymour Parkway to the Parkgate Village Shopping Centre, then turn left at Mount Seymour Road. Halfway up Seymour Mountain, you'll find a lookout point from which to view Simon Fraser University, Indian Arm and the wilderness beyond. Hiking trails begin farther up where the road ends in the top parking lot.

VIEW FROM DEEP COVE CULTURAL CENTRE

Returning downhill, turn left at Mount Seymour Parkway and watch for the close-up view of Indian Arm, nestled in mountains shrouded in mist. Turn left onto Deep Cove Road for the short drive into the forested cove. At the Deep Cove Cultural Centre residents are invited to participate on stage or backstage.

The Seymour Art Gallery features local artists, and the Shaw Theatre, the Deep Cove Heritage Association and Arts in the Cove provide opportunities for artists of all ages and aspirations. From Deep Cove Lookout at the foot of Gallant Avenue, see weekenders stocking up for a cruise up Indian Arm. Join them on a rental paddle from Deep Cove Canoe and Kayak Centre and view waterfront homes on Panorama Drive.

LONSDALE QUAY MARKET

A public footpath follows the shore to Panorama Park where live music fills summer evenings. The Baden Powell hiking trail begins just north of the park. This forty-eight-kilometre trail links Deep Cove to Horseshoe Bay across the North Shore mountains.

LYNN CANYON SUSPENSION BRIDGE

North Vancouver is well equipped for local culture. Live theatre is offered at Presentation House. Upstairs, the Presentation House Gallery is renowned for its photography exhibitions. North Vancouver Museum and Archives focuses on local history of logging, shipbuilding and early community development and features a walking tour of historic houses. Just down the hill is Lonsdale Quay Market where you can buy live crabs, salmon, fresh pasta, vegetables, flowers and specialties from Everything Garlic and Out of Africa Global Culture. Children can blow off steam in the upstairs ballroom. The Lonsdale Quay Hotel overlooks the Cates tugboat operation. The Seven Seas Floating Seafood Restaurant is housed in North Vancouver Ferry No. 5, the last ferry to make the once-popular run to Vancouver in 1958. Nowadays the SeaBus, a modern commuter ferry, links North Vancouver with downtown Vancouver from its Lonsdale Quay terminal.

OUTDOOR FUN

Whytecliff Park offers rocky views to Bowen Island and the passing ferries, picnic sites and a climb up Whyte Islet, accessible at low tide. The stoney beach is popular for divers as marine life is protected in the underwater reserve.

Porteau Cove (twenty-five kilometres north of Horseshoe Bay off Highway 99) is one of the few

POINT ATKINSON LIGHTHOUSE

places you can camp alongside Howe Sound. An artificial reef of shipwrecks at the cove provides interest for divers. Walking trails lead through the picnic area to a small hill with a lookout. Skiing is no more than thirty minutes away from downtown Vancouver at three different mountains. From Highway 1, take Exit 8 and follow Cypress Bowl Road to Cypress Provincial Park for downhill and cross-country skiing, snowboarding and snowshoeing day and night. The seventy-year-old rustic Hollyburn Lodge serves homemade chili, bakes its own bread and during ski season, Saturday night bluegrass or folk music packs the house. Whatever the season, the Highview Lookout provides a tremendous view of the city of Vancouver, the Fraser Valley, Richmond, the Strait of Georgia and the Gulf Islands beyond. Summer hiking on Cypress Mountain ranges from Yew Lake Trail, an easy interpretive loop that is wheelchair and stroller accessible, to the rugged thirty-kilometre Howe Sound Crest Trail.

Grouse Mountain offers excellent downhill skiing and snowboarding on twenty-two runs. Sleigh rides through alpine meadows, outdoor skating, snowshoeing and the latest, showshoe running, are also offered. Hiking in the summer includes the Grouse Grind, a steep climb up beneath the Skyride. At the top, Grouse offers guided walking tours and paragliding for the ultimate view.

Mount Seymour provides natural terrain that's ideal for learning to ski or snowboard. There's snowshoe trails and snow tubing as well.

In North Vancouver, Lynn Canyon Park is a wilderness not far from civilization. The Suspension Bridge, less well known than its well-promoted cousin the Capilano Suspension Bridge, is just as spectacular in a more natural setting. The Ecology Centre reveals how civilization affects the natural environment. There's also good fun for kids with puppets and animal displays.

Lighthouse Park (off Beacon Lane at Marine Drive, West Vancouver) offers trails through the old-growth forest of giant Douglas firs, pines, hemlocks and arbutus trees that look as if they're peeling rust red bark. Stroll to Point Atkinson lighthouse, built in 1912 and still operating. When fog rolls in, the foghorn is very loud. The rocks are a great vantage point for English Bay freighters, fish and sailboats.

INSIDE THE ECOLOGY CENTRE

VICTORIA

Hotels:
1. Admiral Motel
2. Bedford Regency Hotel
3. Best Western Carleton Plaza
4. Best Western Inner Harbour
5. Chateau Victoria Hotel
6. Clarion Hotel Grand Pacific
7. Coast Victoria Harbourside Hotel and Marina
8. Days Inn on the Harbour
9. Empress Hotel
10. Executive House Hotel
11. Green Gables Inn.
12. Harbour Towers Hotel
13. Laurel Point Inn
14. Magnolia Hotel
15. Ocean Pointe Resort Hotel and Spa
16. Queen Victoria Inn
17. Ramada Huntingdon Manor Inn
18. Strathcona Hotel
19. Swans Hotel
20. Travellers Inn Downtown
21. Victoria Plaza Hotel
22. Victoria Regent Hotel

Restaurants
1. Barb's Place
2. Blue Crab Bar and Grill
3. Bond Bond's
4. Café Brio
5. Canoe Club
6. Cassis Bistro
7. Empress Room
8. Foster's Eatery
9. Herald St. Café
10. Hugo's Brewpub Lounge
11. J & J Wonton Noodle House
12. Paradiso di Stelle
13. Re-bar
14. Restaurant Matisse
15. Suze Restaurant and Lounge
16. Swans
17. Victorian Restaurant
18. Zambri's

EXPLORING VICTORIA

D. C. REID

More British than the British, Victoria lines its streets with 3,000 hanging baskets every summer. Even in February, residents count the flowers for the benefit of snowbound Canada, recording well over 1 billion blooms some balmy winters.

Compact and pretty, Victoria lies at the southern end of Vancouver Island. Vehicle traffic arrives from the Swartz Bay ferry terminal north of town as well as the Inner Harbour terminal, with scheduled arrivals from Seattle and Port Angeles. Air travellers land at Victoria International Airport and take the scenic Pat Bay Highway by taxi or shuttle bus.

LOTS TO SEE AND DO

Once settled into your downtown hotel, hitch a ride in a human-powered Kabuki cab, or lounge back in a horse-drawn carriage. Double-decker English buses whisk patrons to the world-famous Butchart Gardens. Historical interest trips leave from the Inner Harbour bound for Beacon Hill Park and surrounding neighbourhoods. Or, for something completely different, head to the Oak Bay Marina, where you can feed wild seals by the docks.

SMALL INNER HARBOUR FERRIES

The centrepiece of this Tudor and granite city lies at the corner of Belleville and Government streets. The ivy-covered Empress Hotel opens onto the causeway, Carillon Tower and Royal British Columbia Museum. Famed for its exhibits of natural history, aboriginal lore and gold-rush paraphernalia, the museum ranks high with visitors. Completing the corner are the grey granite Parliament Buildings with green-weathered copper domes.

A few blocks away, Fort Street houses antique shops and book dealers. Bastion Square marks the site of the original Fort Victoria, and the McPherson Playhouse offers music and plays throughout the year. One block farther, Victoria's Chinatown once rivalled San Francisco for size.

You can get around Victoria on BC Transit's 200 buses, which serve thirty-nine Greater Victoria routes seven days a week. The city runs a system of small ferries in the Inner Harbour, where you can take a pleasant walk along the Songhees boardwalk and by the Dungeness crab displayed at Fisherman's Wharf. For adventure, sail out to view the killer whales in Juan de Fuca Strait.

If you don't know where to begin, visit the Tourism Victoria office on Wharf Street. Alternatively, there are several sightseeing companies in the city to take you on guided bus, carriage or walking tours.

A BRIEF HISTORY

D. C. REID

THE EMPRESS HOTEL

In 1843, James Douglas arrived aboard his ship the *Beaver* to become chief factor for the Hudson's Bay Company. His new Fort Victoria owed its origin to American territorial ambitions. At the time, Great Britain and the United States disputed control of the Pacific Northwest. Shrewdly judging that the forty-ninth parallel ultimately would become the border between the two nations, the Hudson's Bay Company sent Douglas from its Columbia River depot to set up operations on Vancouver Island's southernmost tip, thereby solidifying trade in beaver and sea otter pelts.

Douglas wrote, "The place itself appears a perfect Eden in the midst of the dreary wilderness." Through the Hudson's Bay Company, he leased the entire area of Vancouver Island for a mere seven shillings a year. This move forestalled American expansionism.

AMOR DE COSMOS

THE GOLD RUSH

The 1858 Fraser River gold rush transformed Victoria from a sleepy village of 500 inhabitants to a bustling, brawling settlement of 25,000 gold seekers. Seeking to keep Victoria ahead of Vancouver in development, Douglas declared the town a free port and taxed all traffic in goods.

When British Columbia joined Canada in 1871, Confederation Day marked a glorious binge in taverns and streets with speeches and naval guns saluting. In the same year the quintessential B.C. artist, Emily Carr, was born. At the time, her stark, savage style earned nothing but hostility.

Victoria's growing prosperity proved short-lived. The gold rush crash resulted in plummeting land values and the population shrank to 1,500 souls. Amor de Cosmos, the West's first radical newspaper baron, railed against the

government, criticizing the law-and-order-prone James Douglas as a species of cockroach. When Arthur Kennedy succeeded Douglas as governor, de Cosmos won election to the House of Assembly.

ECONOMIC CHANGE

Matching the theatricality of its new Legislature, Victoria's free port status conferred control over all B.C. trade in mining, lumbering, fishing, land sales, brewing and shipbuilding. By 1900, Victoria's population had tripled to 20,000 and business boomed. Francis Mawson Rattenbury, soon to become the province's most famous architect, designed the Provincial Legislature (commonly, but erroneously, called the Parliament Buildings) in 1898 and The Empress Hotel soon after.

But again the good times were short-lived. A fire during the First World War devastated the city core. The collapse of the seal hunt resulted in financial ruin for 80 percent of Victorians. Salmon canneries and shipbuilding factories were moved to Vancouver. The Canadian government outlawed the opium trade. Victoria's economics changed from business and finance to government and tourism.

TOURISM

Fortunately Victoria's lingering financial demise received a restorative tonic: prohibition was declared in the United States. In the 1930s, whiskey from downtown factories moved through Smugglers Cove at night and sped to nearby American ports.

After the Second World War, retirees discovered Victoria, bringing with them over $50,000,000 per year. Construction of new Legislature wings, banks, law courts, power authorities, retail space and a refurbished City Hall altered the skyline for good. Along with the arrival of old money came the stability of the government payroll and the expanding tourist trade.

Capitalizing on Victoria's tourist potential, The Royal British Columbia Museum was completed in 1970 along with the Carillon Tower, producing an atmosphere of quiet opulence. Since 1971, the sixty-two-bell tower, largest of its type in Canada, has tolled the arrival of visitors every fifteen minutes during its summer and fall season and visit they do: *Travel & Leisure* magazine ranks Victoria second on the continent and ninth in the world as a holiday destination.

ROYAL BC MUSEUM AND FIRST PEOPLES MASK

TOP ATTRACTIONS

LESLEY KENNY

THE PARLIAMENT BUILDINGS AT NIGHT

Here are the top things to see and do in Victoria.

THE PARLIAMENT BUILDINGS

The name of this key Victoria landmark is a misnomer. The only Canadian House of Parliament is in Ottawa. In Victoria, the Parliament Buildings (named after a bill was passed in the 1890s) actually house the Provincial Legislature, where the members of the legislative assembly sit. Tours run every day in the summer and when the house is in session, you can sit in the galleries and watch the ad-libbed performances. The Parliament Buildings are on Belleville Street, adjacent to The Empress Hotel, overlooking the Inner Harbour.

In 1856, Governor James Douglas, the first governor of the colony of Vancouver Island, issued a proclamation to elect a House of Assembly. Seven members were elected from four districts. Governor Douglas didn't believe that the common folk had much to say about how they were governed so he added a catch: all voters had to own at least twenty acres of land. This meant that in the first so-called democratic election, forty people were allowed to vote for the seven representatives. All of the elected reps had ties to the Hudson's Bay Company. Three just happened to be enemies of Governor James Douglas.

GOVERNOR JAMES DOUGLAS

The first legislative assembly had little power. The only source of money it had was through the sale of liquor licenses. The Hudson's Bay Company was the legislative assembly's rival for authority, with vast amounts of money at its disposal from trading profits and land sales. In the beginning, the assembly was basically a place for public criticism of the Douglas administration. The assembly didn't have money for much-needed roads, nor did it have the authority to levy taxes or give grants. Meanwhile, the downtown core of Victoria was expanding, largely because of the gold rush, which was attracting immigrants from all over the world.

The first government buildings were built by a German immigrant, Herman Otto Tiedmann. These were built between 1859 and 1864 and called the Bird Cages for their design. The Bird Cages replaced the old colonial offices inside Fort Victoria. After Confederation with Canada, in 1871, the first parliament of British Columbia met in the Bird Cages. Most of these structures were demolished in 1898 to make way for the stone and marble buildings you see today.

The Parliament Buildings were designed by Francis Mawson Rattenbury, a twenty-five-year-old architect from Leeds, England. The buildings were under construction from 1893 until their completion in 1898, all for less than $1 million. The stones were cut locally. The slate for the roofs was brought in from Jervis Inlet, off Vancouver Island. Inside the four-level buildings, the marble in the assembly hall was brought in from Italy, while the marble in the rotunda was imported from Tennessee.

The diamond jubilee celebration of Queen Victoria was scheduled before the completion of the Parliament Buildings. To show its appreciation, the government decided to honour the anniversary by hooking up thousands of tiny lights to the outside of the buildings. The buildings were like this for special occasions until 1956. From then onward, the lights have been turned on every day at dusk and turned off at midnight. There are more than 3,300 bulbs outlining the buildings, giving them a faintly Disney-esque look.

But there's more behind this manicured façade than meets the eye. Soon after he designed the Parliament Buildings, Francis Rattenbury became the Canadian Pacific Railway's Western architect. He designed The Empress Hotel, Victoria Crystal Gardens (on Douglas Street, behind The Empress Hotel) and numerous banks and mansions in Victoria and Vancouver. His affair with Alma Pakenham, thirty years younger than himself, resulted in his being snubbed by polite Victoria society. He left his wife and moved to England with Alma. This move proved fatal.

THE PARLIAMENT BUILDINGS

THE INNER HARBOUR
(ABOVE AND BELOW)

After their move, the new Mrs. Rattenbury took a new lover, George Stoner, the family's eighteen-year-old chauffeur. In 1935, Stoner was charged with the bludgeoning murder of the famous architect. He was sentenced to death, though after public outcry he was given life in jail. Alma, thinking that her lover was going to be executed and realizing that her life in society was over, committed suicide by stabbing herself and then falling into a river where she drowned.

THE INNER HARBOUR AND FISHERMAN'S WHARF

Directly in front of The Empress Hotel and the Parliament Buildings, is Victoria's Inner Harbour. Walk down the steps either from Government or Belleville streets, and you'll find an eclectic group of buskers and artisans offering their talents and wares. If you've spent the day shopping, you could sit on one of the benches or stone steps and watch the boats come into dock or small aircraft taxi along the water for a mid-harbour launch. If you sit by the window at Milestone's restaurant on Wharf Street, you can enjoy a harbour view.

You're welcome to walk around the dock and look at the privately owned boats. On occasion you will see a meticulously restored sailboat or a reproduction of a historic explorer's ship. If the urge to get on the water overtakes you, there's always the ten-minute taxi-boat ride

over to the West Bay Marina in Esquimalt. From there you could walk back along a boardwalk beside the ocean. You'll also pass by Spinnakers, one of Victoria's fine micro-breweries and pub, with patio seating looking out at the Inner Harbour.

All around the Inner Harbour, on Government and Belleville streets, horse-carriage rides

are available, as well as double-decker bus tours. The carriages and buses leave frequently for guided tours of the city. On the other side of the Inner Harbour is Fisherman's Wharf, where the commercial fishing boats dock. From both harbours, you can see the *Princess Marguerite* ferry on its way to and from Seattle (passengers and cars), or the speedier hovercraft, also destined for Seattle. No matter which way you face, the Inner Harbour is within five minutes' walking distance from some of the major tourist attractions as well as the boutique shops along Government Street.

HORSE-CARRIAGE DOWNTOWN

THE EMPRESS HOTEL

Probably one of the most photographed Victoria landmarks, The Empress Hotel grandly overlooks the Inner Harbour, adjacent to the Royal British Columbia Museum and the Parliament Buildings. The Empress is one of a series of château-style luxury hotels in major cities across Canada. Designed by Francis Rattenbury (architect of the Parliament Buildings), it was built in 1908 for 1 million dollars. The Empress was restored to the tune of $45 million in the late 1980s when it was closed for six months and completely gutted on the inside. The grand-style hotel, its towering brick walls semi-covered in ivy, has 460 rooms and thirty-three suites on seven floors, with an eighth floor being added soon. There are eighty different room configurations, some with vaulted ceilings, some with interesting nooks and all with down-filled duvet covers. In 1999, *Travel & Leisure* magazine rated The Empress Hotel number three in North America, and number thirty-five in the world.

THE CRYSTAL BALLROOM

There's no shortage of luxury extras here. The Crystal Ballroom shows off its eighteen crystal chandeliers and mirrored ceiling. The two restaurants offer regional cuisine and the Bengal Lounge (one of two lounges) is known for its curry buffet. There are sauna rooms, a swimming pool and a whirlpool, as well as a modern fully equipped health club, complete with massage therapy. The hotel expects to add a $5.5-million health spa in the near future.

ON GOVERNMENT STREET

On a typical summer day, The Empress Hotel registers 1,200 visitors. The Queen of England does not stay here, but she does come for tea when she's in town. In fact, afternoon tea at The Empress is open to everyone. There are four seatings a day in the summer. For $42, you can have tea and sandwiches with 400 other diners in the elegant main lobby.

Some of the employees of The Empress Hotel have worked there for more than thirty-five years, some for almost fifty years. The strangest thing that appeared in the lost and found, reported one, was jewellery worth a quarter of a million dollars. It eventually found its way back to an amazed owner.

Double-decker bus tours leave frequently in front of the hotel on Government Street. Boutique shops in the downtown core are just a block away. The concierges at the front desk are well versed in tours and travel plans.

CHINATOWN

GATE OF HARMONIOUS INTEREST

The two blocks that make up Victoria's Chinatown may seem small, but once you pass through the arched Gates of Harmonious Interest, at Fisgard and Government streets, you could easily spend an entire afternoon browsing, shopping and eating. At one time, this "forbidden city" covered several city blocks and bustled with more than 100

businesses, three schools, a hospital, two churches, five temples and two theatres. It is Canada's oldest Chinatown. Until the late 1800s, it was the largest Chinese settlement north of San Francisco.

The elaborate red-and-gold-tiled archway was the first permanent Chinese arch in Canada. In 1981, it was dedicated to symbolize the spirit of cooperation between the two cultures. Two hand-carved stone lions stand guard over the entrance, a gift from Victoria's twin city, Suzhou, China.

Modern Chinatown may be smaller than it was at the turn of the century, but the variety of food and shopping still holds its appeal. The merchants are out early each morning, setting up their outdoor vegetable markets. That hard-to-explain craving you have for wonton soup can be satisfied at almost any hour of the day. Walk along this street carefully so you don't miss Fan Tan Alley. This narrow passage — some say the narrowest street in Canada — is home to several artist studios and boutiques. Its more exotic history is that this was home to opium dens at the end of the nineteenth century.

FAN TAN ALLEY

An enjoyable way to spend a Sunday morning is at dim sum. This traditional Chinese brunch feast is served to you one delicious course at a time. Polish this down with a pot of Chinese tea and you're ready for your walk back downtown.

SHRINE AT THE ART GALLERY OF GREATER VICTORIA

THE ART GALLERY OF GREATER VICTORIA

The only Shinto shrine outside Japan sits in the Asian Garden of the Art Gallery of Greater Victoria. If you walk up Fort Street from downtown for one and a half kilometres, you'll come to Moss Street. The art gallery is tucked in just around the corner. Although some of the art gallery is housed in a historic mansion built in 1889, from the outside the main building looks more like a high school. The gallery's main base is Gyppeswick mansion, built by the Spencer family and donated in 1951. Although the gallery has grown in size, the mansion is a significant part of the tour, from the tile painting of the Arthurian legend, Knights of the Round Table, to the large dollhouse in the wooden hallway. The dollhouse is complete with tiny perfect furnishings. This house is perfect in more ways than one: it's under glass, so there are no dusting chores for its tiny occupants.

EXTERIOR AND INTERIOR OF THE ART GALLERY OF GREATER VICTORIA

Step outside the mansion into the Asian garden. This is a peaceful spot, more subtle than colourful. A wooden Shinto shrine lends a reflective quality. The shrine was found abandoned in Japan and was rescued in 1987 and brought to the gallery.

There are six gallery spaces devoted to the works of B.C. artist Emily Carr. Her passionate nature paintings are compared to those of Georgia O'Keeffe and Vincent van Gogh. Some seniors in Victoria remember that Emily Carr herself was a visitor of the Spencer family, in the very mansion that is now the home of much of her original paintings. Also in these galleries are the works of contemporary Canadian artists, North American and European historical artists and traditional and contemporary Asian artists. There are more than thirty-five exhibits per year. Inside, the permanent collection of more than 15,000 pieces (the largest in B.C.) includes some of the finest examples of Japanese art in Canada. Most of these items are not on display every day, but one of the permanent exhibitions is a fourteenth-century Buddha head. The City of Victoria's Ming dynasty bell was moved here from Beacon Hill Park in 1990, perhaps because local kids of all ages figured out that if you curled your body up just right, and placed your hands and feet just so, you could hide inside the dangling bell.

Once a year, in the summer, the art gallery turns itself inside out for The Moss Street Paint-In. From the art gallery on Moss Street, all the way down to the beach at Dallas Road, artists line the sidewalks with their palettes and easels and thousands of people turn out to watch them at work. The gallery also offers several community programs on a regular basis including drop-in discussion groups twice a month. Tours run every day and there are lecture series throughout the year as well as art appreciation programs for children and a popular children's festival in September.

The gallery offers selected paintings for rent, private or business use, and some of these paintings are for sale. There's also a gift shop. From the art gallery you are only a short walk away from Craigdarroch Castle or the gardens at

MING DYNASTY BELL

Government House (open to the public year round).

THE ROYAL BRITISH COLUMBIA MUSEUM

Between The Empress Hotel and the Parliament
Buildings, one of the most renowned museums in
North America is open 363 days a year. The Royal
British Columbia Museum, founded in 1886, sits on
the corner of Belleville and Government streets.
More than 100 full-time staff and 335 volunteers
run the dozens of exhibits and three large galleries.
In the 26,000-square-foot-building, more than 10 million
items document the human and natural history of British
Columbia (though only a fraction of these are on display at
any one time).

The Royal B.C. Museum is designed to allow you to
experience British Columbia history through your senses.
Of course, you can read the printed materials, or take the
time to study all the accompanying display legends and
documentation, but even if you just strolled through each
room and hall, looking and listening, you would pick it up
by osmosis. Perhaps a good gauge of the museum's success
and popularity is the evidence at the entrance gate:
thousands of Victoria locals return each year, alone, with
guests or with their kids, to see the latest exhibit or spend
an afternoon examining the items on all three floors.

Although each of the exhibits are in themselves worth
seeing, it is the three galleries that have drawn the
acclamation of curators and visitors from all over the
world.

In the Gallery of Natural History, lifelike dioramas of

**LIVING LAND,
LIVING SEA EXHIBIT**

forest and beach scenes
complete with taxidermied
animals and audiotaped
sounds of the outdoors are
strangely real. The trees, rocks
and sand look inviting, except
for the large grizzly hunting
for fish and the stuffed
mountain cat looking hungry
himself. The history of
settlement and development
are documented with artifacts,
pictures and scenes behind
glass which, using a series of
timed spotlights, literally
illuminate the progress and
struggle over the centuries.
Many of the halls, all softly
lit, pipe in a running dialogue
discussing the items behind
glass. But beware the child
who keeps pressing the
"repeat" button.

The First Peoples Gallery,
founded in 1970 with the
support of the local First
Nations community,
documents their triumphs and

TOTEM GALLERY, FIRST PEOPLES EXHIBIT

tragedies. Enlarged reproductions of early photographs, along with artifacts, video and audio, lead you through aboriginal history. Spend a contemplative moment in the Big House, still used for ceremonial purposes on occasion. In fact, the Big House is owned by the local First Nations community. That gives it the unusual distinction of being the only space in the museum that isn't government property. At the side of the museum building in Thunderbird Park is a longhouse, also used for ceremonial purposes.

In the Modern History Gallery you can walk along a nineteenth-century cobble-stoned road and look in the windows of old-time businesses: the saloon, the Chinese herbalist, the dressmaker. There's a 1913 Model T car named Elizabeth in the garage. You can see a miniature mill at work in the logging section as you eventually work your way to the 20th Century Hall. In this exhibit, a living room scene has been replicated for each decade of the twentieth century, incorporating technological and design developments. Compare the history of the telephone, from a big wooden box on the wall to a cordless phone.

The Open Ocean exhibit offers a thirty-minute simulation of a submarine voyage to the depths of the ocean. This is not for the claustrophobic or the faint of heart. During this "trip" you are taken into the depths in a submarine with a very large picture window. Actually, several windows. As you pass by each one, you watch the underwater film footage of an actual 1930s deep-sea dive complete with all manner of West Coast marine species floating before you.

From the tiny to the gigantic, the museum has something interesting or weird for everyone. For the bug collector, there are insect larvae and strange little critters that once roamed the territory where mega-stores now

HMS *DISCOVERY*

stand. Contrast with the giant woolly mammoth, the

THE MARITIME
MUSEUM OF BRITISH
COLUMBIA (ABOVE
AND BELOW)

museum's unofficial symbol and mascot, but don't embarrass yourself by asking who shot him. The woolly mammoth died in B.C. some 9,000 years ago.

Quite fascinating is the tiny, intricately decorated Chinese slipper-shoe, once worn by a woman who had her feet bound. You can't help but wonder if she embroidered it herself. And of course history includes things that some of us actually remember, such as John Lennon's 1965 psychedelic Rolls Royce. It's owned by the museum though it's often travelling (on loan for a mere $20,000).

In 1998, National Geographic opened an IMAX theatre in the museum. This is a movie theatre with a six-storey screen and steeply pitched seats for 400. All movies are about countries or wildlife and they run several times a day. You can buy a combined pass for the museum and the IMAX theatre.

Museum staff suggest you take three or four hours to experience all the galleries and exhibits available. After your trek through history, relax in the cafe next door to the three gift shops.

THE MARITIME MUSEUM OF BRITISH COLUMBIA

The Maritime Museum of British Columbia is in the middle of downtown Victoria, between Government and Wharf streets in Bastion Square. Located in Victoria's original 1889 provincial courthouse, the museum is

home to a collection of more than 5,000 artifacts that tell the story of B.C.'s oceangoing history. Through its many precision-built models and antique nautical equipment, the galleries at this museum pay tribute to the Royal Canadian Navy from its early days. As well, they document the era of the elegant *Empress* steamships, vessels of the same vintage as the *Titanic*. The economy-class version is also represented in the paddle wheelers that once steamed

**FIRST FLOOR
GALLERIES AT THE
MARITIME MUSEUM**

through the province's inland waterways.

Although most items are under glass, there are a few things you are actually encouraged to touch and operate. There's an 1864 torpedo and some other nasty hardware you can play with (under supervision, of course). The old cage lift elevator, still there since the building was the provincial courthouse, was installed for one of the rather portly judges. It seems that there was some doubt as to whether he could continue to walk up the three flights of stairs to his courtroom without risking a heart attack. Today, you can climb into the elevator and get a ride to the third floor where you can watch a movie of a trip around Cape Horn, from the perspective of a four-masted sailing vessel in a storm. When you return to either the second or first floor, depending on the skill of the lift operator, you may have to take a small step up, or down, into the room.

The courthouse on the third floor is occasionally used for hearing cases today when the new court on Broughton Street gets jammed. But be warned: ghosts of cases past may be haunting these rooms. The original gallows were just a short distance from the courthouse and the executed were buried in paupers' graves in the courtyard. The remains of nine such unlucky citizens have been found during upgrading, but it is believed that there are still three graves somewhere under what is now the museum.

Museum staff have invented a treasure hunt for kids. There are written clues scattered throughout the building and the winners are rewarded with a treat. This is nice for kids, and great for parents.

If you'd like to take home a book for your nautical library, the museum's bookstore offers a comprehensive selection of maritime books on Vancouver Island, as well as the other items you find in most museum gift shops. After your trip through the museum, you can walk across the square for a pint to talk about your own seafaring days and then wander down towards the water where you may just look at the Inner Harbour in a new light. The museum is open seven days a week with extended daytime hours in the summer.

EMILY CARR HOUSE

EMILY CARR HOUSE

A few short blocks behind the Parliament Buildings, at 207 Government Street, you'll find Emily Carr House, built in 1864. Emily Carr, Canada's first independent artist and writer, was born here in 1871, just a few months after British Columbia became the newest province in Canada. At the time, the house was located in a rural setting. The architecture of the artist's family home is described as both San Francisco Victorian

and English Gingerbread. You can tour the restored rooms and see some of Carr's own pottery and sculpture as well as some of the family's original possessions.

HELMCKEN HOUSE

Later in life, Emily Carr was an ingenious housekeeper. She rigged up a rope-and-pulley system and tied it to her sitting room chairs. When she didn't want visitors, she'd haul the chairs to the ceiling. Imagine as well her household menagerie, including her beloved pet monkey, Woo, and her griffon dogs.

In contrast to the Victorian artifacts, a modern convenience has been added. A computer terminal is available in the house for guests to look up information about the life and work of Emily Carr. One of the other rooms is called The People's Gallery and is used to present the works of Canadian artists. These changing exhibits can be viewed from May to September. Parking in this area is cramped at best, so the ten-minute walk from downtown is your best bet.

HELMCKEN HOUSE

Helmcken House is the oldest house in British Columbia on its original site. It was built in 1852 for Dr. John Sebastian Helmcken, after he married the daughter of Governor Sir James Douglas. Dr. Helmcken was a surgeon with the Hudson's Bay Company who went on to become a statesman and helped negotiate B.C.'s entry into Canada.

Originally, Helmcken House was a three-room log house. As the family grew, so did the house. Today there are guided tours through the restored rooms, which are set up with many of the original Victoriana nicknacks and furniture pieces in an attempt to make the house feel lived in. Although there are velvet ropes keeping you out of most of the rooms, you can sit on the reproduction sofa in the parlour, formerly the room where ladies entertained. Upstairs in the attic, there are old trunks and books and wooden toys you can examine. Dr. Helmcken's original nineteenth-century medical kit is on display on the top

POINT ELLICE
HOUSE PARLOR

floor in the newest part of the house added in 1883.

Helmcken House is right beside the Royal British Columbia Museum and adjacent to Thunderbird Park, where you can sometimes watch totem poles being carved.

POINT ELLICE HOUSE

In the middle of an industrial area, in what seems like the heart of a wrecking lot, there is a little oasis called Point Ellice House. Caroline and Peter O'Reilly owned Point Ellice House in the late 1800s. Both

POINT ELLICE HOUSE

emigrated from England in the 1850s, Caroline after having spent some time in India looking for a British officer to marry. Instead, she married Peter O'Reilly in 1863 and they spent the next few years in Victoria and on the mainland. After the birth of her second child, Caroline wanted to settle in Victoria to be near her own family. When they established their home at Point Ellice House, she was the quintessential lady of the house, organizing dinner parties and social events. Point Ellice House quickly became the place to be for local schmoozers.

Peter O'Reilly, after emigrating to Canada at the age of 31, was employed as a justice of the peace, a magistrate, a gold commissioner, a collector of revenue, an assistant commissioner of lands, an Indian agent and a coroner. From 1864 to 1881 he served on the British Columbia Legislative Council as magisterial appointee. In 1881, he retired as a judge.

The gardens at Point Ellice House have been restored according to the meticulous notes kept by daughter Kathleen O'Reilly. Some of the heritage varieties of plants here are not often found in modern gardens. Today, the English-garden atmosphere is often used for private functions such as weddings, company parties and special anniversaries.

Inside the house, more than 10,000 original O'Reilly items have been catalogued by conservators and are on display, touted as the largest collection of Victoriana in its original setting. There is an audio tour of the house narrated by the "house boy," which no doubt makes

POINT ELLICE HOUSE DINING ROOM

Caroline O'Reilly turn in her grave.

Point Ellice House is located at 2616 Pleasant Street. If you travel west over the Bay Street Bridge and turn north on Pleasant Street, you'll see the large Point Ellice House sign. You can also get there from the Inner Harbour by taking a small Harbour Ferry across the water.

CRAIGDARROCH CASTLE

Though magnificent, it isn't really a castle. The Gaelic translation of Craigdarroch is "rocky oak place." Certainly the Dunsmuir family, who built Craigdarroch, couldn't have imagined how apt this name would be.

Craigdarroch was built in the late 1880s. Robert Dunsmuir and his wife, Joan, had emigrated from Scotland and before moving to Victoria, lived in Nanaimo (a 1.5-h drive north of Victoria today). In Nanaimo, Robert Dunsmuir began to make what became his fortune in mining. As mine superintendent for the Hudson's Bay Company, Robert discovered his own coal seam and started his own company, exporting the coal to San Francisco. In 1882 the family moved to Victoria, where Robert served as the representative for Nanaimo in the provincial legislative assembly.

The stone mansion built for the Dunsmuir family was built on the highest point in Victoria. Originally, there was a lake, a bridge, streams, an orchard, tennis courts, a coach house, stables and a gazebo on the estate. All that's left today is the mansion, the south lawn and its original stone wall. Robert Dunsmuir died shortly before completion of Craigdarroch, but his wife moved in with some of her daughters (she had eleven children) and grandchildren. Presumably they lived comfortably in the thirty-nine rooms on four floors with seventeen fireplaces. The mansion was designed, even then, with gas lighting, electricity, plumbing and the new telephones.

BUTCHART ROSE GARDEN

The interior panelling and woodwork of Craigdarroch was prefabricated and sent from Chicago. Inside the mansion you will be treated to the best collection of residential stained and leaded glass on the West Coast. In the grand entrance hall, the white oak staircase and sandstone fireplace greeted visitors to Craigdarroch, after they parked their coaches under the porte-cochère. On the second floor, two of the bedrooms are restored to their original Victorian state. In the Billiard Room, on the third level, you can stand on the Douglas fir floor and get a good view of the Juan de Fuca Strait and the Olympic Mountain range in Washington State. But the best view is from the tower, with its blue dome ceiling and curved doors and windows with circular stained-glass windows fitted above the doors. From here you can see for twenty-five miles across to Victoria and the surrounding ocean and mountains.

Some years after Robert Dunsmuir died, his two sons began legal proceedings against their mother for control of their generous trust funds. When one son died, he left his estate to his brother, who continued to engage Mrs. Dunsmuir in a legal battle that made newspaper headlines across Canada. Some reports say that Joan Dunsmuir was a recluse during the last eighteen years of her life, spending most of her time on the second floor of "rocky oak place."

BUTCHART GARDENS

Butchart Gardens is not a botanical gardens; it's just for show. But what a show it is. Butchart Gardens is 21 km (thirteen miles) north of Victoria, halfway between the Swartz Bay ferry terminal and Victoria. In the early 1900s, this 130-acre estate was the site of a rock quarry, where Robert Pim Butchart built his successful cement factory. Today, there are fifty acres of garden in the meticulously well-kept estate. The five main areas are the Sunken Garden, the Japanese Garden, the Rose Garden, the Concert Lawn and Ross Fountain.

Robert Butchart was born in 1856, the oldest of eleven

children in a Scottish family living in Owen Sound, Ontario. In his early twenties he formed a partnership with some friends and began to manufacture Portland cement. The successful twist to his entrepreneurial idea was that Robert packaged and transported his cement in sacks, rather than the cumbersome barrels used at the time. As urban Canadian centres sprang up, the demand for cement increased as did Robert Butchart's business. The young man went west.

In 1902, Robert moved to Victoria where a nearby limestone deposit at Tod Inlet provided him with the materials needed for his business: limestone, clay, fresh water and the possibility of transportation by sea. Shortly thereafter he established the Tod Inlet Cement Plant, on the grounds of what is now Butchart Gardens. His Toronto-born wife, Jennie Foster Butchart, and their two daughters, moved to the site and set up their home. Mrs. Butchart was a certified chemist and sometimes worked in the cement factory — presumably for love, and not money. To hide the unsightly factory from view, Jennie Butchart planted some trees and shrubs. When their formal residence was complete, she turned her hand to the construction of a Japanese garden, with the help of Japanese landscape artist Isaboru Kishida.

In 1908, the limestone supply from the quarry was exhausted and the quarry was abandoned. The story goes that an offhand comment made to Jennie Butchart by a friend — "Even you would be unable to get anything to grow in there" — was the inspiration of what is now the famous Sunken Gardens. Jennie had tons of topsoil brought in by horse and cart from nearby farms and she used a bosun's chair to lower herself down the sides of the quarry where she tucked ivy into the crevices, knowing it would one day cover the bleak walls. Rock gardens were made with the unearthed stones. A deep part of the three-and-a-half-acre quarry was lined and filled with water from a

JAPANESE GARDEN

145

natural spring, forming a lake forty feet deep in places. The Sunken Garden took nine years to make, and was completed in 1921.

The Italian Garden, the most formal of all the gardens, was completed in 1926. The bronze girl-and-dolphin statue in this garden was purchased in Italy, by the Butcharts. The Rose Garden was completed in 1930, and here too the centrepiece wrought-iron wishing well was imported from Florence, Italy. As her gardens grew, Mrs. Butchart hosted hundreds and then thousands of curious guests, offering them tea and showing them around the gardens for free. In the 1930s, she and her husband were honoured with citizenship awards from the City of Victoria.

In 1939, thirty-five years after starting their garden work, the Butcharts presented the gardens to their grandson, Ian Ross, who continued to devote the same care until his death in 1997. It was Ian Ross who oversaw the illumination project in the 1950s. At the time, it was one of the largest underground wiring projects in North America. Hundreds of miles of electrical cords were laid in the ground so that specially hidden lights would show off the gardens at night. Ross Fountain, at the far end of the gardens, was named for Mr. Ross, and the patterns made here by the lights and the 21-metre-high spray continue for many hours before they are repeated.

Every year 400,000 new bulbs are planted by the fifty full-time gardeners. On summer nights, there are fireworks choreographed to music and concerts featuring local actors, singers and dancers. Throughout the gardens there are teak benches, strategically placed. (Some of these benches were made from the decking of British sailing ships). You can have afternoon or high tea (more substantial) in what was the original Butchart residence, but it's not free anymore.

If you're driving, follow Blanshard Street as it becomes Highway 17, and turn left on Keating Cross Road (about 21 km north of Victoria). From there, follow the signs to the gardens. Public transit and private tour buses will also get you there. Everybody knows where the Butchart Gardens are.

FOUNTAIN IN BEACON HILL PARK

BEACON HILL PARK

Beacon Hill Park is just south of The Empress Hotel and across from the greatest soft ice cream drive-through in town (The Dairy Queen on Douglas Street). Beacon Hill Park is the oldest and largest park in Victoria. When the city was granted Beacon Hill Park in trust in 1882, the council introduced by-laws regulating the use of the park. To this day, you may not graze your cattle here or discharge firearms. Nor should

WATERFOWL AT BEACON HILL PARK

you use the grass to clean your carpets.

You get the strange sense that Beacon Hill Park is made up of different rooms, each one with an ambiance of its own. You can roll up your pant legs and paddle in the wading pool on a hot day, or you can stroll through one of the more shady "rooms" and watch the ducks and swans from one of the wooden bridges, arched over a stream. The swans have a royal pedigree from the first ones shipped from The Royal Swannery on the Thames in the 1940s. There is an English-style rose garden as well as exotic eucalyptus and palm trees and the gnarled native Garry Oak.

Starting as early as February, the daffodils and crocuses spring up everywhere. Their bright yellows and purples complement the blue-green plumage of the peacocks you encounter on your walk. Bird watchers have recorded more than 150 species of birds in the park. If you are accompanied by a child, you can wander around the petting zoo with the goats and sheep, piglets, chickens and a pony (open in summer only). If you come on the right day, you may catch an outdoor concert, a Shakespeare-in-the-park or the harmonies of a tenor and his diva in the bandshell. Or, on a Saturday morning, you might take in some cricket on the outskirts of the park. Beacon Hill Park is a no-commercial zone, so bring your own picnic lunch.

If you walk up the hill, past the 350-year-old Chinese Bell, you can rest in the Checker House where you'll get a great view of the Olympic Mountain range south of the border. It was on this hill that two beacons were set up in the mid-1800s to guide ships and it was for these beacons that officers of the Hudson's Bay Company named the park. On the other side of the hill, towards Dallas Road and the ocean, is the official "Mile 0" of the Trans-Canada highway. If you cross the street here, you can follow the path along the cliffs or climb down the steps to one of the beaches. If you're driving, or biking, the route along Dallas Road is probably the most spectacular in Victoria. You'll pass several scenic lookout points along the ocean and some prize-winning neighbourhood gardens.

OAK BAY

About three kilometres east of downtown Victoria lies the

FORT STREET ANTIQUES (ABOVE) AND SHOP (BELOW)

village of Oak Bay. If you drive up Fort Street and veer right onto Oak Bay Avenue, follow the road into this British-style shopping district. It has a bookstore, gift stores, women's clothing stores as well as a mews with various eccentric items on both sides of the street (from lingerie to children's toys).

At the corner of Oak Bay Avenue and Hampshire, the Blethering Place is a cosy English-style teahouse in which to rest your feet. Amidst lace-covered tables and English memorabilia, you can treat yourself to a platter of crustless sandwiches and enjoy scones with cream and raspberry jam and your favourite black (or herbal) tea. It's a better value for your dollar than afternoon tea at The Empress, though the atmosphere is a tad more modest.

If you follow Oak Bay Avenue past the shops, curve to the right, take a left on Windsor Street and you will come to the Oak Bay Marina on Beach Drive. (If you take a right, you can have tea or a big dinner at the charming Windsor House Tearoom, 2540 Windsor Street). There's a decent cafeteria at the marina as well as the more posh restaurant. Either one gives you a view of the boats in the harbour through the large windows. If you walk along the path beneath the restaurants, you have a good chance of getting up close and personal with one of the many seals that hang around waiting for scraps of fish from the daily catch.

Willows Beach is just a short drive east along Beach Drive from the marina (turn right when you leave the parking lot). This sandy beach and play area for kids is lively in the summer, especially if you're young and have the latest in fashion swimwear. Admire the great view of Mount Baker, a mountain and extinct volcano in the State of Washington.

If you turn left as you leave the marina, you'll find the Oak Bay Beach Hotel on Beach Drive. Inside this Tudor-style hotel is The Snug, an English-style pub where you can relax with a beer and a decent meal. If there's room, you can sit on the patio overlooking the gardens and the ocean.

SHOPPING

MELANEY BLACK

INSIDE MARKET SQUARE

Downtown Victoria, or Old Town Victoria, can be covered on foot in about an hour — a little longer if you stop at one of the many world-famous attractions nestled among fine examples of turn-of-the-century architecture. Lucky for you, one of these buildings, The Empress Hotel, is also a good place to start your shopping tour.

EMPRESS HOTEL/VICTORIA CONVENTION CENTRE

For most shoppers, Victoria begins here. The Empress, a historic Canadian Pacific hotel, holds centre stage in Victoria's signature Inner Harbour. This elegant setting tempts travellers with objets d'art, designer clothes and exotic chocolates in shopping areas throughout the upper and lower hotel reception areas. Pewter and porcelain collectibles, sculpture and English woollens are all part of The Empress shopping experience. Aboriginal art and masks can be found in the Art of Man gallery at the back of the hotel where it joins the Victoria Convention Centre. Among the convention centre stores on adjacent Douglas Street, you will find Collections of Madison Avenue, a fine clothes retailer, and the renowned Stephen Lowe Art Gallery.

GOVERNMENT STREET

Moving up Government Street from The Empress front entrance, you'll find Harbour Trading Company at the corner of Government and Wharf Street. This holds a compendium of Canadian and international gifts: art prints, blown glass, fleece sports apparel and collectibles.

Government Street abounds with treasures for the discriminating shopper. For those with a penchant for chocolate, try Rogers Chocolates or Purdy's Chocolates.

MERCHANDISE AT SYDNEY REYNOLDS

CHINA AT SYDNEY REYNOLDS

EATON CENTRE

Irish Linen Stores boasts a wide assortment of table linens and home goods as well as some women's clothing. For lovers of fine British tweeds, British Importers has a complete selection of men's clothing and accessories. Similarly, W&J Wilson offers Aran and Payne sweaters and several lines of men's apparel.

If you love fine china, head for Sydney Reynolds for Spode, St. George, Royal Victorian and Brown Dorset. From here, you can stroll to Copithorne and Row, which features Waterford crystal and Wedgwood and Dresden figures. You'll also appreciate its Belleek and Swarovski china and quality giftware.

No less than three Victoria stores are devoted exclusively to Christmas decorations and novelties, and two of these can be found on Government: The Spirit of Christmas and the Original Christmas Village. One block west towards the water is Christmas House. If you're looking for beautifully made decorations, ornate Christmas gift items and a variety of Christmas icons, these elves' workshops are open year round.

A major landmark in Old Town Victoria is the very contemporary Eaton Centre Mall, a four-tiered shopping area built around a central courtyard, fountain and clock, spanning the entire 1,000-block of Government Street from Fort Street to View Street. Those searching for the familiar will find it in Bryan's women's apparel, La Senza lingerie, Mariposa, Bentley, Aldo Shoes, Tabi International, Boutique of Leathers and the Body Shop.

Across the street from Eaton's is historic Munro's Books, nestled in a 1909 building. You'll find books

for every special or general interest. Next door is a B.C. icon, world-famous Murchie's Tea and Coffee, where you can buy Olde English and exotic teas, local coffee blends and gifts for caffeine connoisseurs. To complete the European flavour of the area, consider Crabtree & Evelyn for English toffee, soaps and scents and the finer things in life.

Wharf Street, one block west, primarily features restaurants that appeal to a variety of palates. If, however, you'd like to buy an interactive gift for those at home, you could have your pseudo-historical picture taken at Grandpa's Antique Photo on Wharf and Yates streets, choosing from a selection of costumes to suit your personality.

SHOP ON FORT STREET

YATES STREET

If you appreciate and/or collect blown glass, shoppers can walk east up Yates to Broad Street and drop in on a live glass-blowing demonstration at Starfish Glassworks. Many of the artists sell their wares in the studio, where you will find everything from traditional forms to avant-garde expressions of the art in a myriad of colours.

Yates Street is also the place for those with a sweet tooth for British confections. The British Candy Shoppe teases taste buds with British toffee, biscuits and grocery items. A block farther up you'll find the English Sweet Shop, offering a similarly tempting array of English chocolates and sweets.

STARFISH GLASSWORKS

First Nations art is very popular in Victoria. While the Art of Man deals in large-scale art works on canvas or soapstone sculptures, the Cowichan Trading Company features locally designed and knit Cowichan sweaters, small carvings and a wide assortment of less formal crafts. Across the street, the Sa-Nuu-Kwa Gallery offers fine silver aboriginal jewellery and elegant pieces crafted by members of the three tribes that traditionally inhabit Vancouver Island. Hill's Indian Crafts also sells gold and silver jewellery, as well as moccasins, carvings and Inuit art.

FIRST NATIONS ARTS AND CRAFTS

MARKET SQUARE

Market Square, a collection of specialty stores built around a central courtyard, has something for all ages. Out of Hand features the work of local artists, ranging from intriguing fountains to elegant objets d'art and framed acrylics, while Marigold Galleria is bursting with ceramic sculpture, glass and contemporary collectibles. For the young or the young at heart, try Foxglove Toys or sample the latest bestsellers at Griffin Books. There's even a store — Waffles, A Doggie Diner — for your favourite canine friend.

You'll find exotic gifts at Hoi Polloi and La Cache, and cafes to suit every taste. You can also sample the decadent pleasures of Fat Phege's Fudge Factory. Bricks of your favourite fudge flavours are created while you watch.

CHINATOWN

The Gates of Harmonious Interest at the corner of Government and Fisgard streets mark the entrance to the smallest Chinatown in Canada. Here you'll find an eclectic mix of east and west. Quonley's combines groceries and gifts in bamboo, wicker and brass. Nestled among the open-air markets, restaurants and exotic aromas on Fisgard is the Chinatown Trading Company, offering hand-painted ceramics, mats, bamboo, affordable gift items and housewares. Next to the Chinatown Trading Company is the entrance to Fan Tan Alley, a hodgepodge of storefronts that cater to more global interests. From musical instruments to artists' studios to African clothing and jewellery, these close quarters provide a unique shopping experience. Back on Fisgard beyond the alley is Fan Tan Gallery, a sensual array of textures and colours, batik, woods, glass and folk art from around the world.

ANTIQUE ROW

ANTIQUE ROW

Packed into two city blocks on Fort Street, Antique Row draws those who appreciate the beauty of history. Each vendor has a particular specialty. Period furniture is found at Charles Baird and Faith Grant. Look for china, depression glass or pottery at The Glass Menagerie and the Old Vogue Shop. You'll find silver and jewellery at Maggie Dove and a little bit of everything at Recollections. Whatever you're looking for, Antique Row offers a rich assortment of pre-millennium artifacts.

DINING

GARY HYNES

BENGAL LOUNGE AT THE EMPRESS HOTEL

Although the Victoria dining scene is generally more laid-back and sedate than its trendy Vancouver cousin, an influx of younger chefs over the last few years is proving it has more to offer than the places on the Inner Harbour tourist beat. The city now offers many good restaurants, bistros and cafes. Neighbourhoods such as Cook St. Village and Antique Row are catering to an increasingly sophisticated crowd who are demanding quality and good service at affordable prices.

Compared to other major Canadian cities, high-quality dining is generally less expensive. Start your culinary tour in the city first and take in the charms of the heritage buildings and colourful gardens of Victoria. Then, if you're willing to take a short drive into the country, you will find many top tables set amidst spectacular West Coast surroundings. Dine at the Aerie Resort, high atop a mountain overlooking the long fiord-like Finalyson Arm, or make a pilgrimage to Sooke Harbour House, one of Canada's gastronomic treasures.

FINE DINING

Fine dining in Victoria in most cases means an emphasis on what is local and in season. The valleys and coastal areas of Vancouver Island are a haven for small farmers, many of them escapees from the big cities on the mainland. Many chefs scour the farm gates of the Cowichan Valley, Metchosin Valley or Saanich Peninsula trying to outdo their rivals in sourcing out the most flavourful blackberries or the rarest heirloom tomatoes. Throw in the catch from the sea, such as local spot prawns, Dungeness crab, sablefish and a variety of wild salmon, and why would they want to cook with faraway global ingredients anyway?

153

In town, for four-star dining and impeccable service, there's The Victorian Restaurant in the Ocean Pointe Resort and Spa. This sleek, contemporary room has the best seats for viewing the city's skyline across the waters of Inner Harbour, including the Parliament Buildings, which are lit up at night. Chef Neil Antolin excels at creating flavoured oils, chutneys and compotes for ostrich, venison and other game. Slightly up town along the newly hot Antique Row, Cafe Brio serves up some of the best food in town. The art-filled room may be loud for some but the kitchen sources its juicy salad greens from a local farm; the staff is warm and knowledgeable and Greg Hayes' wine list always features a rare find or two. The cooking is contemporary Pacific Northwest and chef Sean Brennan excels at creating multi-textured food combinations. In a more classic mode, the new Matisse Restaurant at the bottom of Yates Street is all traditional French cuisine and pretty yellows in a cosy dining room. Try the duck, it's second to none.

CAFE BRIO (TOP); MATISSE (ABOVE)

The most sumptuous restaurants, however, are to be found just outside of town. No one visiting Victoria should miss one of Canada's top restaurants, the Sooke Harbour House. Fredrica and Sinclair Philip started this country inn nineteen years ago and have been receiving accolades ever since. Dazzlingly innovative, delightfully eccentric, the kitchen remains a crucible for modern Canadian regional cuisine.

THE VIEW FROM OCEAN POINTE

At the far tip of Saanich Peninsula, near the ferries to

Vancouver, chef Pierre Koffel has been turning out some of the most sophisticated dishes to be found in the province. There's fresh foie gras flown in from Quebec, truffle soup, scrambled eggs with caviar and a cellar full of vintage Bordeaux and Sauternes.

BISTROS, CAFES

Victorians are an out-of-doors lot and prefer not to dress up if they can help it. Therefore, the most popular destinations are the bistros and cafes springing up all over the city. John and Lisa Hall work very hard to make their Cassis Bistro a welcoming spot. Casual and unpretentious, big portions of contemporary bistro fare such as locally caught rockfish

DESSERT AT THE HERALD ST. CAFE

paired with Japanese ponzu sauce or pork tenderloin in a rich brandied cream and mustard sauce round out an exciting dining experience. Another husband-and-wife team look after Paprika Bistro on Estevan in the city's tony Oak Bay area. Here, George Szasz' Hungarian background combines with his ability to present light, yet vividly flavoured dishes to make a night out in this intimate room a pleasure.

Recently, the whisk has been passed from mother to son at the Herald St. Cafe in the Olde Towne area. Son Paul Bell is breathing new life into this beloved Victoria institution. It was Herald St. Cafe that first brought modern dining to this city. It's still the locals' first choice when taking an out-of-town guest to dinner. The new, long bar annex is a great place for late-night eating. Suze Restaurant and Lounge has the downtown buzz of the martini set and is the place to go for people watching and international, casual fare. At Rebar, a funky, quirky downtown cafe, you never knew health food could be so good. You'll find inventive, delicious and guilt-free food.

TEAROOM ON FORT STREET

Victoria is also a city on the go and cafes where quick lunches and the best coffees keep its denizens well fuelled never lack patrons. Zambri's, located downtown in a tiny strip mall behind a London Drugs, holds the title as best Italian cafe. Order from Peter Zambri himself as he stands cooking at the stove in his small open kitchen. He'll size you up and tell you what you should have. You can't go wrong with the Illy espresso. There's suave Foster's Eatery by the Eaton Centre for designer sandwiches and Paradiso di Stelle on Bastion Square for gelato. Bond Bonds, the city's top bakery, serves simple, fresh lunches. Of course, Barb's Fish & Chips at Fisherman's Wharf is the spot for reliable fish and chips, hauling in both Victorians and visitors to this funky dockside take-out.

WITH TEA AT THE
EMPRESS

SEAFOOD

Good seafood is harder to find than you would think for this coastal city, but three restaurants come to mind when the urge for fresh fish hits. The Blue Crab Bar & Grill in the Coast Harbourside Hotel is Pacific Northwest casual with a great water view. Check out the blackboard for the specials of the day and don't skip the desserts here. They're delicious. The Marina Restaurant at the Oak Bay Marina is just the nautical setting to sample fine naturally smoked Black Cod braised in local Merridale cider. Or try chef Mel O'Brien's modern take on retro dishes like rare-grilled Ahi Tuna or Steak Diane. Twenty minutes outside the city, in Sidney, at another marina, Dock 503 keeps the focus finely tuned on the freshest seafood. After dinner take the time to explore Sidney's many used bookstores.

BREW PUBS

Since owner Paul Hadfield got an act of parliament to allow pubs to brew their own beer, Victoria has been a leader in craft brewing in Canada. Popular brews include his light and lemony Hefeweizen wheat beer and a smoky Dunkleweizen. Do try the hot and sour soup, which is made from Spinnaker's own India Pale Ale malt vinegar. Other brew pubs worth a visit are Hugo's, the Canoe Club and Swans.

A SPOT OF TEA

For many, Victoria and English High Tea are synonymous. The Empress Hotel holds court as the queen of teas. It isn't cheap, but the chance to sit amid such splendour sipping on properly steeped and poured tea and munching on dainty sandwiches and flaky scones is worth the price of admission. Another fine spot for tea is Butchart Gardens outside of town on picturesque Brentwood Bay. It is especially refreshing after a tramp around the spectacular gardens of Victoria's number one attraction.

CHINATOWN

ETHNIC EATERIES

Vancouver Island is also a melting pot where different culinary cultures come together to add spice and nuance to the eating scene. Victoria's Chinatown, with its colourful history and other Asian influences, is shoulder-to-shoulder with grocery stores overflowing with the exotic and restaurants often serving the freshest fish in town. The always busy J & J Won Ton Noodle House, a simple noodle shop with always tasty Chinese chow, is worth a visit.

EXCURSIONS

WHISTLER

CONSTANCE BRISSENDEN

**WHISTLER AND
BLACKCOMB
MOUNTAINS**

It's astonishing to realize that just over thirty-five years
ago, Whistler Resort was serviced by just one ski lift.
Travelling from Vancouver, 120 kilometres away, took
seven hours on a rugged, unpaved road. By 1975,
responding to tremendous growth, the Resort Municipality
of Whistler, British Columbia's first and only resort
designation, was created. Today, Whistler is an
international mega-star, voted the number one ski resort in
North America. It's proof that spending billions of dollars
in continual development, upgrading, improvements and
marketing does pay off.

Some miss the rough-and-ready early days, but for
everyone else the response is enthusiastic. Whether winter
or summer, the two tandem mountains of Whistler and
Blackcomb are now world-class, the food and shopping are
memorable and the amenities deluxe. Yet you can easily
spend time here and not blow your budget.

**SKIERS AND
SNOWBOARDERS IN
WHISTLER**

More than 2 million people visited
Whistler Resort in 1999. For eight months of
the year, there's action on the slopes: skiing
and snowboarding on Whistler and
Blackcomb from late November to mid-June
(on Blackcomb to April 30), and again on
Blackcomb from mid-June to mid-August on
Horstman Glacier. The resort's extensive lift
system is capable of carrying over 59,000
skiers and riders per hour. With fifteen high-
speed lifts (out of a thirty-three-lift system),
Whistler/Blackcomb boasts the most high-
speed lifts at a single resort in North America.
Above and beyond downhill skiing and
snowboarding, try cross-country skiing,
snowmobiling, heli-skiing, heli-snowboarding,
wildlife viewing, snowshoeing and sleigh

rides. Ski lessons for adults and children are offered on both mountains.

Ironically, summer was the area's first tourist season. In 1914, Alex and Myrtle Philip opened the Rainbow Lodge and soon had visitors backpacking in to canoe and fish the five local lakes. The historic lodge on Alta Lake burned down in 1978 but you can still visit the site at present-day Rainbow Park. In 1966, when the first ski lift opened on Whistler Mountain, summer took a back seat, but it is now back as a major draw. Whistler is promoted as a four-season destination although in spring and fall, visitors can expect to find a number of attractions closed. On the other hand, some visitors prefer the off-peak prices, ample parking and the quieter atmosphere of the hotels, restaurants and cafes.

Whistler can be reached by scheduled bus, train and air service as well as charter bus service, taxis, limousines and charter air service. If you drive, take Highway 99 from Vancouver. Remember that this mountain highway can be treacherous, and drive with care.

With the help of the Whistler Activity and Information Centre, it's easy to plan your itinerary whatever the season. You can call or visit their office, located just off Village Gate Boulevard. Resort Reservations Whistler assists with bookings in hotels, condominiums and bed and breakfasts.

They can also create a customized vacation package to include lift tickets, air tickets and ground transportation to and from Vancouver International Airport, including express coach service. For overall information, visit Tourism Whistler's website.

In addition to accolades for its two mountains, Whistler Resort has been praised for best overall resort design. The resort combines ski-in, ski-out convenience with distinctive Nouveau European architecture. The original Whistler Village is now joined by the Upper Village at the foot of Blackcomb Mountain and Village North off Lorimer Road. All three are within easy walking distance of one another.

The resort offers a complete range of services, including the Whistler Medical Centre, Whistler Public Library and the Whistler Museum and Archives. As befits an international resort, both dining and shopping are exceptional. There are

SLEIGH RIDE IN WHISTLER

more than ninety restaurants, cafes and pubs, including mountain-peak gastronomic experiences on both Whistler and Blackcomb. Visitors can also enjoy a variety of live entertainment. Eight art galleries tempt visitors, who may want to take home a First Nations carving or finely designed jewellery as a keepsake. Luxurious winter wear is also a highlight.

WHISTLER MOUNTAIN

Thirty-five years have made a tremendous difference to London Mountain. For one thing, it's now known as Whistler Mountain, a name with far more panache.

Consider for a moment the thrill of the mountain's longest run, a satisfying eleven kilometres. The mountain offers 1,500 hectares (3,657 acres) of skiable terrain, with 25 percent designed for beginners, 55 percent for intermediate skiers and 20 percent for advanced to expert skiers. Choice is the name of the game. Ski from the Whistler Gondola or Whistler Creekside. A third access point was added in 1999 with the Fitzsimmons Quad, installed between the Blackcomb Excalibur Gondola and Whistler Gondola. It connects with the new Garbanzo Express that goes up, up, up with the greatest vertical rise of any chair on either mountain. On your way to the top, don't forget to count the more than 100 marked runs below.

Whistler Mountain also attracts enthusiastic snowboarders, with options for all. The Terrain Park is now ten and a half hectares of snowboarding freedom, ideal for newer riders. Expert boarders can start at the top at the Peak and Harmony Express and work their way down to intermediate and beginner levels.

Tucked at the base of Whistler Mountain are two impressive European-style tourist areas. The pedestrian-only Whistler Village opened in 1980 around Village Square. Today it offers a choice of hotels, restaurants, pubs, shops, the Whistler Conference Centre, banks and tour companies. More recently, Village North has taken shape in a ten-year expansion of a twenty-four-hectare site. Already completed in Village North is the Whistler Town Plaza and Marketplace, a $25-million shopping plaza with the resort's first major grocery store. You can buy gourmet groceries or stamps, order Chinese food or a hamburger, stock up a liquor cabinet, bank or buy a condo here.

To satisfy culinary cravings, several restaurants are located on Whistler Mountain. The

WINTER IN WHISTLER VILLAGE

newest is Chic Pea at the top of Garbanzo Express, a rustic 300-seater serving pizzas, soups and humongous cinnamon buns. Old favourites include the huge 1,740-seat Roundhouse Lodge at the top of Whistler Express Gondola, with a full fast-food menu, and Pika's at the top of Whistler Express Gondola with cafeteria-style offerings. The Raven's Nest at the top of the Creekside Gondola boasts spectacular views and outdoor seating as well as New York-style deli sandwiches. Located at the Whistler Creek Base (base of Creekside Gondola), the World Cup Cafe and Dusty's take you from breakfast to après-ski fun.

BLACKCOMB MOUNTAIN

Blackcomb's nickname is the Mile-High Mountain. Launched in 1980 as a brand-new facility, Blackcomb rivalled Whistler until the merger of both mountains in 1996 under the Intrawest name.

Blackcomb is serviced by three base areas: Excalibur Village Station, Upper Village Blackcomb Base (known as the Daylodge) and Excalibur Base II Station. There are more than 100 marked runs. Fifteen percent are designed for beginners, 55 percent for intermediate skiers and 30 percent for the advanced and expert group. A few seasons back, the mountain unveiled its superb Excalibur gondola system, featuring ninety-seven, eight-passenger sit-down cabins capable of carrying 2,600 skiers an hour. Combined with the Excelerator high-speed quad chair and the Glacier Express, skiers can climb from village to glaciers in nineteen minutes.

SNOWMOBILER AT DUSK (TOP); DOWNHILL SKIER (ABOVE)

KIDS AT WHISTLER RESORT

Snowboarding also has a niche in Blackcomb's challenging 6.5-hectare snowboard Terrain Park, accessible by its own lift, the Catskinner Triple Chair.

Dining on the mountain is a must. For a warm-up, grab a freshly brewed coffee at the Rendezvous or lunch at the Mountain Grill, both located at the top of Solar Coaster. Horstman Hut, at the top of 7th Heaven,

serves pasta, pizza and chili. Crystal Hut, with its 1950s theme, offers trout fillets, baked beans and freshly baked pies. Glacier Creek, at the base of the Jersey Cream and Glacier Express quad chairs, is Blackcomb's largest dining facility. It offers 360 degree views and accommodates 1,496 diners. Upstairs is River Rock Grill with ten food market areas; downstairs is Glacier Bite, a take-away bistro-style counter. For fine dining, head for Christine's in the Rendezvous with its view of Wedge Mountain and Armchair Glacier.

Blackcomb Benchlands is a mix of hotels, shops, restaurants and condominiums centred in and around Château Whistler Resort. The Château, built in the grand Canadian Pacific Railway style, features stone-clad fireplaces and domed ceilings painted with gold leaf. Just walking through is a vicarious pleasure.

ALTA LAKE CANOERS (TOP); WHISTLER RESORT RIDERS (MIDDLE)

SUMMER ACTIVITIES

You can still canoe down the River of Golden Dreams in Whistler, a favourite of Alex Philip in the 1920s. The mountains, and the resort's five lakes (Alpha, Nita, Alta, Lost and Green) are still there. What has changed is the way you experience them — whether by helicopter or floatplane flights, glider rides, paraglides, valley bus tours, four-wheel drive vehicles, in-line skating, horseback riding and hayrides, white-water rafting, jet boating, kayaking, mountain biking or good old, unadorned mountain hiking. Golfing is also a favourite, with four designer courses in awe-inspiring settings. The Whistler Activity and Information Centre (932-2394) is the place to go to arrange any activity.

Boredom is truly not an option in summer. When you need a break from all that healthy physical stuff, take in some culture. Street entertainers, band concerts, art shows, jazz, blues and even symphony concerts will entertain you and your family. Throughout the summer, annual festivals add energy to the scene, from the Whistler Arts Festival in June to Cornucopia, a food and wine festival in mid-November.

BLACK BEAR AT REST

Kids also get plenty of attention. They can swim at the Meadow Park Aquatic Centre or ice skate at the Meadow Park Arena. At the five local lakes, swimming, picnicking, fishing and canoeing are options. Château Whistler runs the Tennis Tigers camp daily in July and August. First-run movies are shown at the Rainbow Theatre. As well as nature walks, families can challenge the easy-going Valley Trail on rented bikes, skateboards and in-line skates. For more information on children's activities, call the Whistler Activity and Information Centre.

GULF ISLANDS

ANNE SMART

TRIBUNE BAY IN HORNBY ISLAND

In 1792, Captain George Vancouver, exploring the waters between the mainland and what is now Vancouver Island, believed himself to be in a gulf rather than a continuous body of water. The numerous islands and islets in the Strait of Georgia therefore became — erroneously — the Gulf Islands. Nestled in the lee of Vancouver Island, they exert an irresistible charm, luring both visitors and immigrants from around the world.

In the 1850s, some of the earliest settlers were slaves from south of the border. Others, naturally, were European. Altogether, the settlers formed an eclectic mix: the Hudson's Bay Company, which had previously controlled the area, developed trading outposts and some of their Hawaiian employees also settled here. Japanese families, often originally engaged in small fishing operations, came later. Several developed market gardens. Chinese settlers were not uncommon. These early families worked hard to clear the forest and establish farms on the 160 acres they could claim in the new British Colony. Logging, farming, fishing and attempts to mine were the earliest occupations. With a mild year-round climate on their side, some of the islands soon supplied a major part of the Canadian fruit market, until the province's Okanagan Valley on the mainland took over the role. Old orchards are still very evident throughout the islands.

Early settlers faced many challenges. Some were confronted by First Nations bands, who came seasonally to the shores to fish and gather shellfish. Local transportation in canoes and rowboats resulted in drowning deaths. Cougars were rampant and children frequently had to be protected from these hungry predators. Living in the islands today, by contrast, is idyllic. Good paved roads abound and ferries run to many of the most populated

SIDNEY ISLAND

islands. Some even have scheduled air transportation, to small airstrips or harbour facilities. Some residents of the closer islands, with good ferry facilities, commute to work on Vancouver Island. More frequently, except for those who retire to the kind climate of the islands, islanders tend to work at home. Jobs on the islands are scarce and many people choose to live simply and pursue their talents, selling the varied artistic results in local stores and markets, as well as from their own studios.

STOPOVERS

Accommodation resources are varied on most of the larger islands, from bed and breakfasts, hotels, lodging rooms and cabins. There are also several places to camp in provincial parks or on private campgrounds. Although the islands are lovely in wintertime quietness, gorgeous during blossom-bedecked spring months and magnificent in fall colours, most visitors come in the summertime. It's a good idea to arrange your summer accommodations ahead of time with the help of the local tourism agencies, accessible now by mail, phone or Internet.

Most people arrive by ferry, perhaps watching for sea life, such as seals raising their heads in curiosity, or otters running the rocks of the shores in search of shellfish. Baldheaded eagles and herons swooping over the water are frequently seen. Some vacationers seek the tranquillity of isolation. They come simply to enjoy quiet walks in the woods with only the songs of birds for background noise. Others will want a strenuous hike first, earning peaceful contemplation of a Gulf Island panorama from a fragrant mountain meadow.

If you like mingling with fellow visitors and locals, the islands offer craft shops, markets and local pubs and restaurants. Those who like to fish can spend leisured time at a freshwater lake well stocked with trout, or in an oceangoing boat taking a chance at hooking a mighty salmon. Hikers, bikers, paddlers, sailors, golfers, shoppers

HELLIWELL PARK ON HORNBY ISLAND

and the downright lazy all have their ideal image of the perfect holiday. These varied islands can please them all. Here is a sampling of the many Gulf Islands that await you.

SALTSPRING ISLAND

The largest of the thirteen major Gulf Islands, with several freshwater lakes, Saltspring (also spelled Salt Spring) is also the most heavily populated. Irregularly shaped and about twenty-seven kilometres long, it has a population of approximately 10,000 residents. Saltspring boasts the only hospital facilities and the only high school in the Gulf Islands. It also has three ferry terminals. Accommodations here are plentiful and range widely in cost and type.

SALTSPRING ISLAND'S ECOLOGICAL RESERVE

You'll find three distinct villages on the island, each with stores, restaurants and a pub. Fulford Harbour in the south, and Vesuvius in the northerly section, are more residential. Ganges in the narrowed mid-section is the commercial centre. Each village has its own distinct personality and all can be explored on foot. Some residences date back to the early settlers. Some are barely more than a cabin, and some are of recent vintage and far more elaborate. Note the sturdy and sometimes eccentric fencing around the vegetable gardens, designed in various formats to discourage deer, those prolific and voracious vegetarians.

Allow plenty of time to explore the treasures to be found in Saltspring's numerous craft shops, galleries and studios. Before leaving the island, stroll the Ganges sea walk to enjoy the views of the chain of islands in the long harbour and the yachts at moorage and anchor.

GALIANO ISLAND

GALIANO ISLAND

Some people consider Galiano the most scenic of the Gulf Islands, with its shoreline ranging from high bluffs to sandy beaches. Nearly as long as Saltspring Island, Galiano is often less than two kilometres wide, but boasts seven parks. The nature of the land and the lack of water have made farming on Galiano a challenge, and fishing has historically been a more important industry.

The population here grows very slowly, compared to most Gulf Islands. For some time, it has stood at little more than 1,000 residents. This small group is fiercely independent, exerting recent political action

to preserve their island from clear-cutting. Several accommodation options are available on Galiano, including camping. Montague Harbour Park in the south end has white shell beaches and a lagoon that can be explored by a trail system. Dionisio Point Park, in the north end, features natural sandstone sculptures along the shoreline.

GABRIOLA ISLAND

This island can be circumnavigated by bike in several hours. Many of its several thousand residents commute daily to Nanaimo on Vancouver Island to work, since it's only a twenty-minute ferry run between Descanso Bay and downtown Nanaimo. Gabriola is an easy place to visit for a day if you're exploring Vancouver Island.

DIONISIO POINT PARK ON GALIANO

Here too there are a variety of places to stay, eat and shop, as well as several provincial parks with picnic facilities, hiking trails and beautiful views. Sandwell Provincial Park offers petroglyphs for view at low tide. Drumberg Provincial Park has interesting sculptured sandstone formations.

MAYNE ISLAND

GABRIOLA ISLAND'S DRUMBEG PARK

Orchards are still to be found everywhere on Mayne Island, reminding visitors of an earlier time when the island was a major fruit producer. Although one of the earliest islands to be settled, with deeds dating back to 1859, the population is only about 900. With more than a dozen different accommodation facilities, the residents are a hospitable group.

SATURNA ISLAND

Think Saturna, think annual Lamb Barbecue each July 1, Canada's birthday. The entire population of about 350 residents work together tirelessly to invite the world at large to come and celebrate with them. With a choice of ten places to stay, visitors can cycle, hike or paddle past galleries of sandstone sculptures.

SUNSHINE COAST

KEVIN BARKER

The misty fiords immediately north of Greater Vancouver have endured many misconceptions since old George Gibson first weighed anchor in Gibsons Harbour some 100 years ago. But none is more enduring than the mistaken belief of just about everyone that the Sunshine Coast is an island.

Although a forty-minute ferry ride from Horseshoe Bay to Langdale is required to reach it, the region is not an island but part of the mainland of British Columbia. It is in fact a ribbon of highway that winds past seaside communities like Gibsons, Roberts Creek and Sechelt. When you finally reach the rocky shores of Jervis Inlet, you can embark on yet another ferry to Powell River and the northern terminus of Highway 101.

Sunshine is indeed more plentiful on the Sunshine Coast. Unspoiled beaches like Bonniebrok and Davis Bay are in abundance, along with excellent hiking trails such as Cliff Gilker Park. Socially, the Sunshine Coast is a land of duelling bumper stickers. You can enjoy a genteel evening at the Raven's Cry Theatre in Sechelt or the Gumboot Gardens Cafe in Roberts Creek. For a livelier evening, join in on the rather frequent hometown dances at the Roberts Creek Hall located near the corner of Roberts Creek Road and Highway 101.

Most visitors are sufficiently enamoured of the seaside town of Gibsons, located about two kilometres from the Langdale ferry, to inquire about house prices. Several realtors work along Marine Drive, so just drop in and ask for a tour. Before you move along, check out Molly's Lane for antiques and the Sunshine Coast Maritime Museum. It's right behind Molly's Reach, an ancient maritime hotel and the setting for CBC's long-running television series, The Beachcombers.

SECHELT AND SURROUNDING AREA

A few kilometres past Gibsons is Cliff Gilker Park with an excellent network of trails adjacent to the Sunshine Coast

Golf and Country Club. In Roberts Creek, turn left on Roberts Creek Road and drive to the Gumboot Gardens Cafe at the crossroads; the lunch menu is delectable and the conversation is especially good on Sundays when the intelligentsia gather to discuss everything from sometime-resident Joni Mitchell to the healing properties of obscure fungi.

Travelling northwest from "The Creek" one crosses a series of rivers before arriving in the mid-coast town of Sechelt, a narrow isthmus separating the Strait of Georgia from Sechelt Inlet. Downtown fronts a lovely sandy beach, with Snickett Park forming the west perimeter. Rockwood Lodge is a restored heritage house on Cowrie Street that hosts the Annual Festival of the Written Arts in mid-August. The Sunshine Coast Arts Centre at the nearby corner of Trail and Medusa has local and off-coast visual arts. Local muse Peter Trower and author Jim Christy are known to read from their own works here. Note the unusual log construction of the building designed by pioneer builder Clarke Stebner.

Farther up the road, Halfmoon Bay's rustic General Store suggests an earlier time when steamers made daily stops at the pier to drop off mail and pick up passengers. Situated on a picturesque bay, it is reached from Redrooofs Road, which detours off the highway and winds past Sargeant Bay and Coopers Green (great picnicking) before meeting the highway a stone's throw from the bay itself. Homesite Road farther along features local old growth forest and great hikes.

The coastline gets progressively rockier towards Secret Cove and finally Pender Harbour, where communities lie clustered in tiny coves linked by secondary roads and the meandering coastline. Madeira Park, Garden Bay and Irvines Landing are centered around the waters of Pender Harbour itself. The Ruby Lake Resort enroute to Earls Cove is ideal for boating and fishing.

If weather permits, take the Egmont turnoff just before Earls Cove and hike to Skookumchuk Narrows, where tidal forces weave the placid waters into gigantic eddies and whirlpools. Check the tide table for the best viewing times.

ISLAND ALTERNATIVES

Foot passengers arriving at the Langdale ferry dock from Horseshoe Bay are welcome to board the tiny *Dogwood Princess* to visit Keats or Gambier islands across Howe Sound. Both offer day-trippers excellent trails, beaches, and kayaking routes. Keats Island enjoys a commanding view of the Strait of Georgia. Gambier is home to the cutest general store in Christendom complete with home-baked goodies, a curlicued façade and a rugged mountain backdrop. Boaters should try to arrive at dusk when the harbours and coves are at their most exquisite. Keats Island has excellent moorage at Plumpers Cove on the northwest side.

CANADA GOOSE AND GOSLING

LISTINGS: CONTENTS

Getting There 170

VANCOUVER
170 By Air
170 By Sea
170 By Car
170 By Bus
170 By Rail

VICTORIA
171 By Air
171 By Sea
171 By Car
171 By Bus
172 By Rail

Travel Essentials 172

172 Money
172 Passports
172 Customs
172 Taxes

Getting Acquainted 173

173 Time Zone
173 Climate, Rain and Snow
173 Guides and Information

Getting Around 174

174 Public Transit
175 Cars and Rentals
176 Tours

Accommodation 177

VANCOUVER
177 Hotels: Vancouver
    International Airport
178 Hotels: Downtown Vancouver
182 Bed and Breakfasts
183 Hostels and Educational

VICTORIA
184 Hotels: Victoria International
    Airport
184 Hotels: Downtown Victoria
    and Inner Harbour
186 Bed and Breakfasts
189 Hostels and Educational

Dining 189

VANCOUVER
189 Asian
191 French and Italian
191 Pacific Northwest
192 Fine Dining and Hotel Dining

192 Specialty

VICTORIA
193 Fine Dining
194 Bistros and Cafes
194 Seafood
194 Brewpubs
194 Tea
195 Ethnic

Top Attractions 195

195 Vancouver
196 Victoria

Galleries and Museums 196

VANCOUVER
196 Galleries
198 Museums

VICTORIA
199 Museums

Vancouver Entertainment 199

199 Clubs
199 Theatre
200 Music

Parks and Gardens 200

Sports and Activities 201

201 Sports
201 Outdoor Activities

Kids' Stuff 202

202 Indoors
202 Outdoors
203 Waterplay
203 Children's Culture
204 History and Living Culture

Vancouver Annual Events 204

Excursions 206

206 Whistler
206 The Gulf Islands
206 The Sunshine Coast

Shopping 206

206 Vancouver
210 Victoria

Index 211

GETTING THERE

VANCOUVER

On the brink of the Pacific Ocean, at the foot of the mountains, Vancouver is well-served by air, land and sea routes.

BY AIR

Vancouver International Airport (YVR) is located south of Vancouver, approximately 15 minutes away in Richmond. A new international terminal was opened in 1996 as part of an expansion that included a new control tower and third runway. Together with the old terminal handling domestic flights, YVR serves 19 major carriers, 11 regional and local airlines and several charter companies. General inquiries are taken at 604 276-6101. More information on the YVR can be found at its website www.vancouverairport.com

An Airport Improvement Fee (AIF) is levied from passengers departing from Vancouver: $5 when travelling within BC and Yukon Territory; $10 when travelling to other North American destinations; and $15 when travelling to destinations outside North America. Children under two and passengers on same-day connecting flights are exempt.

From the airport, buses, shuttles and taxis are available curbside. Take Translink, the city's public transit system (#100 - New West Stn, transferring at Granville and West 71st Ave. to #8 - Fraser; $2.25 from Richmond to downtown Vancouver), or the Airporter buses (604 946-8866 or 1-800-668-3141), which offer service to major downtown hotels, cruise ship terminal and bus depot for $10 one way, $17 round trip.

AirportLink buses (604 878-1290) run to outlying areas such as South Surrey, Langley, Aldergrove and Chilliwack for $7 to $10, depending on the destination. Courtesy shuttles are available to many hotels. A cab ride downtown costs about $25; Black Top and Checker Cabs (604 731-1111), MacLure's Cabs (604 683-6666), Vancouver Taxi (604 871-1111) and Yellow Cab Company (604 681-1111 or 1-800-898-8294) are the main taxicab companies. Car rental companies operating from YVR include Avis, Alamo, Budget, Hertz, National and Thrifty.

BY SEA

BC Ferries (604 444-2890 in Victoria and outside BC; other parts of BC call 1-888-724-5223) offers regular passenger and vehicle service from Vancouver Island, the Gulf Islands and many other parts of BC. One-way fares in peak season (June 29 to September 10) are: $9 per adult; $4.50 per child; $41 per car and driver. Check www.bcferries.com for information on sailing and current fares.

BY CAR

Three major highways connect Greater Vancouver to the rest of British Columbia, Canada and the United States. Highway 99 connects the north end of the city to Whistler before joining Highway 97, BC.'s main north-south highway. To the south, Highway 99 also connects Vancouver to Washington's Interstate 5 and Seattle. The TransCanada Highway (Highway 1) runs into Vancouver through the Lower Mainland and Fraser River Valley from the rest of Canada, where its feeders include Highway 97 and various connectors and highways from the U.S.

BY BUS

Pacific Central Station (1150 Station St.) is Vancouver's bus station. Visitors from many U.S. and Canadian cities can get to Vancouver on Greyhound buses (604 482-8747 or 1-800-661-8747 in Canada, 1-800-231-2122 in the U.S.). Maverick Coach Lines (604 669-5200) will bring in visitors from Nanaimo, the Sunshine Coast, Squamish and Whistler. Seattle travellers can catch the Quick Shuttle (604 244-3744 or 1-800-665-2122).

BY RAIL

Pacific Central Station is also the city's train station. VIA Rail (1-800-561-8630) has transcontinental service from Toronto via Jasper three times a week. BC Rail (604 984-5246 or 1-800-663-8238 in Canada and the U.S.) serves North Vancouver, Whistler, Lillooet and Prince George. Travellers from Seattle may choose Amtrak Cascades (1-800-872-7245), which operates one round-trip per day between Seattle and Vancouver.

VICTORIA

Two main options are available to the traveller:

- Fly to Vancouver, then transfer to a plane or a bus plus a ferry.
- Fly to Seattle, then transfer to a plane or a ferry.

BY AIR FROM VANCOUVER

Thirty-five minute flights to Victoria from Vancouver are offered by the following:

- Harbour Air Seaplanes (250 384-2215 in Victoria; 604 688-1277 in Vancouver; 1-800-665-0212 toll-free). Twin Otter seaplane service from downtown Vancouver and YVR to Victoria's Inner Harbour.
- Helijet Airways (250 382-5222 in Victoria; 604 273-1414 in Vancouver). Helicopter service from downtown Vancouver or YVR to Victoria's Ogden Point.
- Westcoast Air (604 688-9115). Float plane service from downtown Vancouver to Victoria's Inner Harbour.
- AirBC, (250388-4521 in Victoria; 604 273-2464 in Vancouver). Flights on small planes from airport to airport.

BY AIR FROM SEATTLE

- Horizon Air (1-800-547-9300). Direct (35 min.) and nondirect (75 min.) flights to Victoria International Airport.
- Kenmore Air (206 486-1257 in Seattle, 1-800-543-9595 in the U.S. and Canada). Fifty-minute seaplane flights from downtown Seattle (shuttles from Seattle-Tacoma Airport available in summer) to Victoria's Inner Harbour.

The Victoria International Airport is located near Sidney, about 30 minutes from the downtown area. From the airport, the Victoria International Airporter (250 386-2525) and PBM airport buses (250 475-2010) run to all hotels, motels and downtown on

the half-hour, for $13 one way. Taxis are run by Victoria Taxi (250 383-7111), Empress Taxi (250 381-5577) and Blue Bird Cabs (250 384-1155). Fares are about $40.

BY SEA FROM VANCOUVER

BC Ferries (604 669-1211 in Vancouver; 250 386-3431 in Victoria; 1-888-223-3779 toll-free) traverses the Strait of Georgia between Vancouver and Victoria. Ferries make the journey from Tsawwassen (Vancouver) to Swartz Bay (Victoria) in approximately 95 minutes. Board as a walk-on passenger ($9 in high season) or by car ($41 in peak season for car and driver). Different rates apply to motorcycles, bicycles and oversize vehicles. Pacific Coach Lines runs buses directly from YVR onto the ferry and into downtown Victoria. Call 1-800-661-1725, 604 662-8074 (Vancouver) or 250 385-4411(Victoria) for rates and more information.

BY SEA FROM SEATTLE

Victoria Clipper offers three marine choices. The slower ferry leaves from Seattle's Pier 48 and arrives at Victoria's Ogden Point in about four and a half hours. Call 1-800-683-7977 in the U.S. and 1-800-668-1167 in Canada for rates and more information. From Pier 69, high-speed catamarans make the trip in three hours, and turbojets in just 11/2 hours. Rates and information on the faster services can be found at 1-800-888-2535, 206-448-5000 (Seattle) and 250-382-8100 (Victoria).

BY CAR

Driving to Victoria from any place off the Island involves taking a ferry. Allow extra time to make your selected sailing in peak season. From the Swartz Bay Ferry Terminal (and the Victoria International Airport) take Highway 17 south into the city.

BY BUS

Pacific Coach Lines runs buses directly from YVR onto the ferry and into downtown Victoria. Call 1-800-661-1725, 604 662-8074 (Vancouver) or 250 385-4411(Victoria) for rates and more information.

BY RAIL

The E & N Railiner runs a scenic route between Victoria and Courtenay, with several stops on the way: Duncan, Chemainus, Nanaimo, Parksville, Qualicum Beach. Call 1-800-561-8630 or 1-250-953-9000 ext. 5800 for more information.

TRAVEL ESSENTIALS

MONEY

Canadian cash consists of $1 (loonies) and $2 (twoonie) coins and differently coloured $5, $10, $20, $50, $100 and $1000 bills. Main branches of Canadian chartered banks can exchange foreign currency, although small local branches may not exchange currency other than U.S. dollars directly. Several foreign banks have offices in Vancouver, and will handle some foreign currencies directly. Banking hours in general are 9:30 a.m. to 4:30 p.m., Monday to Friday, with extended hours and weekends at some branches. Most banks have automatic teller machines posted in various locations around the city; these can be accessed 24 hours a day with bank cards on international banking networks such as Cirrus, Plus and Interac. Currency can also be exchanged at the many commercial money exchange outlets in each city.

Most businesses accept all major credit cards such as American Express, Diners Club, EnRoute, MasterCard and Visa. Smaller businesses, however, may accept only one or two of these cards. Traveller's cheques can be cashed in major hotels, some restaurants and large stores.

PASSPORTS

Citizens and permanent residents of the United States can cross the border with a birth certificate or voter's registration card. A current U.S. driver's licence is not accepted as proof of citizenship. Naturalized American citizens should carry naturalization certificates. Visitors from countries other than the United States must have a valid passport and may require other documentation such as a visa or alien card allowing entry. Check with the nearest Canadian Consulate well in advance of travel.

CUSTOMS

Arriving

Travellers entering Canada must declare all goods. Reasonable amounts of personal effects and food are admitted free of duty. Special restrictions or quotas apply to certain specialty goods, especially to plant-, agricultural- and animal-related materials. Each visitor over the age of 19 may bring into Canada up to 40 ounces (1.1 litres) liquor or wine, or 288 ounces (8.5 litres) of beer or ale. Visitors over the age of 19 may also bring up to 50 cigars, 200 cigarettes and 8 ounces (200 grams) of tobacco. Revolvers, pistols, and fully automatic firearms are not allowed into Canada. All other weapons (such as hunting rifles and shotguns) must be declared. For more information contact:
Revenue Canada, Customs and Excise
    Regional Office
    333 Dunsmuir Street,
    Vancouver, BC,
    V6B 5R4 Canada
    604 666-0545 available 24 hours
    Dial "0" for an officer available
    8 a.m. - 4:15 p.m., Monday - Friday

Departing

Before visiting B.C., contact a U.S. Customs office, where copies of the U.S. customs information brochure "Know Before You Go" are available, to find out customs rules for entering or re-entering the United States. Visitors from other countries should check their own customs regulations before leaving home as well.

TAXES

The Federal Goods and Services Tax (GST) of 7% is applied to most goods and services. Visitors from outside of Canada can obtain a GST rebate on most goods taken out of Canada and on accommodation for a stay of less than 30 days. For an instant GST rebate of up to $500 upon exiting Canada, submit receipts and a one-page form to participating duty-free shops. Alternatively, visitors can have original receipts validated by duty-free shop staff or customs officials, and file for a GST rebate (reimbursement by cheque) from home. Visitors departing by air, rail, charter-bus or ferry must include boarding passes or a carrier ticket with the claim.

A non-refundable provincial sales tax (PST) of 7% applies to all retail purchases. Liquor is taxed at 10%. For more information or assistance, call (920) 432-5608 (outside Canada) or 1-800-668-4748 (inside Canada).

GETTING ACQUAINTED

TIME ZONE

Vancouver and Victoria are in the Pacific Standard Time Zone.

CLIMATE, RAIN AND SNOW

These are the average high and low temperatures in Vancouver (source Environment Canada, based on data from 1937 to 1990):

January	5.7°C to 0.1°C
	42°F to 32°F
February	8.0°C to 1.4°C
	46°F to 34°F
March	9.9°C to 2.6°C
	50°F to 37°F
April	12.7°C to 4.9°C
	55°F to 41°F
May	16.3°C to 7.9°C
	61°F to 46°F
June	19.3°C to 11.0°C
	67°F to 52°F
July	21.7°C to 12.7°C
	91°F to 55°F
August	21.7°C to 12.9°C
	71°F to 55°F
September	18.4°C to 10.1°C
	65°F to 50°F
October	13.5°C to 6.4°C
	56°F to 44°F
November	9.0°C to 3.0°C
	48°F to 37°F
December	6.1°C to 0.8°C
	43°F to 33°F

Average temperatures are:

12.0C (54°F) in spring
16.3C (61°F) in summer
6.5C (44°F) in fall
4.7C (40°F) in winter

Average annual rainfall:

1117.2 mm (44.0 inches)

Average annual snowfall:

54.9 cm (21.6 inches)

The average high and low temperatures in Victoria, near the water are (source Environment Canada, based on data from 1967 to 1990):

January	6.7°C to 1.6°C
	44°F to 35°F
February	8.4°C to 2.4°C
	47°F to 36°F
March	10.1°C to 3.0°C
	50°F to 37°F
April	11.9°C to 4.3°C
	53°F to 40°F
May	14.2°C to 6.7°C
	58°F to 44°F
June	16.4°C to 8.8°C
	62°F to 48°F
July	18.2°C to 9.9°C
	65°F to 50°F
August	18.6°C to 10.1°C
	65°F to 50°F
September	17.1°C to 8.8°C
	63°F to 48°F
October	13.1°C to 6.2°C
	56°F to 43°F
November	9.3°C to 3.8°C
	49°F to 39°F
December	6.9°C to 2.0°C
	44°F to 36°F

Average temperatures are:

10.4C (51°F) in spring
14.0C (57°F) in summer
6.9C (44°F) in fall
5.4C (42°F) in winter

Average annual rainfall:

1197.7 mm (47.2 inches)

Average annual snowfall:

29.3 cm (11.5 inches)

GUIDES AND INFORMATION

B.C. has established a Visitor's Info Network with Visitor Info Centres in many communities to assist travellers throughout the province. Tourism BC's official website can be found at www.hellobc.com. Visitors can call 1-

800-435-5622 in North America, 604 435-5622 in Vancouver and 250 387-1642 internationally, for reservations and help with accommodations and other travel plans.

VANCOUVER

• Tourism Vancouver - The Greater Vancouver Convention and Visitors Bureau, 210-200 Burrard St., Vancouver BC V6C 3L6; 604 682-2222, Fax: 604 682-1717.
• Vancouver Tourist Info Centre, Plaza Level, 200 Burrard St., Vancouver BC V6C 3L6; 604 683-2000, Fax: 604 682-6839, Website: www.tourismvancouver.com Source for current information on the Greater Vancouver area, guides and maps. Visitors can make reservations for many accommodations, sightseeing, transportation and outdoor adventures.

VICTORIA:

• Tourism Victoria, Administration, 31 Bastion Square, 4th Floor, Victoria BC V8W 1J1; 250 414-6999, Fax: 250 361-9733.
• Victoria Visitor Info Centre, 812 Wharf St., Victoria BC V8W 1T3; 250 953-2033, Fax: 250 382-6539, Website: www.tourismvictoria.com Source for current information on seeing Victoria, with guides, maps and other travel services.

GETTING AROUND

PUBLIC TRANSIT

VANCOUVER

The TRANSLINK public transit system is a network of buses and ferries (SeaBus) under the Coast Mountain Bus Company and light rapid transit (SkyTrain). Fares for buses, SkyTrain and SeaBus are the same: travel in one zone costs $1.50 for adults and $1.00 for teenagers, children over 5 and seniors; travel in two zones costs $2.25/$1.50; and in three zones, $3.00/$1.00. Discount fares (single-zone amount for all zones) apply after 6:30 p.m. weekdays and all day weekends and holidays. Daypasses cost $6.00/$4.00. Faresaver books of 10 tickets

($13.75) are available at many convenience stores. Schedules can be found at the Vancouver Tourist Info Centre, public libraries, SkyTrain stations and City Hall.

Buses on most routes run until 1 a.m., with some major routes running until 3 a.m. Drivers carry no change, so bring exact fare. A transfer is given as proof of payment and allows passengers to transfer between buses, SkyTrain and SeaBus until the time shown (90 minutes). Blue Buses serve West Vancouver and leave downtown at the corner of Granville and Georgia. The same fares and transfers apply. Call 604 985-7777 for more information on Blue Buses.

SkyTrain is an automated rapid-transit line that runs on mostly elevated tracks from Vancouver's westernmost Waterfront Station through the municipalities of Burnaby and New Westminster to Surrey. These operate from 5 a.m to 1 a.m. Additional SkyTrain lines are being built. Tickets can be purchased or validated at machines in each station.

The SeaBus carries passengers (and bikes) only. Leaving Waterfront Station every 15-30 minutes daily, the ferry crosses Burrard Inlet and arrives 12 minutes later at Lonsdale Quay in North Vancouver.

Many buses are wheelchair lift-equipped or have low floors for easy access. SkyTrains, SeaBus ferries and Seabus terminals are wheelchair accessible. All SkyTrain stations except Granville Station have elevators. HandyDART (604 540-3400) provides service for passengers who can't use the lift-equipped buses or who are not on accessible routes.

For route and schedule information, call 604 521-0400, or visit www.translink.bc.ca

VICTORIA

The Victoria Regional Transit System operates over two zones. Adult fares are $1.75 for one zone, $2.50 for two zones; concession fares for seniors, children over five years of age and students are $1.10 for one zone, $1.75 for two zones. Exact change must be given on buses, and transfers are valid for one-way travel only. Sheets of 10 tickets may be purchased in advance from many stores. Daypasses are also available.

The Victoria Regional Transit System is increasing wheelchair accessibility with low floor buses. For passengers who are not on accessible routes, HandyDART service can be booked at 250 727-7811. For route and schedule information call the 24-hour information line at 250 382-6161 or visit the website at www.transitbc.com/victoria

CARS AND RENTALS

Most foreign drivers' licences are valid in British Columbia. Check with a B.C. Motor Vehicle Branch to find out specific requirements. Visiting motorists should bring registration documents and have insurance in place before driving. Insurance is available as an option in most car rental contracts, and Visitor to Canada Insurance can be purchased through the British Columbia Automobile Association (BCAA) in B.C. United States motorists should have a Canadian Non-Resident Interprovince Motor Vehicle Liability Insurance Card, available only in the U.S. For more information or to obtain a copy of B.C.'s "rules of the road," contact Driver Services Centre, 254-800 Hornby St., Vancouver, BC; 1-800-950-1498 (within North America), Website: www.icbc.com

Speed limits within Vancouver and Victoria are 50 km/h (30 mph) unless otherwise posted. The use of seat belts, child restraints and motorcycle helmets is mandatory. Vancouverites and Victoria residents believe in the pedestrian's right of way. Distances, speed limits, and fuel measurements are indicated in metric units. To convert kilometres to miles, multiply by 0.6; to convert miles to kilometres, multiply by 1.6. One litre equals about 1/3 of an American gallon or 1/5 of an Imperial gallon.

VANCOUVER

- Alamo Rent A Car, 1132 West Georgia St.; 604 684-1401, 1-800-462-5266 or 1-800-327-9633; Vancouver International Airport; 604 231-1400, 1-800-462-5266 or 1-800-327-9633, Email: international@goalamo.com, Website: www.goalamo.com
- Avis, 757 Hornby St.; 604 606-2869, 1-800-272-5871; Vancouver International Airport; 604 606-2847, 1-800-272-5871, Website: www.avis.com
- Budget Rent A Car, 501 West Georgia St.; 604 668-7000, 1-800-268-8900; Vancouver International Airport; 604 668-7000, 1-800-268-8900, Website: www.budget.com
- EZ Car and Truck Rentals, 750 Terminal Ave.; 604 806-6210, 1-888-806-6210; 1087 Hornby St.; 604 662-8543, 1-888-806-6210; Website: www.ez-car.com
- Hertz, 1128 Seymour St.; 604 606-3782, 1-800-263-0600; Vancouver International Airport, 604 606-3782, 1-800-263-0600, Website: www.hertz.com
- Lo Cost Rent A Car Ltd., 1105 Granville St.; 604 689-9664, 1-888-556-2678 or 1-800-986-1266, Website: www.locost.com
- National Car Rental - Downtown, 1130 West Georgia St.; 604 609-7150, 1-800-227-7368; Vancouver International Airport, 604 207-3730, 1-800-227-7368, Website: www.nationalcar.com
- Rent-A-Wreck, 1083 Hornby St.; 604 688-0001, 1-888-665-3777, Website: www.rentawreck.ca
- Thrifty Car Rentals, Century Plaza Hotel, 1015 Burrard St; 604 606-1666, 1-800-847-4389; Landmark Hotel, 1400 Robson St; 604 681-4869, 1-800-847-4389; Vancouver International Airport; 604 606-1655, 1-800-847-4389, Website: www.thrifty.com

VICTORIA

- Avis, 2507 Government St.; 250 386-8468; Victoria International Airport; 250 656-6033, Website: www.avis.com
- Budget Rent A Car, 757 Douglas St.; 250 953-5300, 1-800-268-8900; Victoria International Airport, 250 953-5300, 1-800-268-8900, Website: www.budget.com
- Enterprise Rent-A-Car, Victoria International Airport, 250 656-4808, 1-800-325-8007
- Hertz, 655 Douglas St.; 250 360-

2822; Victoria International Airport, 250 656-2312, Website: www.hertz.com
- Rent-A-Wreck, 2634 Douglas St.; 250 384-5343
- National, 767 Douglas St.; 250 386-1213 or 250 381-1115; Victoria International Airport; 250 386-1213 or 250 381-1115, Website: www.nationalvictoria.com
- Thrifty Car Rentals, 625 Francis Ave.; 250 383-3659, 1-800-847-4389, Website: www.thrifty.com

Check the Telus Yellow Pages for more listings under Automobile renting.

TOURS

VANCOUVER

- Landsea Tours. Guided tours of Vancouver, Victoria, Whistler and the North Shore. 875 Terminal Dr.; 604 255-7272 or 604 669-2277, 1-877-669-2277, Email: landseatours@orca.bc.ca, Website: www.vancouvertours.com
- Stanley Park Horse-Drawn Tours. One-hour narrated, horsedrawn tours. Stanley Park; 604 681-5115, Email: tours@stanleypark.co, Website: www.stanleyparktours.com
- Gray Line of Vancouver. A wide variety of sightseeing, packages, group charters. 255 East 1st Ave.; 604 879-3363, 1-800-667-0882, Email: vancouver.info@grayline.com, Website: www.grayline.ca/vancouver
- Walkabout Historic Vancouver. A walk into Vancouver's past. 342-6038 Imperial St.; 604 439-0448, Email: walkabout_van@bc.sympatico.ca
- Vancouver Trolley Company. A loop showing off 16 attractions in Vancouver with on/off privileges. 875 Terminal Ave.; 604 801-5515, 1-888-451-5581, Email:info@vancouvertrolley.com, Website: www.vancouvertrolley.com
- West Coast City and Nature Sightseeing. Tours of Vancouver, Grouse, Whistler and Victoria in mini-coaches. 3945 Myrtle St. (Burnaby); 604 451-1600, Email: westcoast@vancouversightseeing.com,

Website: www.vancouversightseeing.com
- Champagne Cruises. Yachts for charter cruises and special occasions. 100-1676 Duranleau St.; 604 688-6625, Email: cruises@smartt.com, Website: www.champagnecruises.com
- Harbour Cruises. Sunset dinner cruises, harbour tours, luncheon cruises, day trips. North Foot Denman St.; 604 688-7246, 1-800-663-1500, Email: tours@boatcruises.com, Website: www.boatcruises.com
- Pride of Vancouver Charters. Charters for luncheons, tours, carol ship dinners, fireworks viewing. 141-757 West Hastings St.; 604 687-5533, Email: info@vancouvercharters.com, Website: www.vancouvercharters.com
- Vancouver Yacht Charters. Yacht touring and cruises. 750 Pacific Blvd.; 604 682-2070, Email: info@boatcharters.net, Website: www.boatcharters.net
- Velo-City Cycle Tours Inc. Mountain bike tours. 2256 Chapman Way (North Vancouver); 604 924-0288, Email: velocity@direct.ca, Website: www.velo-city.com
- Gastown Business Improvement Society. Summer walking tours of Gastown. 107-131 Water St.; 604 683-5650.
- Rockwood Adventures. Walking tours of Chinatown and Granville Island. 1330 Fulton St. (West Vancouver); 604 926-7705.

VICTORIA:

- Gray Line of Victoria. Popular tours include Grand City Drive, Butchart Gardens and Whale Watching and Nature Tour. 700 Douglas St.; 250 388-6539, 1-800-663-8390, Email: victoria.info@grayline.ca, Website: www.grayline.ca/Victoria
- Kabuki Kabs. Pedicabs with friendly and knowledgeable drivers. Generally downtown tours, but some operators have specialized tours. 613 Herald St.; 250 385-4243, Email: info@kabukikabs.com, Website: www.kabukikabs.com

- Tallyho Tours. Horse-drawn carriage tours carrying up to 20 people. 180 Goward St.; 250-383-5067.
- Black Beauty Carriages. Private horse-drawn tours for six. 180 Goward St.; 250 361-1220.
- Victoria Harbour Ferries. Full tours of the Gorge and Inner Harbour, moonlight cruises or short hops to points in the harbour. 4530 Markham St.; 250 708-0201, Website: www.vhfc@islandnet.com
- Enchanted Tours. Butchart Gardens, city tours. 3408 Seymour Pl.; 250 975-3396.
- Victoria Bobby Walking Tours. One and a quarter hours of talk and touring of old town Victoria. 414-874 Fleming St.; 250 995-0233.
- Victoria's Secret Gardens. A guided look into private gardens in Oak Bay. 3150 Midland Rd.; 250 595-5333, 1-877-595-5333, Email: Dale_Frank@telus.net
- Fantasea Charters. Luxurious covered yacht for whale-watching or sightseeing. 1243 Miramar Dr.; 250 658-6052.
- Life's a Beach Tours. Guided gourmet picnic tours of Victoria's beaches. 2801 Dewdney Ave.; 250 595-4271, Email: rondaeden@home.com

ACCOMMODATION

In both Vancouver and Victoria, a multitude of lodgings has evolved, both to accommodate the varied tastes of world travellers and to showcase the allure of the West Coast. The major and minor hotels and motels, most located in the downtown areas, put the traveller in each city's heart, while a host of charming bed and breakfasts beckon from quieter, residential streets.

What follows is a cross-section of the hotels, bed and breakfasts, and budget establishments to be found in each city. Maps are provided at the beginning of this book. Prices indicated are approximate, based on the costs quoted at the time of publishing, for two people staying in a double room (excluding taxes) during peak season: $ = $50-$90; $$ = $90-$180; $$$ = above $180. Many establishments offer special Internet rates and online reservation services. HELLO BC (604 435-5622 or 1-800-435-5622) is a free service providing access to over 700 Tourism BC approved lodgings and trip planning services.

VANCOUVER

HOTELS: VANCOUVER INTERNATIONAL AIRPORT

Most of Vancouver's hotels are within a short drive's reach of the airport. The following, however, are considered the closest:

- Best Western Abercorn Inn, 9260 Bridgeport Rd., Richmond BC V6X 1S1; 604 270-7576, 1-800-663-0085, Fax: 604 270-0001, Website: www.bestwestern.com Styled as a Scottish country inn, with antiques and fresh flowers. Spacious rooms, restaurant. $$.
- Best Western Richmond Inn, 7551 Westminster Hwy., Richmond BC V6X 1A3; 604 273-7878, 1-800-663-0299, Fax: 604 278-0188, Website: www.bestwestern.com Two restaurants, four nightspots. Welcomes pets. $$.
- Comfort Inn, 3031 #3 Rd., Richmond BC V6X 2B6; 604 278-5161, 1-800-228-5750, Fax: 604 207-2380. Location allows easy access to casino, Fraser River trails and malls. Welcomes pets. $$.
- Delta Pacific Resort and Conference Centre, 10251 St. Edwards Dr., Richmond BC V6X 2M9; 604 278-9611, 1-800-268-1133, Fax: 604 278-6876. Three towers of rooms with excellent children's programs. Pools, tennis, playground. Welcomes pets (with deposit). $$.
- Delta Vancouver Airport Hotel and Marina, 3500 Cessna Dr., Richmond BC V7B 1C7; 604 278-1241, 1-800-268-1133, Fax: 276-1975. Older hotel on nine landscaped acres overlooking the Fraser River. Heated pool. Welcomes small pets. $$.
- Executive Inn Airport Plaza and Conference Centre, 7211 Westminster Hwy., Richmond BC V6X 1A3; 604 278-5555, 1-888-388-3932, Fax: 273-3024, Website: www.executiveinnhotels.com.

Large rooms and suites. Heated pool, whirlpool. Two restaurants, lounge. $$.

- Fairmont Vancouver Airport, 3111 Grant McConachie Way, PO Box 23798, Vancouver BC V6X 1A1; 604 207-5200. Newly opened, world-class hotel brings sophistication to the concept of airport accommodation. Globe@YVR Restaurant, Jetside Lounge, pool, fitness centre. Offers in-room airline check-in service. Welcomes pets. $$-$$$.
- Four Points Hotel Vancouver Airport, 8368 Alexandra Rd., Richmond BC V6X 4A6; 604 214-0888, 1-800-325-3535, Fax: 604 214-0887, Website: www.fourpoints.com. Modern hotel in Richmond's shopping and entertainment district. Heated pool, restaurant, lounge. $$.
- Hilton Vancouver Airport, 5911 Minoru Blvd., Richmond BC V6X 4C7; 604 273-6336, 1-800-445-8667, Fax: 604 273-6337. Restaurant, lounge, pool, fitness centre, tennis courts. $$.
- Holiday Inn Vancouver Airport, 10720 Cambie Rd., Richmond BC V6X 1K8; 604 821-1818, Fax: 604 821-1819. Suites include themed, kid-friendly suites with bunkbeds, video games. $$.
- Quality Inn Airport, 725 S.E. Marine Dr., Vancouver BC V5X 2T9; 604 321-6611, 1-800-228-5151, Fax: 604 327-3570. Casino, bowling alley, liquor store and sports bar onsite. $$.
- Radisson President Hotel and Suites, 8181 Cambie Rd., Richmond BC V6X 3X9; 604 276-8181, 1-800-333-3333, Fax: 279-8381, Website: www.radisson.com. Home to Western-style and Chinese seafood restaurants. Heated pool, whirlpool. Welcomes small pets. $$$.
- Stay 'n Save Motor Inn, 10551 St. Edwards Dr., Richmond BC V6X 3L8; 604 273-3311, Fax: 273-9522. Well kept and comfortable. Exterior corridors, restaurant. Welcomes small pets. $$.
- Travellodge, 3071 St. Edwards Dr., Richmond BC V6X 3K4; 604 278-5155, 1-877-278-5155, Fax: 278-5125. Comfortable setting.

Heated pool, whirlpool, restaurant, lounge. $$.
- Vancouver Airport Marriott 7571 Westminster Hwy., Richmond BC V6X 1A3; 604 276-2112, 1-800-228-9280, Fax: 604 273-0112, Website: www.marriotthotels.com/YVRSA Caters to corporate travellers, with spacious desks in comfortable rooms. Heated pool. Welcomes small pets. $$.

HOTELS: DOWNTOWN VANCOUVER

In downtown Vancouver, over 10,000 rooms, from budget hostels to luxury hotels, can be found amid myriad shops, restaurants and a bustling business district:

- Best Western Chateau Granville Hotel, 1100 Granville St., Vancouver BC V6Z 2B6; 604 669-7070, 1-800-528-1234, Fax: 604 669-4928, Website: www.bestwestern.com. Downtown hotel bordering the business and shopping districts. Wheelchair access, babysitting, restaurant and lounge. Complimentary passes to nearby health club. $$$.
- Best Western Downtown Vancouver, 718 Drake St., Vancouver BC V6Z 2W6; 604 669-9888, 1-888-669-9888, Fax: 604 669-3440, Email: welcome2@bestwesterndowntown. com, Website: www.bestwesterndowntown.com Built in 1997 to take advantage of great views. Rooftop fitness centre, sauna, Jacuzzi. Complimentary downtown shuttle. $$$.
- Blue Horizon Hotel, 1225 Robson St., Vancouver BC V6E 1C3; 604 688-1411, Fax: 604 688-4461, Email: bluehorizon@ibm.net Distinctive comfort with oversized corner rooms and private balconies in all rooms. Harbour and city views, heated pool. $$$.
- Bosman's Hotel, 1060 Howe St., Vancouver BC V6Z 1P5; 604 682-3171, 1-888-267-6267, Fax: 604 684-4010, Email: info@bosmanshotel.com, Website: www.bosmanshotel.com Newly upgraded older hotel. Dining room, piano lounge, outdoor pool. $$.
- Century Plaza Hotel and Spa, 1015

Burrard St., Vancouver BC V6Z 1Y5; 604 687-0575, 1-800-663-1818, Fax: 604 682-5790, Email: reserve@century-plaza.com, Website: www.century-plaza.com Oversized suites with panoramic ocean, mountain and city views. Seafood restaurant, lounge, cappuccino bar and day spa, steam room, pool. $$-$$$.

- Crowne Plaza Hotel Georgia Vancouver, 801 West Georgia St., Vancouver BC V6C 1P7; 604 682-5566, 1-800-663-1111, Fax: 604 642-5579, Email: hgsales@hotelgeorgia.bc.ca, Website: www.hotelgeorgia.bc.ca Magnificently restored to reflect its 1920s roots. Full service, with dining room serving afternoon tea. Lounge, fitness centre. Multilingual staff. $$$.

- Days Inn Vancouver Downtown, 921 West Pender St., Vancouver BC V6C 1M2; 604 681-4335, 1-800-325-2525, Fax: 604 681-7808, Email: welcome2daysinn-van.com, Website: www.daysinnvancouver.com. 1914 English-style heritage building, renovated 1998. Views restricted by neighbouring buildings. Restaurant, lounge. $$.

- Empire Landmark Hotel and Conference Centre, 1400 Robson St., Vancouver BC V6G 1B9; 604 687-0511, 1-800-830-6144 Email: ehl@asiastandard.com, Website: www.asiastandard.com Vancouver's tallest, featuring the Cloud Nine Revolving Restaurant and Lounge. Sauna and whirlpool, fitness room, business centre and convention space. $$$.

- Executive Inn Hotel - Downtown Vancouver, 1379 Howe St., Vancouver BC V6Z 2R5; 604 688-7678, 1-888-388-3932, Fax: 604 688-7679, Website: www.executiveinnhotels.com Contemporary deluxe rooms and fully-furnished condos. $$-$$$.

- Four Seasons Hotel, 791 West Georgia St., Vancouver BC V6C 2T4; 604 689-9333, 1-800-268-6282, Fax: 604 689-3466, Website: www.fourseasons.com. Luxurious hotel with the exclusive Chartwell Restaurant atop the shops of Pacific Centre. $$$.

- Georgian Court Hotel, 773 Beatty St., Vancouver BC V6B 2M4; 604 682-5555, 1-800-663-1155, Fax: 604 682-8830, Email: info@georgiancourt.com, Website: www.georgiancourt.com. Intimate, European-style hotel, well-known William Tell Dining Room. Deluxe guestrooms and suites. Welcomes small pets. $$$.

- Greenbrier Hotel, 1393 Robson St., Vancouver BC V6E 1C6; 604 683-4558, 1-888-355-5888, Fax: 604 669-3109, Email: greenbrierhotel@aol.com, Website: www.vancouver-bc.com /greenbrierhotel. Smallish hotel. Business centre, full kitchens in suites. $$.

- Hampton Inn and Suites, 111 Robson St., Vancouver BC V6B 2A8; 604 602-1008, 1-877-602-1008, Fax: 604 602-1007, Email: info@hamptoninnvancouver.com, Website: www.hamptoninnvancouver.com New, West-Coast themed hotel. Breakfast buffet, daily newspaper, local calls, rooftop entertainment and exercise facilities. $$$.

- Holiday Inn Vancouver Downtown Hotel and Suites, 1110 Howe St., Vancouver BC, V6Z 1R2; 604 684-2151, 1-800-465-4329, Fax: 604 684-4736, Email: hidtvan@intergate.bc.ca, Website: www.hi-vancouver.bc.ca. Offers some suites with extra-long beds. Unsupervised Kids PlayCentre with video games, jungle gym. Welcomes small pets. $$$.

- Hotel Vancouver, 900 West Georgia St., Vancouver BC V6C 2W6; 604 684-3131, 1-800-441-1414, Fax: 604 662-1929, Email: reserve@hvc.cphotels.ca, Website: www.cphotels.ca. Heritage landmark that is home to the renowned restaurant 900 West. Beautiful guestrooms and suites. Indoor pool, healthclub, spa, business centre, free local calls. $$$.

- Howard Johnson Hotel, 1176 Granville St., Vancouver BC V6Z 1L8; 604 688-8701, 1-800-446-4656, Fax: 604 688-8335, Email: info@hojovancouver.com, Website: www.hojovancouver.com Beautifully renovated boutique hotel. Swing bar, continental breakfast. Free passes to Fitness World. $$.

- Hyatt Regency Vancouver, 655 Burrard St., Vancouver BC V6C 2R7; 604 683-1234, 1-800-233-1234, Fax: 604 689-3707, Website: www.hyatt.com. Luxury tower connected to Royal Centre plaza. Two restaurants, coffee bar and lounge, health club, outdoor pool. Multilingual staff. $$$.

- Jolly Taxpayer Hotel, 828 West Hastings St., Vancouver BC V6C 1C8; 604 681-3550, Fax: 604 682-2160. Small and intimate, with British-style pub downstairs. $.

- Landis Hotel and Suites, 1200 Hornby St., Vancouver BC; 604 681-3555, Fax: 604 681-9222. Large, fully equipped apartments perfect for families on long stays. $$$

- Listel Vancouver, 1300 Robson St., Vancouver BC V6E 1C5; 604 684-8461, Fax: 604 684-7092, Email: moreinfo@listel-vancouver.com, Website: www.listel-vancouver.com Features two Gallery floors showcasing original work by regional and international artists. Restaurant and Bar with live jazz on weekends. $$$.

- Lord Stanley Suites on the Park, 1889 Alberni St., Vancouver BC V6G 3G7; 604 688-9299, 1-888-767-7829, Fax: 604 688-9297, Website: www.lordstanley.com Location at entrance to Stanley Park offers unobstructed views of the water, mountains, and the city. Private workrooms, washer and dryer available. $$$.

- Marriott - Residence Inn, 1234 Hornby St., V6Z 1W2; 604 688-1234, 1-800-663-1234, Fax: 604 689-1762, Website: www.residenceinn.com/YVRRI Furnished suites with kitchen facilities. Fitness centre, indoor pool whirlpool, café, complimentary downtown transportation. $$$.

- Metropolitan Hotel, 645 Howe St., Vancouver BC V6C 2Y9; 604 687-1122, Fax: 604 689-7044, Email: reservations@metropolitan.com, Website: www.metropolitan.com. Sumptuous surroundings, full service rooms. Hosts elegant Diva at the Met Restaurant. Sports court. Welcomes small pets. $$$

- Pacific Palisades Hotel, 1277 Robson St., Vancouver BC V6E 1C4; 604 688-0461, Fax: 604 891-5104, Email: sales@pacificpalisadeshotel.com, Website: www.pacificpalisadeshotel.com All-suite hotel. Kitchens in some suites, health club with pool, sauna. Complimentary shoe shine and daily newspaper. Welcomes small pets. $$$.

- Pan Pacific Hotel, 300-999 Canada Place, Vancouver BC V6C 3B5; 604 662-8111, 1-800-663-1515, Fax: 604 685-9690, Email: reservations@panpacific-hotel.com, Website: www.panpac.com. One of the city's best luxury hotels. Part of a complex shared by the cruiseship terminal, convention centre, and the celebrated Five Sails Restaurant. Racquetball court, harbour and mountain views, full service. Welcomes small pets. $$$.

- Quality Hotel - The Inn at False Creek, 1335 Howe St., Vancouver BC V6Z 1R7; 604 682-0229, 1-800-663-8474, Fax: 604 662-7566, Email: quality@qualityhotelvancouver.com Website: www.qualityhotelvancouver.com Mexican tile, pottery and rugs contribute to a Sante Fe atmosphere. Heated outdoor pools, complimentary access to nearby fitness centre. Offers excellent "passport" featuring 50% savings at 35 Vancouver attractions, restaurants and entertainment. $$-$$$.

- Ramada Inn and Suites Downtown Vancouver, 1221 Granville St., Vancouver BC V6Z 1M6; 604 685 1111, 1-888-835-0078, Fax: 604 685-0707, Email: sales@ramadavancouver.com, Website: www.ramadavancouver.com Situated in the Granville Entertainment district, with Granville Island just an Aquabus ferry away. Restaurant, lounge, airport shuttle. $$-$$$.

- Renaissance Vancouver Harbourside, 1133 West Hastings St., Vancouver BC V6E 3T3; 604

689-9211, 1-800-905-8582, Fax: 604 689-4358, Website: www.renaissancehotels.com. Guestrooms and suites with harbour and city views. Restaurant, heated pool, convention space. Welcomes small pets. $$$.

- Robsonstrasse Hotel, 1394 Robson St., Vancouver BC V6E 1C5; 604 687-1674, 1-888-667-8877, Fax: 604 685-7808, Email: info@robsonstrassehotel.com Boutique hotel offering studio and deluxe suites with kitchenette. Personalized voice mail, modem hookup, free covered parking. $$$.

- Rosedale on Robson, 838 Hamilton St., Vancouver BC V6B 6A2; 604 689-8033, 1-800-661-8870, Fax: 604 689-4426, Email: roseresv@direct.ca, Website: www.rosedaleonrobson.com Vancouver's newest all-suite hotel offers one- or two-bedroom suites. Recreation facilities, restaurant, lounge. $$$.

- Royal Hotel, 1025 Granville St., Vancouver BC V6Z 1L4; 604 685-5335, 1-877-685-5337, Fax: 604 685-5351, Email: frontdesk@attheroyal.com, Website: www.attheroyal.com Newly renovated boutique-style hotel. Complementary tea/coffee in lobby, popular gay pub The Royal onsite. Some pet-friendly rooms. $$$.

- Sheraton Vancouver Wall Centre Hotel, 1088 Burrard St., Vancouver BC V6Z 2R9; 604 331-1000, 1-800-663-9255, Fax: 604 873-7200, Email: wallcentre@intouch.bc.ca Website: www.sheratonwallcentre.com Luxurious guestrooms and suites, first-class service. Expansion planned for 2001. $$$.

- St. Regis Hotel, 602 Dunsmuir St., Vancouver BC V6B 1Y6; 604 681-1135, 1-800-770-7929, Fax: 604 683-1126, Website: www.stregishotel.com. Recently restored and renovated (1997) in the boutique style. Steakhouse, bar and grill, breakfast lounge. $$.

- Sutton Place Hotel, 845 Burrard St., Vancouver BC V6Z 2K6; 604 682-5511, 1-800-961-7555, Fax: 604 682-5513, Email: info@vcr.suttonplace.com, Website: www.suttonplace.com. Attentive staff, understated elegance. Home to the award-winning Fleuri Restaurant of chocoholic bar fame. $$$.

- Sylvia Hotel, 1154 Gilford St., Vancouver BC, V6G 2P6; 604 681-9321, Fax: 682-3551, Website: www.syviahotel.com. A charming, ivy-covered heritage building immortalized by the children's book *Mister Got To Go*. Welcomes pets. $$.

- Terminal City Club Tower Hotel, 837 West Hastings St., Vancouver BC, V6C 1B6; 604 681-4121, Fax: 604, 488-8604, Email: hotel@tcclub.com, Website: www.tcclub.com. Full service hotel offers to the public the privileges of the members-only Terminal City Club. Conference facilities, two restaurants, pub, billards, fitness club, pool. $$$.

- Waterfront Centre Hotel, 900 Canada Place Way, Vancouver BC V6C 3L5; 604 691-1991, Fax: 604 691-1999, Email: reserve@wfc.cphotels.ca, Website: www.fairmont.com. Waterfrontage, terraced gardens. Concourse shops and an enclosed walkway links hotel to Vancouver Convention and Exhibition Centre and Cruiseship Terminal. Heated pool. Welcomes small pets. $$$.

- Wedgewood Hotel, 845 Hornby St., Vancouver BC, V6Z 1V1; 604 689-7777, 1-800-663-0666, Fax: 604 608-5348, Email: info@wedgewoodhotel.com, Website: www.wedgewoodhotel.com Intimate and stylish European boutique hotel. Attentive staff, award-winning Bacchus restaurant. Afternoon tea, lounge, cigar room. $$$.

- Westin Bayshore Resort and Marina Vancouver, 1601 West Georgia St., Vancouver BC V6G 2V4; 604 682-3377, Fax: 604 687-3102, Email: bayshore@westin.com, Website: www.westin.com. Luxury in a waterfront resort setting. Two restaurants, two lounges, whirlpool, masseur, pools, some environmentally-friendly rooms. Welcomes small pets. $$$.

- YMCA Hotel, 955 Burrard St., Vancouver BC V6Z 1Y2; 604 681-0221, Fax: 604 681-1630, Email: vancouver_hotel@ymca.ca, Website: www.ymca.vancouver.bc.ca Clean, affordable co-ed accommodations. Daily maid service, shared bathrooms, café, cafeteria, complete fitness facility including pools, workout equipment, aerobics, racquetball and gym. $.
- YWCA Hotel/Residence, 733 Beatty St., Vancouver BC V6B 2M4; 604 895-5830, 1-800-663-1424, Fax: 604 681-2550, Email: hotel@ywcavan.org, Website: www.ywcahotel.com. Built in 1995 for women and men. Air-conditioning, private, shared or hall bathrooms, shared kitchen, laundry room. Complimentary access to YWCA Health and Wellness Centre with pool, steam room whirlpool, gym, fitness and aquatics drop-in classes. $-$$.

BED AND BREAKFASTS

Bedding down in one of Vancouver's bed and breakfasts gives travellers a glimpse of the enviable, everyday lifestyle of the West Coast. Best Canadian Bed and Breakfast Reservations (free service, 604 738-7207), Canada-West Accommodations B&B Registry (604 990-6730 or 1-800-561-3223), and Old English B&B Registry (604 986-5069) are reservation services that can help sort through the many choices.

- Albion Guest House, 592 West 19th Ave., Vancouver BC V5Z 1W6; 604 873-2287, Fax: 604 879-5682, Email: albion@direct.ca. Four rooms in a renovated, turn-of-the-century house. Hot tub in courtyard, full breakfast, tennis rackets and bicycles. French spoken. No smoking, street parking only. $$.
- Arbutus House, 4470 Maple Crescent, Vancouver BC V6J 4B3; 604 738-6432, Fax: 604 738-6433, Website: www.arbutushouse.com. Five rooms in a 1920s Shaughnessy character house with leaded windows, oak floors, cove ceilings. Guest rooms with sitting areas, one with private deck. Full breakfast, no pets, smoking outdoors. $$.
- Camilla House Bed and Breakfast, 2538 West 13th Ave., Vancouver BC V6K 2T1; 604 737-2687, Fax: 604 737-2586, Email: info@vancouver-bb.com, Website: www.vancouverbb.com /camilla.html. Five rooms in a private home with oriental touches in public areas. Breakfast plan. $$.
- Chelsea Cottage Bed and Breakfast, 2143 West 46th Ave., Vancouver BC V6M 2L2; 604 266-2681, Fax: 604 266-7540, Email: info@vancouver-inn.com Website: www.vancouver-inn.com. Four rooms in a 1925 character house in leafy Kerrisdale. Ceiling fans, telephones, TVs. Full breakfast. No pets, street parking only, no smoking. $$.
- Cherub Inn, 2546 West 6th Ave., Vancouver BC V6K 1W5; 604 733-3166, 1-899-733-3166, Fax: 604 733-3106, Email: info@cherubinn.com, Website: www.cherubinn.com. Four rooms in a restored and updated 1913 Craftsman house. Anaglyphic wallpaper, stained glass, high ceilings, wood panelling, English and Belgian antiques. Chocolates and morning paper, full breakfast. $$.
- Columbia Cottage, 205 West 14th Ave., Vancouver BC V5Y 1X2; 604 874-5327, Fax: 604 879-4547, Email: info@columbiacottage.com, Website: www.columbiacottage.com. Four rooms in a 1929 Tudor-style cottage, Fairview area close to city Hall. Full breakfast, no smoking. $$.
- Johnson Heritage House Bed and Breakfast, 2278 West 34th Ave., Vancouver BC V6M 1G6; 604 266-4175, Fax: 604 266-4175, Email: fun@johnsons-inn-vancouver.com, Website: www.johnsons-inn-vancouver.com. Three rooms in a 1920s home restored in the Craftsman style. Lots of whimsy in antique furniture, Persian carpets, carousel horse, gramophone and themed bathrooms. Breakfast plan. No smoking, no pets. $-$$.
- Jolie Maison, 1888 West 3rd Ave.,

Vancouver BC V6J 1K8; 604 730-8010, Fax: 604 730-8045, Email: skelly@direct.ca. Four rooms in a restored 1901 house, Kitsilano district. Breakfast served. French, Dutch, German spoken. $$.

- O Canada House, 1114 Barclay St., Vancouver BC V6E 1H1; 604 688-0555, Fax: 604 488-0556. Five rooms in a beautifully restored 1897 home, where the national anthem O Canada was written in 1909. Fans, designated smoking area, breakfast. Wheelchair accessible. $$-$$$.
- Penny Farthing Inn, 2855 West 6th Ave., Vancouver BC V6K 1X2; 604 739-9002, Fax: 604 739-9004, Email: info@pennyfarthinginn.com, Website: www.pennyfarthinginn.com. Two rooms, two suites in a renovated 1912 house. Guest living room, guest fridge, guest business room with computer, scanner, printer, email connection, fax, photocopier. Full breakfast. The four resident cats aren't permitted in guest rooms or suites. $$.
- West End Guest House, 1362 Haro, Vancouver BC V6E 1G2; 604 681-2889, Fax: 604 688-8812. Eight period rooms in a pink Victorian-era home. Resident ghost, designated smoking areas, breakfast plan. $$-$$$.
- Windsor House, 325 West 11th Ave., Vancouver BC V5Y 1T3; 604 872-3060, Fax: 604 873-1147. Ten rooms, simple décor. Designated smoking areas, breakfast plan. $-$$.

HOSTELS AND EDUCATIONAL

Hostels offer Spartan but economical alternatives for accommodation. In the summer, a few educational institutes open their residences to travellers as well.

- C & N Backpackers Hostel, 927 Main St., Vancouver BC V6A 2V8; 604 682-2441, 1-888-434-6060, Fax: 604 682-2441, Email: nasser@cnnbackpackers.com, Website: www.cnnbackpackers.com. A 1926 heritage building with a renovated interior near SkyTrain, bus terminal, train station. International staff speaks English, French, German, Spanish, Korean, Portuguese, Farsi, Turkish. Fully equipped kitchen, several showers per floor, laundry facility. Internet, ESL school, guest phones, fax. $.

- Cambie International Hostels and Saloons, 300 Cambie St., Vancouver BC V6B 2N3; 604 684-6466, Fax: 604 687-5618, Email: gastown@cambiehostels.com, Website: www.cambiehostels.com Gastown hostel features a pub, general store, and bakery/café. Full laundry, bike storage, email and Internet. Shuttle bus to bus station and airport. $.
- Cambie International Hostels and Saloons II, 515 Seymour St., Vancouver BC V6B 2H6; 604 684-7757, Fax: 604 687-5618, Email: seymour@cambiehostels.com, Website: www.cambiehostels.com Downtown location. Features a pub, general store, and bakery/café. Full laundry, bike storage, email and Internet. Shuttle bus to bus station and airport. $.
- Hostelling International Vancouver Downtown, 1114 Burnaby St., Vancouver BC V6E 1P1; 604 684-4565, 1-888-203-4302, Fax: 604 684-4540, Email: van-downtown@hihostels.bc.ca, Website: www.hihostels.bc.ca Shared and private rooms with fully equipped kitchens. Internet, TV room, game room, and organized activities. Library/reading room, laundry room, bike rental/storage, limited parking. $.
- Hostelling International Vancouver Jericho Beach, 1515 Discovery St., Vancouver BC V6R 4K5; 604 224-3208, 1-888-203-4303, Fax: 604 224-4852, Email: van-jericho@hihostels.bc.ca, Website: www.hihostels.bc.ca. Shared and private rooms with fully equipped kitchens. Internet, TV room with movie library, pool table, licensed cafeteria. Laundry, bike rental, free shuttle making loop from Jericho Beach to Pacific Centre, bus and train stations, to downtown HI hostel. $.
- St. George's Conference Centre, 4175 West 29th Ave., Vancouver BC V6S 1V6; 604 224-1304, Fax: 604 224-7066, Email:

summer@stgeorges.bc.ca, Website: www.stgeorges.bc.ca. Open July up to the third week of August. Three-story dorm facilities built in 1993. Student lounges with TV, VCR, table tennis, minimal kitchen with refrigerator, microwave, sink (no cooking facility). Public phones, shared and central washrooms and showers. Limited housekeeping, no smoking. Minimum three-night stay. $.

- UBC Conference Centre, 5961 Student Union Blvd., Vancouver BC V6T 2C9; 604 822-1000; Fax: 604 822-1069, Email: reservation@brock.housing.ubc.ca, Website: www.conferences.ubc.ca The UBC Conference Centre arranges accommodation and meeting space at the following four residences on campus:
- Gage Court Suites. Available year round. Court suites with private washrooms, kitchenette, phone, TV, limited parking. $$.
- Gage Tower Suites and Apartments. Available May 10 to August 26. Single and double tower suites with kitchenette, phone, TV, shared or private bath. Single occupancy. $$.
- Place Vanier. Available July 1 to August 20. Single and twin dorm-style rooms. Shared washrooms. Bring own soap, towels. No cooking facilities. TV lounge, pay phone. $.
- Totem Park Residences (May 11 to August 26). Single and twin dorm-style rooms with shared washrooms. Bring own soap, towels. No cooking facilities. TV lounge, pay phone. Modified housekeeping can be arranged. Hot or cold breakfast served. $.
- Vancouver School of Theology, 600 Iona Drive, Vancouver BC V6T 1L4; 604 822-9031, Fax: 604 822-9212, Email: vstconf@vst.edu, Website: www.vst.edu/housing Year-round guest accommodation on scenic part of University of BC campus. Dorm-style rooms with sink and hall baths/showers, double rooms with shower ensuite. $.

VICTORIA

HOTELS: VICTORIA INTERNATIONAL AIRPORT

Because the Victoria International Airport is located on the Saanich Peninsula away from the city, Victoria itself has no "airport hotels." However, the towns bordering the airport extend a number of lodgings to serve travellers too tired to make the 30-minute drive to the core of Victoria:

- Best Western Emerald Isle Motor Inn, 2306 Beacon Ave., Sidney BC V8L 1X2; 250 656-4441, 1-800-315-3377, Fax: 250 655-1351, Website: www.bestwestern.com Huge guest rooms. Sauna, whirlpool, restaurant. $$.
- Super 8 Motel Victoria/Saanichton, 2477 Mt. Newton X Road, Saanichton BC V8M 2B7; 250 652-6888, 1-800-800-8000, Fax: 250 652-6800. Modern comfort, economically styled. Restaurant. Welcomes pets. $$.
- Travelodge Victoria Airport Sidney, 2280 Beacon Ave., Sidney BC V8L 1X1; 250 656-1176, 1-888-515-6375, Fax: 250 656-7344, Website: www.travelodge.com. Older but remodeled digs. Courtyard, heated outdoor pool. Welcomes small pets. $$.
- Waterfront Hotel Sidney, 2537 Beacon Ave., Sidney BC V8L 1Y3; 250 656-1131, 1-888-656-1131, Fax: 250 656-9396, Email: waterfront@hotelsidney.com Website: www.hotelsidney.com The hotel's location on the Sidney Harbour means access to whale-watching, fishing and other water-related activities. Some rooms with harbour views, kitchens. $$.

HOTELS: DOWNTOWN VICTORIA AND INNER HARBOUR

Victoria's downtown and Inner Harbour hotels perfectly situate the traveler in the thick of the city's attractions:

- Admiral Motel, 257 Belleville St., Victoria BC V8V 1X1; 250 388-6267, 1-800-236-4722, Fax: 250 388-6267, Email: alan@admiral.bc.ca, Website:

www.admiral.bc.ca Well-equipped rooms and suites in a harbourside hotel-class accommodation. Complimentary local calls, parking, continental breakfast and coffee. English and French-speaking staff. Welcomes pets. $$-$$$.

- Bedford Regency Hotel, 1140 Government St., Victoria BC V8W 1Y2; 250 384-6835, 1-800-665-6500, Fax: 250 386-8930, Email: bedford@victorialoc.com, Website: www.victoriabc.com/accom/bedford.html Architectural details lend old-world charm to this small but elegant 1800s hotel. Wood-burning fireplaces in some suites. Off-site parking only. Restaurant serving breakfast only.$$-$$$.
- Best Western Carleton Plaza, 642 Johnson St., Victoria V8W 1M6; 250 388-5513, 1-800-663-7241, Fax: 250 388-5343, Website: www.bestwesterncarleton.com Refurbishing has made for bright and spacious rooms. Air conditioning, restaurant. $$-$$$.
- Best Western Inner Harbour, 412 Quebec St., Victoria BC V8V 1W5; 250 384-5122, 1-800-383-2378, Fax: 250 384-5113, Email:bestwest@victoriahotels.com, Website: www.bestwestern.com Spacious, renovated rooms, all with private balconies. Jacuzzi, sauna, heated outdoor pool. $$-$$$.
- Chateau Victoria Hotel, 740 Burdett Avenue, Victoria BC V8W 1B2; 250 382-4221, 1-800-663-5891, Fax: 250 380-1950, Email: reservations@chateauvictoria.com, Website: www.chateauvictoria.com Full-service boutique hotel hosting Victoria's only rooftop restaurant. English, Chinese, German, Portuguese, Spanish and Swiss spoken. Lounge, heated pool. $$-$$$.
- Clarion Hotel Grand Pacific, 450 Quebec St., Victoria BC V8V 1W5; 250 386-0450, 1-800-663-7550, Fax: 250 380-4475, Email: reserve@hotelgrandpacific.com, Website: www.hotelgrandpacific.com. Rooms all have private balconies, air conditioning. Pool, whirlpool, sauna, workout facilities, squash and racquetball courts. Chinese, English, French, German, Spanish,

Punjabi spoken. $$$.
- Coast Victoria Harbourside Hotel and Marina, 146 Kingston St., Victoria BC V8V 1V4; 250 360-1211, 1-800-663-1144, Fax: 250 360-1418, Website: www.coasthotels.com/hotels/vic.htm. Waterfrontage with indoor and outdoor pools and health club. Award-winning Blue Crab Bar and Grill, lounge. $$$.
- Crystal Court Motel, 701 Belleville St., Victoria BC V8W 1A2; 250 384-0551, Fax: 250 384-5125, Email: mbscott@vanisle.net. Well-kept, older budget motel with mix of room size and style. Exterior corridors. $.
- Days Inn on the Harbour, 427 Belleville St., Victoria BC V8V 1X3; 250 386-3451, 1-800-665-3024, Fax: 250 386-6999, Email: info@daysinnvictoria.com, Website: www.daysinnvictoria.com The Victoria connection in the Days Inn chain. Restaurant, lounge, heated pool, whirlpool. $$-$$$.
- Empress Hotel, 721 Government St., Victoria BC V8W 1W5; 250 384-8111, 1-800-414-1414, Fax: 250 381-4334, Email: theempresshotel@fairmont.com, Website: www.cphotels.com Unparalleled elegance and service in a restored heritage setting as regal as the name implies. Restaurant and lounge, fitness, whirlpool, heated pool. World-famous afternoon tea. $$-$$$.
- Executive House Hotel, 777 Douglas St., Victoria BC V8W 2B5; 250 388-5111, 1-800-663-7001, Fax: 250 385-1323, Email: executivehouse@executivehouse.com, Website: www.executivehouse.com. Older hi-rise hotel with spacious rooms and suites. Sauna, steamroom, whirlpool, restaurants. Welcomes small pets. $$.
- Green Gables Inn, 850 Blanshard St., Victoria BC V8W 2H2; 250 385-6787, Fax: 250 385-5800. Comfortable and cheerful. English style pub, restaurant. $$.
- Harbour Towers Hotel, 345 Quebec St., Victoria BC V8V 1W4; 250 385-2405, 1-800-663-896, Fax: 250 385-4453, Email: harbour@pacificcoast.net, Website: www.harbourtowers.com. Spacious

rooms. Indoor pool, whirlpool, sauna, full day spa, fitness centre. Restaurant and lounge. $$$.
- Laurel Point Inn, 680 Montreal St., Victoria BC V8V 1Z8; 250 386-8721, 1-800-663-7667, Fax: 250 386-9547, Email: guestservices@laurelpoint.com, Website: www.laurelpoint.com. A downtown hotel in the resort style. Indoor pool, sauna, Jacuzzi. Free local calls and parking. Two restaurants and a lounge, business centre. English, French and Japanese spoken. $$$.
- Magnolia Hotel, 623 Courtney St., Victoria BC V8W 1B8; 250 381-0999, 1-877-624-6654, Fax: 250 381-0988, Email: sales@magnoliahotel.com, Website: www.magnoliahotel.com Boutique hotel exuding opulence with floor-to-ceiling windows and lavish bathrooms. Family suites available. Restaurant, brew pub. $$$.
- Ocean Pointe Resort Hotel and Spa, 45 Songhees Road, Victoria BC V9A 6T3; 250 360-2999, 1-800-667-4677, Fax: 250 360-1041, Email: reservations@oprhotel.com, Website: www.oprhotel.com. The very incarnation of casual elegance. Heated pool, sauna, whirlpool, racquetball courts, tennis courts, full European spa. Home to The Victorian Restaurant. Welcomes small pets. $$-$$$.
- Quality Inn Downtown, 850 Blanshard St., Victoria BC V8W 2H2; 250 385-6787, 1-800-661-4115, Fax: 250 385-5800. Small hotel downtown. Pub, café, complimentary parking. $$.
- Queen Victoria Inn, 655 Douglas St., Victoria BC V8V 2P9; 250 386-1312, 1-800-663-7007, Fax: 250 381-4312, Email: info@queenvictoriainn.com, Website: www.queenvictoriainn.com. Heated outdoor pool, sauna, restaurant. $$-$$$.
- Ramada Huntingdon Manor Inn, 330 Quebec St., Victoria BC V8V 1W3; 250 381-3456, 1-800-663-7557, Fax: 250 382-7666, Email: huntingdon@bctravelcom, Website: www.ramada.com. Full-service hotel with English -style interiors.

Sauna, whirlpool, aromatherapy. Restaurant, bar and grill, ice cream parlour. Home to Artisans Lane. $$-$$$.
- Strathcona Hotel, 919 Douglas St., Victoria BC V8W 2C2; 250 383-7137, 1-800-663-7476, Fax: 250 383-6893, Email: reservations@strathconahotel.com, Website: www.strathconahotel.com. A 1913 building recently refurbished with charisma. Victorian-era pub, nightclub. Rooftop lounge and volleyball court. $-$$.
- Swans Hotel, 506 Pandora Ave., Victoria BC V8V 1N6; 250 361-3310, 1-800-668-7926, Fax: 250 361-3491, Email: help@swanshotel.com, Website: www.swanshotel.com. Restored heritage building with fabulous art collection in Olde Towne. Onsite brew pub, restaurant, club, beer and wine store. $$.
- Travellers Inn Downtown, 1850 Douglas St., Victoria BC V8T 4K6; 250 381-1000, 1-888-254-6476, Fax: 250 381-1001, Email: callus@travellersinn.com, Website: www.travellersinn.com. Spacious rooms. Top floor rooms with small patio deck. Some rooms with kitchen, whirlpools. No pets. $.
- Victoria Plaza Hotel, 603 Pandora Ave., Victoria BC V8W 1N8; 250 386-3631, 1-800-906-4433, Fax: 250 920-5434, Email: jrincon@telus.net, Website: www.vacationsbc.com/victoriaplaza Modern and clean rooms with fine service. $.
- Victoria Regent Hotel, 1234 Wharf St., Victoria BC V8W 3H9; 250 386-2211, 1-800-663-7472, Fax: 250 386-2622, Email: regent@pinc.com, Website: www.regent-hotel.victoria.bc.ca Condominium-style accommodations with sundecks, kitchens and dining areas. English and French spoken. $$-$$$.

BED AND BREAKFASTS

More than any other, the bed-and-breakfast experience evokes the graciousness and hospitality of a bygone era. AA-Accommodations West Reservation Agency (250 479-1986) and Western Canada B&B

Innkeepers Association (250 388-6669) are two reservation services that can help with B&B accommodation in Victoria and other Vancouver Island locations. The following are but a few of the many bed and breakfasts that dot the Victoria area:

- A B&B at a Hidden Garden, 1326 Manor Rd., Victoria BC V8S 2A2; 250 595-2625, 1-877-595-2625, Fax: 250 595-2645, Email: ahiddengarden@home.com, Website: www.ahiddengarden.com Self-contained suites with bathrooms in a 1922 home 15 minutes away from city centre. Breakfast served. No smoking, no pets. $$.

- A B&B at Swallow Hill Farm, 4910 William Head Rd., Victoria BC V9C 3Y8; 250 474-4042, Fax: 250 474-4042, Email: info@swallowhillfarm.com, Website: www.swallowhillfarm.com. Two suites with private baths on an apple farm on the southwest coast. Ocean and mountain views. Sauna. Wildlife viewing, outdoors activities. Farm breakfast served. No pets (resident dog), no smoking. $$.

- A Haterleigh Heritage Inn, 243 Kingston St., Victoria BC V8V 1V5; 250 384-9995, Fax: 250 384-1935, Email: paulk@haterleigh.com, Website: www.haterleigh.com. Six rooms in a 1901 Victorian heritage mansion. Restored, with a mix of modern and antique furnishings. Private Jacuzzis, gourmet breakfast served. No smoking, no pets. $$$.

- Abigail's Hotel, 906 McClure St., Victoria BC V8V 3E7; 250 388-5363, 1-800-561-6565, Fax: 250 388-7787, Email: innkeeper@abigailshotel.com, Website: www.abigails hotel.com. Twenty-two rooms on four floors in a Tudor-style country bed and breakfast inn. Antique furniture, no elevator. Breakfast served, hors d'oeuvres and sherry offered in library. German spoken. No smoking, no pets. $$$.

- Andersen House B&B, 301 Kingston St., Victoria BC V8V 1V5; 250 388-4565, Fax: 250 388-4565, Email:andersen@islandnet.com, Website: www.andersenhouse.com Four suites in an 1897 house with high ceilings, stained glass, hardwood, fireplaces, built originally for a sea captain. Additional suite with shower and two washrooms housed in a classic, 50-foot motor yacht moored five minutes away. Full breakfast served. $$-$$$.

- Beaconsfield Inn, 998 Humboldt St., Victoria BC V8V 2Z8; 250 384-4044, 1-888-884-4044, Fax: 250 384-4052, Email: beaconsfield@islandnet.com, Website: www.islandnet.com/beaconsfield Six rooms, three suites in 1905 manse. Restored rooms reflect Edwardian atmosphere, with 16-ft beamed ceilings, leaded glass windows, mahogany wood floors, fine antiques. Sunroom with cottage garden view. Gourmet breakfast, afternoon tea and sherry served. No pets, no smoking, no elevator (four stories). $$$.

- Cartref Bed and Breakfast, 1345 Readings Dr., Sidney BC V8L 5K7; 250 656-1247, Fax: 250 656-1247, Email: cartref@islandnet.com, Website: www.victoriabc.com/acom /cartref.html Two rooms, shared and private bathrooms, in a new country-style home. An acre of landscaped rock, sunny hillside, knowledgeable hosts especially appealing for gardeners. Guest sitting room. Full or light breakfast served. No smoking, no pets. $$.

- Gatsby Mansion, 309 Belleville St., Victoria BC V8V 1X2; 250 388-9191, 1-800-563-9656, Fax: 250 920-5651, Email: huntingdon@bctravel.com, Website: www.bctravel.com/huntingdon /gatsby.html. A collection of 18 suites in Belleville Park, housed in a restored Queen Anne mansion (1877) and smaller house, both with ocean view. Main house has antiques, frescoed ceilings, stained glass, large verandah. Licensed lounge, restaurant, aromatherapy studio, gift shop. Full Breakfast served. No smoking, no pets. $$-$$$.

- Holland House Inn, 595 Michigan St., Victoria BC V8V 1S7; 250 384-6644, 1-800-335-3466, Fax: 250 384-6117, Email: stay@hollandhouse.victoria.bc.ca, Website: www.hollandhouse.victoria.bc.ca Fourteen rooms in a 1930s residence. Relaxed elegance in large rooms, country antique items, charming library/loung with open-log fire. No elevator, no pets, designated smoking area. Breakfast served. $$-$$$.
- Humboldt House Bed and Breakfast, 867 Humboldt St., Victoria BC V8V 2Z6; 250 383-0152, 1-888-383-0327, Fax: 250 383-6402, Email: rooms@humboldthouse.com, Website: www.humboldthouse.com Five romantic rooms in authentically renovated Victorian-era house. Large whirlpool, wood burning fireplaces. Sherry served in sitting room. Gourmet champagne breakfast delivered to rooms. No smoking. $$$.
- Iris Garden Country Manor Bed and Breakfast, 5360 West Saanich Rd., Victoria BC V9E 1J8; 250 744-2253, 1-877-744-2253, Fax: 250 744-5690, Email: stay@irisgardenvictoria.com, Website: www.irisgardenvictoria.com. Four rooms featuring vaulted ceilings, new fixtures in an elegant country retreat. Three acres of irises, Douglas firs surround the 1960s character home. Guest living room. Full breakfast served. No smoking. $$.
- Oak Bay Guest House, 1052 Newport Ave., Victoria BC V8S 5E3; 250 598-3812, 1-800-575-3812, Fax: 250 598-0369, Website: www.oakbayguesthouse.com Eleven rooms in a restored manor previously owned by the eccentric Oak Bay Philosopher. Charming décor, wood-paneled walls, open wood beams, lush landscape reflect gentility of the Oak Bay suburb. Compact bathrooms. No smoking. $$.
- Orchard house, 9646 Sixth St., Sidney BC V8L 2W2; 250 656-9194. Four rooms in house built in 1914 by Sidney founding family.

Beamed ceilings, built in wood cabinets with leaded glass windows. Close to airport and Vancouver ferries. Full breakfast served. Smoking outdoors, no pets. $.
- Prior House B&B Inn, 620 St. Charles St., Victoria BC V8S 3N7; 250 592-8847, 1-877-924-3300, Fax: 250 592-8223, Email: innkeeper@priorhouse,com, Website: www.priorhouse.com. Six rooms and suites in a restored 1912 manor house built originally for the lieutenant-governor. Lush landscaped grounds, gracious interior with antique furniture, oak-panelled walls, Venetian glass chandelier, wood-burning fireplace. No elevator, smoking outdoors. Breakfast and High Tea served. $$-$$$.
- Ryan's Bed and Breakfast, 224 Superior St., Victoria BC V8V 1T3; 250 389-0012, Fax: 250 389-2857, Email: ryans@bc1.com, Website: www.ryansbb.com. Six rooms in 1892 restored home. Lace curtains, china cabinets, oil paintings in heavy gilded frames. Designated smoking area, small pets only. Breakfast served. $$-$$$.
- Top o' Triangle Mountain, 3442 Karger Terrace, Victoria BC V9C 3K5; 250 478-7853, 1-877-353-6887, Fax: 250 478-2245, Email: lorreen@hospitalityvictoria.com, Website: www.hospitalityvictoria.com Two rooms, one suite in cedar house set among tranquil fir and arbutus atop a small mountain. Spectacular views of Victoria, Juan de Fuca Strait, mountains. Garden and wrap-around deck. Pool table, library, outdoor hot tub. Full hot breakfast served. No pets (resident cat and dog). $-$$.
- Villa Blanca Bed and Breakfast, 4918 Cordova Bay Rd., Victoria BC V8Y 2J5; 250 658-4190, Fax: 250 658-4120, Email: vesta@villablanca.bc.ca, Website: www.villablanca.bc.ca/victoria Four rooms in a private home. Tranquil garden and pond, handmade quilts. Gourmet breakfast served. No smoking. $$.
- White Heather Cottage, 626 Simcoe St., Victoria BC V8V 1M4; 250

383-0152, 1-888-383-0327, Fax: 250 383-6402, Email: rooms@humboldthouse.com, Website: www.humboldthouse.com Two guestrooms in a beautiful 1925 English Cottage. Pine beds, ensuite baths with deep soaking or jacuzzi tubs. Gourmet breakfast served with champagne and chocolate truffles. No pets. $$-$$$.

• Wooded Acres B&B, 4909 Rocky Point Rd., Victoria BC V9C 4G2; 250 478-8172, Email: cabin@lodgingvictoria.com, Website: www.LodgingVictoria.com /countryside. Two suites in a log house built from trees on the 3-acre treed lot. Hot tub, sitting room library. Full country breakfast served. No pets. $$.

HOSTELS AND EDUCATIONAL

For the budget-conscious traveller not looking for pampering, hostels and schools are the accommodation of choice:

• Hostelling International Victoria, 516 Yates St., Victoria BC V8W 1K8; 250 385-4511, 1-888-883-0099, Fax: 250 385-3232, Email: victoria@hihostels.bc.ca, Website: www.hihostels.bc.ca. Shared and private rooms. Equipment storage, self-service kitchen, laundry room. Hostel-based activities and tours. Games/TV room, Internet access. $.

• Ocean Island Backpacker's Inn, 791 Pandora Ave., Victoria BC V8W 1N9; 250 385-1788, 1-888-888-4180, Fax: 250 385-1750, Email: get-it@oceanisland.com Spacious dorms with kitchen facilities. Licensed café, music room, Internet access. Pub crawl, parties, day trips organized. $.

• St. Margaret's School, 1080 Lucas Ave., Victoria BC V8X 3P7; 250 479-7171, Fax: 250 479-8976, Email: stmarg@islandnet.com Modern hotel-like accommodations on 22-acre property. Various meal plans available. $.

• University of Victoria Student Residences, PO Box 1700, Stn CSC, Victoria BC V8W 2Y2; 250 721-8395, Fax: 250 721-8390, Email: vriddell@uvvm.uvic.ca, Website: www.hfcs.uvic.ca/Housing.htm Available May to August. Single

and double rooms with shared bath, coin-operated laundry, pay phones, lounge. Seven suites (Craigdarroch House) with private bath, desk, TV, phone, complimentary breakfast. Fully-furnished townhouses also available at higher rates. $.

• Victoria Backpacker's Hostel, 1608 Quadra St., Victoria BC V8W 2L4; 250 386-4471, Fax: 250 386-4471. Dorm-style and private rooms. Four shared bathrooms, full kitchen facility, laundry room. Parking available. English and French spoken. $.

DINING

Vancouver and Victoria restaurants take full advantage of their setting, poised on the edge of an ocean and surrounded by wilderness. Fresh flavours incorporating indigenous ingredients mark each restaurant, as do the creativity of each chef and the diverse origins of the people they serve. The following lists a select number of the multitude of restaurants in each city. Each listing includes the approximate price range for dinner for two, including a bottle of wine (where served), taxes and gratuity: $ = under $45; $$ = $45-$80; $$$ = $80-$120; $$$$ = $120-$180; $$$$$ = over $180. Keep in mind that many fine restaurants make a wide selection of wines available by the glass as well. Meals served are indicated as: B = breakfast; L = lunch; D = dinner; G = grazing; T-O = take-out; Late = open past midnight. The credit cards accepted by each establishment are also listed: AX = American Express; V = Visa; MC = Mastercard; DC = Diners Club.

VANCOUVER

ASIAN

CHINESE

Most restaurants represent the Cantonese and Mandarin regions. Many other styles, however, are showing up at diverse locations. Dim sum is available at most establishments, with the exception of noodle houses.

- Dynasty Chinese Seafood Restaurant, 102-888 Burrard St.; 604 681-8283. Elevated Chinese dining. L/D, $$$$, AX/V/MC/DC.
- Floata Seafood Restaurant, 400-180 Keefer St.; 604 602-0368. Sets a standard for good food, strong service in a huge venue. Additional location at 1425-4380 #3 Rd. (Richmond); 604 278-8889. L/D/T-O, $$$, AX/V/MC/DC.
- Grand King Seafood Restaurant, Holiday Inn, 705 West Broadway Ave.; 604 876-7855. A small hotel restaurant with a huge Chinese following. L/D, $$$$, AX/V/MC.
- Hon's Wun Tun House, 1339 Robson St.; 604 685-0871. An institution for fast, cheap rice and noodles, potstickers, wun tun, and vegetarian dim sum. Multiple locations: 108-268 Keefer St.; 604 688-0871, 280 Keefer St.; 604 688-0871, 288 East Pender St.; 604 681-8842, 310-3025 Lougheed Hwy. (Coquitlam); 604 468-0871, 408 6th St. (New Westminster); 604 520-6661, 101-4600 #3 Rd.; 604 273-0871. L/D/T-O, $, AX/V/MC/DC.
- Kirin Mandarin Restaurant, 102-1166 Alberni St.; 604 682-8833. Refined dining from China's northern regions. L/D, $$$$, AX/V/DC.
- Pink Pearl Chinese Restaurant, 1132 East Hastings St., 604 253-4316. Come early for the dim sum; come late if you want to see a Chinese wedding banquet. L/D/T-O, $$$, AX, V, MC, DC.
- President Chinese Seafood Restaurant, 2200-8181 Cambie Rd.; 604 279-1997. A hotel restaurant in Richmond's Asia West just has to have authenticity, and it doesn't disappoint. L/D, $$$, AX/V/MC.
- Shanghai Chinese Bistro, 1124 Alberni St.; 604 683-8222. Chinese food, Shanghai-style and a dinner show in the form of noodle-pulling demonstration. L/D/Late, $$, AX/V/MC.
- Sun Sui Wah Restaurant, 3888 Main St.; 604 872-8822. Every visiting food writer makes this stop for seafood and dim sum. Additional location in Richmond at 102-4940 #3 Rd.; 604 273-8208. L/D, $$$-$$$$, AX/V/MC.

- Szechuan Chongqing Seafood Restaurant, 1668 West Broadway Ave.; 604 734-1668. Showcases Chongqing regional cooking style. Additional location at 4519 Kingsway (Burnaby); 604 434-1668. L/D, $$-$$$, AX/V/MC.
- Top Gun Chinese Seafood Restaurant, 2110-4151 Hazelbridge Way (Richmond); 604 273-2883. Features Cantonese-style lobster, crab and fish. L/D, $$-$$$, V.
- Won More Szechuan Cuisine, 201-1184 Denman St.; 604 688-8856. Mainly spicy dishes in a crowded, upstairs space. Bigger version at 1944 West 4th Ave.; 604 737-2889. D, $$, V/MC.

JAPANESE

- Ezogiku Noodle Café, 5-1329 Robson St.; 604 685-8606. For ramen in all its forms (and more). An additional location is under the Rosedale Hotel at 270 Robson; 604 685-9466. L/D/T-O, $, no credit cards.
- Gyoza King, 1508 Robson St.; 604 669-8278. Gyozas galore: meat-based, vegetable-based, seafood-based. Noodle and rice dishes, too. D/Late, $, V/MC.
- Musashi Japanese Restaurant, 780 Denman St.; 604 687-0634. The West End's answer to sensibly priced sushi. D, $, AX/V/MC.
- Suehiro Japanese Restaurant, Delta Pacific Resort, 10251 Saint Edwards Dr. (Richmond); 604 276-1163. For the teppan-yaki experience. L/D, $$$$, AX/V/MC/DC.
- Taka Sushi, 2059 West 4th Ave.; 604 734-4990. Great quality and fair prices in a surprising, Zen-meets-Art Deco décor. No lunch weekends, closed Monday. L/D, $$, AX/V/MC/DC.
- Tojo's Restaurant, 202-777 West Broadway Ave.; 604 872-8050. The ultimate in sushi springs from the hands of chef Hidekazu Tojo. Closed Sunday. D, $$$$, AX/V/MC/DC.

SOUTH ASIAN

- Heaven & Earth India Curry House, 1754 West 4th Ave.; 604

732-5313. Hot (and not so hot) curries and more in a warm, relaxed setting. D, $$, AX/V/MC.

- Rubina Tandoori, 1962 Kingsway; 604 874-3621. Deceptively plain exterior hides a sophisticated and skillful kitchen. Closed Sundays, no lunch Saturday. L/D/T-O, $$$, AX/V/MC.
- Sami's, 986 West Broadway Ave.; 604 736-8330. Highly rated "progressive Indo-American" food. Closed Sunday, L/D, $$-$$$, V/MC/DC.
- Vij's Restaurant, 1480 West 11th Ave.; 604 736-6664. Expect lineups (no reservations are taken) for Vij's BC-influenced Indian dishes. Closed Sunday. D, $$$, AX/V/MC/DC.

THAI

- Chili Club Restaurant, 1018 Beach Ave.; 604 681-6000. The view is distracting, but the cooking commands your attention. L/D, $$$, AX/V/MC/DC.
- Montri's Thai Restaurant, 3629 West Broadway Ave.; 604 738-9888. Authentically hot, in every sense of the word. D, $$$, V/MC.

OTHER ASIAN

- Phnom Penh, 955 West Broadway Ave.; 604 734-8898. A Vietnamese-Cambodian-Chinese mix of dishes in a family-run establishment. Additional location at 244 East Georgia St.; 604 682-5777. Closed Tuesday. L/D, $$, AX/MC.
- Singapore Restaurant, 546 West Broadway Ave.; 604 874-6161. Bargain-priced dishes, spice-rated, and a cosy atmosphere. L/D, $-$$, V/MC.
- Tropika Malaysian Cuisine, 3105 West Broadway Ave.; 604 737-6002. Authentic Malaysian fare. L/D, $$-$$$, MC.

FRENCH AND ITALIAN

- Borgo Antico, 321 Water St.; 604 683-8376. Enter Tuscany, aka Borgo Antico. L/D, $$$-$$$$, AX/V/MC/DC.
- Café de Paris, 751 Denman St.; 604 687-1418. Both the setting and fare bring to mind the classic Paris bistro. No lunch weekends. L/D, $$$, AX/V/MC.
- Cioppino's Mediterranean Grill, 1133 Hamilton St.; 604 688-7466. Light, fresh dishes melding Italian, French and Spanish flavours. L/D, $$$-$$$$, AX/V/MC.
- Il Giardino di Umberto, 1382 Hornby St.; 604 669-2422. A seaside villa recreated, serving excellent pasta and game. Closed Sunday, no lunch Saturday. L/D, $$$$, AX/V/MC/DC.
- Le Crocodile, 909 Burrard St.; 604 669-4298. Offers the full, real Alsace experience. Closed Sundays, no lunch Saturday. L/D, $$$$, AX/V/MC.
- Pastis Restaurant, 2153 West 4th Ave.; 604 731-5020. Satisfying bistro classics plus some lighter plates. D, $$$-$$$$, AX/V/MC.
- Piccolo Mondo, 850 Thurlow St.; 604 688-1633. Traditional cooking from Northern Italy. Closed Sunday, no lunch Saturday. L/D, $$$$, AX/V/MC/DC.
- Quattro on Fourth, 2611 West 4th Ave.; 604 734-4444. Mosaic and mahogany and marvellous food. D, $$$-$$$$, AX/V/MC/DC.
- Smoking Dog Bar and Grill, 1889 West 1st Ave.; 604 732-8811. Simple French fare in the perfect people-watching place. No lunch weekends. L/D, $$-$$$, AX/V/MC.
- Villa Del Lupo, 869 Hamilton St.; 604 688-7436. Generous and contemporary cooking in a charming old house. D, $$$$, AX/V/MC/DC.

PACIFIC NORTHWEST

- Liliget Feast House, 1724 Davie St.; 604 681-7044. A rarity: original First Nations cuisine, in a fabulous longhouse setting. D, $$$, AX/V/MC/DC.
- Rodney's Oyster House, 405-1228 Hamilton St.; 604 609-0080. Oysters are the main attraction here, but other seafoods are popular too. L/D, $$$, AX/V/MC/DC.
- Beach House at Dundarave Pier, 150-25th St. (West Vancouver); 604 922-1414. Strong on seafood. By Dundarave Beach, it's a great spot for weekend brunch. L/D, $$$$, AX/V/MC/DC.
- Beach Side Café, 1362 Marine Dr.

(West Vancouver); 604 925-1945. Light, subtle food and stunning views. Brunch on weekends. L/D, $$$$, AX/V/MC.

- The Cannery Seafood Restaurant, 2205 Commissioner St.; 604 254-9606. Promises good seafood, and delivers. No lunch weekends. L/D, $$$$, AX/V/MC/DC.
- The Fish House in Stanley Park, 8901 Stanley Park Dr.; 604 681-7275. Bold and creative seafood. Sunday brunch. L/D, $$$-$$$$, AX/V/MC/DC.
- The Pear Tree, 4120 Hastings St. (Burnaby); 604 299-2772. Inventive food, reasonable prices. Closed Sunday. D, $$$, AX/V/MC/DC.
- Raincity Grill, 1193 Denman St.; 604 685-7337. Ever-changing menu based on what's fresh. Weekend brunch. L/D, $$$$, AX/V/MC/DC.
- Seasons in the Park Restaurant, (Queen Elizabeth Park) Cambie St. and West 33rd Ave.; 604 874-8008. Good, conservative food in an intoxicating garden setting. Weekend brunch. L/D, $$$-$$$$, AX/V/MC.
- Star Anise, 1485 West 12th Ave.; 604 737-1485. Diners are spoiled here, with the attention and unbelievable food. No lunch weekends. D, $$$-$$$$, AX/V/MC/DC.

FINE DINING AND HOTEL DINING

- 900 West Restaurant and Wine Bar, Hotel Vancouver, 900 West Georgia St.; 604 684-3131. Simple, pure preparations. No lunch weekends. L/D, $$$$, AX/V/MC/DC.
- Bacchus Ristorante, Wedgewood Hotel, 845 Hornby St., 604 689-7777. Small, exclusive room with unfailingly good food. Afternoon tea served. B/L/D, Late (lounge), $$$$, AX/V/MC/DC.
- Bishop's Restaurant, 2183 West 4th Ave.; 604 738-2025. Flawlessly prepared food, understated elegance and superb service. No lunch weekends. L/D, $$$$, AX/V/MC/DC.
- C, 2-1600 Howe St.; 604 681-1164. Intriguing dishes and a million-dollar marina view. Sunday brunch served, no lunch Saturday. B/L/D,

$$$$-$$$$$, AX/V/MC/DC.
- Chartwell, Four Seasons Hotel, 791 W. Georgia St.; 604 689-9333. The classic dining choice. No lunch Saturday. B/L/D, $$$$-$$$$$, AX/V/MC/DC.
- Diva at the Met, Metropolitan Hotel, 645 Howe St.; 604 602-7788. Airy space with multi-tiered seating and stylish food preparation. Weekend brunch. B/L/D, $$$$, AX/V/MC/DC.
- Five Sails Restaurant, Pan Pacific Hotel, 300-999 Canada Place; 604 662-8111. Imaginative orchestration of flavours and breath-taking views. D, $$$$, AX/V/MC/DC.
- Fleuri Restaurant, Sutton Place Hotel, 845 Burrard St.; 604 682-5511. A hidden treasure. Afternoon tea, Sunday brunch, Chocoholic Bar. No lunch Saturday. B/L/D, $$$$, AX/V/MC/DC.
- Lumiere, 2551 West Broadway Ave.; 604 739-8185. Classic French preparation with contemporary flair. Tasting menus are superb. Closed Mondays. D, $$$$-$$$$$, AX/V/MC/DC.

SPECIALTY:

HERITAGE:

- Hart House on Deer Lake, 6664 Deer Lake Ave (Burnaby); 604 298-4278. The Tudor-style setting embraces both traditional and more daring fare. L/D, $$$-$$$$, AX/V/MC/DC.
- Teahouse at Ferguson Point, 7501 Stanley Park Dr.; 604 669-3281. Former officers' mess perfectly situated in the midst of one of the world's best and biggest urban parks. Weekend brunch. L/D, $$$$, AX/V/MC.

VEGETARIAN

- Habibi's, 7-1128 West Broadway Ave.; 604 732-7487. Bargain-priced, vegetarian Lebanese fare makes for both a healthy body and a happy wallet. No lunch weekends, closed Sundays. L/D, $, no credit cards.
- The Naam, 2724 West 4th Ave.; 604 738-7180. Vancouver's oldest

vegetarian restaurant offers dishes from around the world. B/L/D/G/Late, $, AX/V/MC.

- Planet Veg, 1941 Cornwall Ave.; 604 734-1001. A warning: lineups form fast for the Indian, Mexican and Mediterranean vegetarian fast foods. L/D/T-O, $, no credit cards.

TAPAS

- Bin 941 Tapas Parlour, 941 Davie St.; 604 683-1246. Generously filled tasting bowls. D/Late, $$-$$$, V/MC.
- Bin 942 Tapas Parlour, 1521 West Broadway Ave.; 604 734-9421. Much like Bin 941, but bigger. D/Late, $$-$$$, V/MC.

CASUAL DINING AND BAKERIES

- Earl's Restaurants, 1601 West Broadway Ave.; 604 736-5663. Fresh and healthy food that's fast, for parents travelling with children. Various additional locations: 901 West Broadway Ave.; 604 734-5995 and 1185 Robson; 604 669-0020 in Vancouver. L/D, $$, AX/V/MC.
- Ecco Il Pane Bakery, 238 West 5thAve.; 604 873-6888. Wide selection of specialty breads, freshly baked. Additional location at 2563 West Broadway Ave.; 604 739-1314. G/T-O, $, MC.
- Nottes Bon Ton Bakery and Confectionary, 874 Granville St.; 604 681-3058. While the tea quenches your thirst and the pastries sate your hunger, the cards reveal your fate. Closed Sunday and Monday. G/T-O, $, V/MC.
- Solly's Bagelry, 189 East 38th Ave.; 604 872-1821. Order from the bagelry and deli, or sit with a coffee and something sweet (the best cinnamon bun in town, perhaps). Additional location at 2873 West Broadway Ave.; 604 738-2121. B/L/G/T-O, $, V.
- Steamworks Brewing Company, 375 Water St., 604 689-2739. Some say the best beer in town is found in Steamworks' onsite brewery. B/L/D/Late, $$, AX/V/MC.
- Subeez, 891 Homer St.; 604 687-6107. Popular industrial-style bistro. B/L/D, $$-$$$, V/MC.

- Terra Breads, 2380 West 4th Ave.; 604 736-1838. A seemingly endless supply of really good bread. Also located in the Granville Island Public Market, 604 685-3102. G/T-O, $, AX/V/MC.
- The Creek Restaurant Brewery and Bar, 1253 Johnston St.; 604 685-7070. Pub, gourmet restaurant, microbrewery and lounge, all in one. No breakfast weekends. B/L/D, $$, AX/V/MC.
- Tomato Fresh Food Café, 3305 Cambie St.; 604 874-6020. Distinctively healthy and colourful comfort food, with the same food available for takeout around the corner (Tomato to Go, 530 West 17th Ave.; 604 873-4697). B/L/D/T-O, $$, AX/V/MC.
- Waazubee Café, 1622 Commercial Dr.; 604 253-5299. Casual and upbeat spot on The Drive. B/L/D, $$, V/MC.
- White Spot Triple O, 1881 Cornwall Ave.; 604 738-3888. The express version of Nat Bailey's famous White Spot. Fries, milkshakes and Vancouver's favourite burgers with legendary Triple O sauce are served fast. Two other Vancouver locations: 805 Thurlow St.; 604 669-7000, 1455 Quebec (Science World); 604 647-0003. B/L/D/T-O, $, V/MC.

VICTORIA

FINE DINING

- Aerie Resort, 600 Ebadora Lane (Malahat); 250 743-7115. French class and quality well worth the price. L/D, $$$$-$$$$$, AX/V/MC/DC.
- Sooke Harbour House, 1528 Whiffen Spit Rd. (Sooke); 250 642-3421. Innovative, even eccentric, one of Canada's gastronomic treasures. D, $$$$$, V/MC/DC.
- Victorian Restaurant, Ocean Pointe Resort and Spa, 45 Songhees Rd.; 250 360-2999. Sleek and contemporary, with impeccable service. D, $$$$, AX/V/MC/DC.
- Café Brio, 944 Fort St.; 250 383-0009. Contemporary Pacific Northwest creations in a lively, art-filled room. No lunch weekends. L/D, $$$-$$$$, AX/V/MC.
- Restaurant Matisse, 512 Yates St.;

250 480-0883. Classic French cuisine in a cozy setting. Closed Monday, Tuesday. D, $$$$, V/MC.

BISTROS AND CAFES

- Barb's Place, 310 St. Lawrence St.; 250 384-6515. Look inside the blue-pained shack for authentic halibut fish and chips. Closed November to March. L/D/G/T-O, $, no credit cards.
- Bond Bond's, 1010 Blanshard St.; 250 388-5377. The city's top bakery makes lunch items, too. Closed Sunday. G/T-O, $, no credit cards.
- Cassis Bistro, 253 Cook St.; 250 384-1932. Welcomes you with big portions of contemporary bistro fare. D, $$$, V/MC.
- Foster's Eatery, 753 Yates St.; 250 382-1131. Designer sandwiches for a quick lunch. B/L/D, $, AX/V/MC.
- Herald St. Caffe, 546 Herald St.; 250 381-1441. Beloved by locals. Sunday brunch, no lunch Monday, Tuesday. L/D, $$$, AX/V/MC/DC.
- Paprika Bistro, 2524 Estevan Ave.; 250 592-7424. Vivid, yet light dishes with a Hungarian history. Closed Sunday. D, $$$, AX/V/MC.
- Paradiso di Stelle, 10 Bastion Sq.; 250 920-7266. The place to go for a gelato fix. Hours and menu undergoing change at press time. V/MC.
- Re-bar Modern Foods, 50 Bastion Sq.; 250 361-9223. Inventive, delicious, healthy food. Kid-friendly. B/L/D, $$, AX/V/MC/DC.
- Suze Restaurant and Lounge, 515 Yates St.; 250 383-2829. The place to go for people-watching and international fare. Sunday brunch. L/D/Late/T-O, $$$, AX/V/MC.
- Zambri's, 110-911 Yates St.; 250 360-1171. Best Italian café in town. L/D, $$, AX/V/MC.

SEAFOOD

- Blue Crab Bar and Grill, Coast Victoria Harbourside Hotel, 146 Kingston St.; 250 480-1999. Look for Pacific Northwest casual and look out for dessert. B/L/D, $$$, AX/V/MC/DC.
- Dock 503 Waterfront Café, 2320 Harbour St. (Sidney); 250 656-0828. Zeroes in on the freshest seafood in Sidney. Breakfast, weekend brunch in summer. B/L/D/G, $$$, AX/V/MC/DC.
- Marina Restaurant, 1327 Beach Dr.; 250 598-8555. The natural setting for a nautical meal. Sunday Brunch. L/D, $$$-$$$$, AX/V/MC/DC.

BREWPUBS

- Harbour Canoe Club, 450 Swift St.; 250 361-1940. A prize location in a restored 1894 heritage powerhouse, homemade brews and a continental menu besides. L/D/Late, $$, V/MC.
- Hugo's Grill and Brewhouse, Magnolia Hotel, 625 Courtney St.; 250 920-4846. Hotel brewpub worth a visit. L/D/Late, $$-$$$,
- Spinnakers Brewpub, 308 Catherine St.; 250 384-6613. Traditional brewery, sausage kitchen, smokehouse and bakery. B/L/D, $$, AX/V/MC.
- Swans Brewpub, Swans Suite Hotel, 506 Pandora St.; 250 361-3310. In house brews and reasonably priced food makes this a popular hangout. B/L/D/Late, $$, AX/V/MC.

TEA

While in Victoria, one must have tea. Keep in mind that many places make a distinction between "Afternoon", or "Light" Tea—small sandwiches, scones, clotted cream, jam, berries and coffee or tea—and High Tea, a more substantial tea with trifles and more of the above. For the list that follows, prices given reflect the following scale, for two people: $ = $5-$10; $$ = $10-$20; $$$ = $20-$30; $$$$ = over $30.

- Butchart Gardens, 800 Benvenuto Ave. (Central Saanich); 250 652-8222. Tea in the garden, a fine idea. Afternoon Tea, AX/V/MC.
- Empress Room, The Empress Hotel, 721 Government St.; 250 384-8111. Afternoon tea served as it should be. Reserve ahead. Dress code in Tea Lobby. High Tea, $$$$, AX/V/MC/DC.
- James Bay Tearoom and Restaurant, 322 Menzies St.; 250 382-8282. A favourite for friendliness and prices. Afternoon Tea, High Tea Sunday, $,

AX/V/MC.
- Blethering Place Tea Room and Restaurant, 2250 Oak Bay Ave.; 250 598-1413. A cozy place in Oak Bay Village. Light Tea, Full Tea, $$, AX/V/MC.
- Point Ellice House, 2616 Pleasant St.; 250 380-6506. Tea served out on the lawn, complete with white wicker, against a heritage house setting overlooking the Gorge. Light Tea, High Tea, $$ per person. AX/V/MC.
- Oak Bay Tea Room and Restaurant, 2241 Oak Bay Ave.; 250 370-1005. Friendly and welcoming tea experience. Full Tea, $$$, AX/V/MC.

ETHNIC

- J & J Won Ton Noodle House, 1012 Fort St.; 250 383-0680. Savory noodles, soups, mein, fun, simply served. L/D, $, V/MC.

TOP ATTRACTIONS

VANCOUVER

The list that follows gives the sights that define Vancouver to the rest of the world. Travellers who've spent even just a weekend here, however, will agree there's much more.
- Vancouver Museum. Fronted by Vancouver's pet stainless steel Crab, this odd structure encloses Vancouver's past. Also hosts visiting and temporary exhibits. 1100 Chestnut St.; 604 736-4431, Website: www.vanmuseum.bc.ca
- H. R. MacMillan Planetarium and Pacific Space Centre. Space comes to Earth with the Space Centre's hands-on galleries, interactive computer displays, multimedia and laser shows and live demonstrations, while the Planetarium snares the stars. 1100 Chestnut St.; 604 738-7827, Website: www.pacific-space-centre.bc.ca
- Vancouver Maritime Museum. A historic ship, Heritage Harbour, the Children's Maritime Discovery Centre and permanent as well as temporary exhibits pay tribute to Vancouver's seagoing heritage. 1905 Ogden Ave.; 604 257-8300,

Website: www.vmm.bc.ca
- Vancouver Aquarium Marine Science Centre. Brings the denizens of different dark sea habitats into close focus through aquatic displays, live shark dives, feedings and killer whale and dolphin shows. Also features the new Pacific Canada Pavilion, behind-the-scene tours, sleepovers and special animal encounters. Stanley Park; 604 659-3474, Website: www.vanaqua.org
- Canada Place/CN Imax Theatre. Five white sails hover over a convention centre, cruise-ship terminal, a first-class hotel, and the CN IMAX theatre, where the steeply-pitched amphitheatre seating, a five-story screen and six-channel IMAX Digital wraparound sound make film-viewing an intense experience. 999 Canada Place Way; 604 682-4629, Website: www.canadaplace.com
- Science World/Alcan OMNIMAX Theatre. Science and entertainment merge in creative, hands-on exhibits inside the mirrored geodesic dome. The Alcan OMNIMAX Theatre runs documentaries to tremendous effect. 1455 Quebec St.; 604 443-7443, Website: www.scienceworld.bc.ca
- Grouse Mountain. Scale Grouse, by hiking or taking the Skyride aerial tram, for panoramic views, fine and casual dining and winter and summer sports at the top. 6400 Nancy Greene Way, North Vancouver; 604 984-0661, Website: www.grousemtn.com
- Capilano Suspension Bridge. A swaying structure of sturdy steel cables high above the forested Capilano River canyon. 3735 Capilano Rd., North Vancouver; 604 985-7474, Website: www.capbridge.com
- Vancouver Art Gallery. The neo-classical building is a permanent home to a collection of works by Emily Carr, among others, and hosts touring exhibitions, demonstrations, lunch-hour concerts and art education programs. 750 Hornby St.; 604 662-4719, Website: www.vanartgallery.bc.ca

- UBC Museum of Anthropology. Research and teaching museum-cum-gallery, with artifacts from around the world and one of the world's finest collections of Northwest Coast First Nations art. Outdoor sculpture garden with totem poles and Haida houses. 6393 N.W. Marine Dr. (University of BC campus); 604 822-5087, Website: www.moa.ubc.ca
- Stanley Park. One thousand acres of urban wilderness. While its rim has been adapted for recreation, its centre is untamed. 2099 Beach Ave.; 604 257-8400 (Vancouver Parks and Recreation Board).
- Dr. Sun Yat-Sen Garden. Classical Chinese garden reflects perfect equilibrium in all elements, from design through use. 578 Carrall St.; 604 662-3207.

VICTORIA

- Parliament Buildings. The seat of the Provincial Legislature. Free tours and a live "performance" when the house is in session. 501 Belleville St.; 250 387-3046, Website: www.parl-bldgs.gov.bc.ca
- Inner Harbour and Fisherman's Wharf. Outdoors where buskers and artisans offer their talents against a view of the harbour. On one side is Fisherman's Wharf, where commercial fishing boats dock. In front of The Empress Hotel and Parliament Buildings.
- The Empress Hotel. Grand, chateau-style heritage hotel. Famed Afternoon Tea. 721 Government St.; 250 384-8111, Website: www.cphotels.com
- Chinatown. Two crammed blocks' worth of browsing, shopping and eating almost hides narrow Fan Tan Alley, current home to artist studios and boutiques, former haven for opium dens. Fisgard St. and Government St.
- Emily Carr House. Artist and writer Emily Carr's family home, restored and updated with computerized information centre and Canadian artists' gallery. 207 Government St.; 250 383-5843, Website: www.emilycarr.com
- Helmcken House. Oldest house in B.C. still on its original site. Douglas and Belleville Streets; 250 361-0021, Website: www.tbcgov.bc.ca/culture/schoolnet/helmcken
- Point Ellice House. Meticulously restored house and garden with unusual collection of Victoriana. 2616 Pleasant St.; 250 380-6506.
- Craigdarroch Castle. Monumental Dunsmuir family stone mansion. 1050 Joan Crescent; 250 592-5323.
- The Art Gallery of Greater Victoria. 1889 mansion attracting internationally-renowned exhibits and housing contemporary B.C. and other Canadian art, North American, European, Japanese and Chinese works. Moss Street Paint-In festival every August. 1040 Moss St.; 250 384-1531 or 250 4101.
- Royal British Columbia Museum. Three permanent galleries — Natural History Gallery, Open Ocean Gallery and The First Peoples and Modern History Gallery — plus multiple exhibits and the National Geographic IMAX Theatre. 675 Belleville St.; 250 387-3701, 1-888-447-7977, Website: www.rbcm1.rbcm.gov.bc.ca
- Maritime Museum of British Columbia. The original 1889 provincial courthouse houses artifacts documenting the oceangoing history of B.C. Treasure hunt for kids. 28 Bastion Sq.; 250 385-4222.

GALLERIES AND MUSEUMS

VANCOUVER

Vancouver's galleries are outlets for the diverse expressions of Vancouver's artistic community. The past finds a place in Vancouver's many small and large museums. Check *The Georgia Straight* and *Queue Magazine* (Vancouver Sun, Thursdays) for details of current shows. *Preview: The Gallery Guide* lists many more galleries; the online version can be found at www.preview-art.com

GALLERIES

- Andrighetti Glass Gallery. Glass

works by member artists. 1751 West 2nd Ave.; 604 731-8652.

- Appleton Gallery. Haida, Kwakiuth and Coast Salish masks, paddles, talking sticks and wall plaques. 1451 Hornby St.; 604 685-1715.
- Art Beatus. Specializes in international and Chinese artists. M1-888 Nelson St.; 604 688-2633.
- Art Emporium. Early modern works. 2928 Granville St.; 604 738-3510 or 604 738-4510.
- Artspeak Gallery. Phototext installations and interactive video. 233 Carrall St.; 604 688-0051.
- Atelier Gallery. Attractive works on a smaller scale. 2421 Granville St.; 604 732-3021.
- Bau-Xi Gallery. One of Vancouver's oldest private galleries. Specializes in the work of Canadian artists including Jack Shadbolt. 3045 Granville St.; 604 733-7011.
- Buschlen Mowatt Gallery. Leading-edge and contemporary art as well as works by international luminaries. 1445 West Georgia St.; 604 682-1234.
- Canadian Craft Museum. Cathedral-like setting and shop for craft artists (entrance fee applies). 639 Hornby St.; 604 687-8266.
- Catriona Jeffries Gallery. Emphasis is on the contemporary. 3149 Granville St.; 604 736-1554.
- Charles H. Scott Gallery. Works reflecting the curriculum areas of painting, sculpture, photography, design and printmaking. 1339 Johnston St.; 604 844-3809.
- Circle Craft Co-op. Jury-selected works by B.C. craft artists. 1-1666 Johnston St., Granville Island; 604 669-8021.
- Coastal People's Fine Arts. Northwest Coast, Inuit and Plains art. 1072 Mainland St.; 604 685-9298.
- Contemporary Art Gallery. Exhibits of vanguard Canadian and international works. 555 Hamilton St.; 604 681-2700.
- Crafthouse Gallery. Non-profit gallery/shop showcases the talents of B.C. craftspeople. 1386 Cartwright St., Granville Island; 604 687-6511.
- Diane Farris Gallery. Industrial style gallery for young and

contemporary local and national artists such as Atilla Richard Lukacs and Janieta Eyre. 1565 West 7th Ave.; 604737-2629.
- Douglas Reynolds Gallery. Works by established and emerging Northwest Coast artists and silver and gold carved jewelry. 2335 Granville St.; 604 731-9292.
- Dundarave Print Workshop. Fine art limited edition prints by members and other artists. 1640 Johnston St., Granville Island; 604 689-1650.
- Eagle Spirit Gallery. Northwest Coast masks, button blankets and bentwood boxes. 1814 Maritime Mews, Granville Island; 604 801-5205.
- Emily Carr Institute of Art and Design Concourse Gallery. Student works. 1339 Johnston St., Granville Island; 604 844-3800.
- Equinox Gallery. A long-established gallery, home to Gathie Falk, Gordon Smith and others. 2321 Granville St.; 604 736-2405.
- Gallery of B.C. Ceramics. Features the pottery of B.C. artists. 1359 Cartwright St., Granville Island; 604 669-5645.
- Grunt Gallery. Specializes in performance art, explorations of gender issues, First Nations art. 116-350 East 2nd Ave.; 604 875-9516.
- Heffel Gallery. Historic stone building houses a gallery partial to Group of Seven works. 2247 Granville St.; 604 732-6505.
- Helen Pitt Gallery. Thought-provoking work by emerging artists. 882 Homer St.; 604 681-6740.
- Images for a Canadian Heritage. Works include Northwest Coast, Inuit, and wildlife art. 164 Water St.; 604 685-7046.
- Inuit Gallery. Museum-quality exhibits of Inuit art. 345 Water St.; 604 688-7323.
- John Ramsey Gallery. Gallery with a roster of contemporary artists. 2423 Granville St.; 604 737-8458.
- Leona Lattimer Gallery. Works and limited-edition prints by Northwest Coast artists. 1590 West 2nd Ave.; 604 732-4556.
- Malaspina Printmakers Gallery. Exhibits fine art limited edition

prints. 1555 Duranleau St., Granville Island; 604 688-1827.

- Marion Scott Gallery. Inuit art by artists living in the tradtional way. 481 Howe St.; 604 685-1934.
- Monte Clark Gallery. Contemporary photography and emerging stars. 2339 Granville St.; 604 730-5000.
- Morris and Helen Belkin Gallery. Formerly known as the UBC Fine Arts Gallery. Changing exhibitions of contemporary art, lectures and special events. 1825 Main Mall, University of B.C.; 604 822-2759.
- Newsmall and Sterling Studio Glass. Hot glass blowing displays and glass works. 1440 Old Bridge St., Granville Island; 604 681-6730.
- Or Gallery. Conceptual showcase for local, emerging contemporary artists. 103-400 Smithe St.; 604 683-7395.
- Simon Patrich Gallery. Distinguished by its Latin American connections. 2329 Granville St.; 604 733-2662.
- Spirit Wrestler Gallery. Finely curated aboriginal works. 8 Water St.; 604 669-8813.
- Third Ave. Gallery. Exhibits recent art grads and emerging artists in various genres. 1735 West 3rd Ave.; 604 738-3500.
- Vancouver Art Gallery. Permanent home to an Emily Carr Collection and others. Hosts touring exhibitions, demonstrations, lunch-hour concerts and art education programs. 750 Hornby St.; 604 662-4719, Website: www.vanartgallery.bc.ca
- Western Front Lodge. A non-profit alternative gallery showing national and international artists in various genres. 303 East 8th Ave.; 604 876-9343.

MUSEUMS

- B.C. Sports Hall of Fame and Museum. Chronicles B.C.'s professional and amateur sports and recreation history through displays, hands-on exhibits and multimedia. Gate A, BC Place Stadium, 777 Pacific Blvd. S.; 604 687-5520.
- Burnaby Village Museum. A turn-of-the-century town with authentically costumed "residents" and restored 1912 carousel called the "Carry-Us-All." 6501 Deer Lake Ave., Burnaby; 604 293-6501.
- Chinese Cultural Centre Museum and Archives. Temporary exhibits Chinese artists, archive of Chinese history in B.C. 555 Columbia St.; 604 687-0282.
- Geology Museum - UBC. Dinosaur bones, crystals, minerals and fossils encompass 4.5 billion years of mineral and fossil history. Free. Geological Science Centre, UBC, 6339 Stores Rd.; 604 822-2449.
- Granville Island Museums. Three international collections: Sport Fishing Museum, Model Trains Museum, Model Ships Museum. 1502 Duranleau St., Granville Island; 604 683-1939, Website: www.sportfishingmuseum.bc.ca
- Hastings Mill Store Museum. A charmingly cluttered museum inside Vancouver's oldest building shelters items such as muskets, Native baskets, period clothes, clocks and a coach. 1575 Alma St.; 604 734-1212.
- UBC Museum of Anthropology. Research and teaching museum-cum-gallery, with artifacts from around the world and Northwest Coast First Nations art. Outdoor sculpture garden with totem poles and Haida houses. 6393 N.W. Marine Dr. (University of BC campus); 604 822-5087, Website: www.moa.ubc.ca
- Vancouver Maritime Museum. A historic ship, Heritage Harbour, the Children's Maritime Discovery Centre and permanent as well as temporary exhibits pay tribute to Vancouver's seagoing heritage. 1905 Ogden Ave.; 604 257-8300, Website: www.vmm.bc.ca
- Vancouver Museum. Vancouver's past plus visiting and temporary exhibits. 1100 Chestnut St.; 604 736-4431, Website: www.vanmuseum.bc.ca
- Vancouver Police Centennial Museum. Crime and crime-fighting paraphernalia, including old photos, gambling displays, artifacts and accounts of ancient unsolved murders. 240 East Cordova St.; 604 665-3346.

VICTORIA

MUSEUMS

- B.C. Aviation Museum. Volunteers restore airplanes and exhibit early engines and aircraft. 1910 Norseman Rd., Victoria International Airport, Sidney; 250 655-3300.
- Maritime Museum of British Columbia. The original 1889 provincial courthouse houses artifacts documenting the oceangoing history of B.C. Treasure hunt for kids. 28 Bastion Sq.; 250 385-4222.
- Oriental Discovery Museum. Exhibits on the sources of many basic inventions and discoveries. 631 Courtney St.; 250 388-6869.
- Royal British Columbia Museum. Three permanent galleries--Natural History Gallery, Open Ocean Gallery and The First Peoples and Modern History Gallery — plus multiple exhibits and the National Geographic IMAX Theatre. 675 Belleville St.; 250 387-3701, 1-888-447-7977, Website: www.rbcm1.rbcm.gov.bc.ca
- Royal London Wax Museum. Wax figures of famous and infamous characters in history, show business and literature. 470 Belleville St.; 250 388-4461, Website: www.waxworld.com

VANCOUVER ENTERTAINMENT

In addition to a well-known film and television production industry, entertainment in Vancouver can be found live at clubs, theatres and arts centres around town. The 24-hour Arts Hotline at 604 684-2787 provides probably the most up-to-date information on current happenings. The Vancouver Cultural Alliance's website (www.culturenet.ca/vca) is a valuable resource, and *The Georgia Straight* publishes weekly events listings as well. Ticketmaster operates an Arts Line at 604 280-3311.

CLUBS:

- The Gérard Lounge (Sutton Place Hotel), 845 Burrard St.; 604 682-5511. Attracts celebrities and a moneyed crowd.
- Richard's On Richards, 1036 Richards St.; 604 687-6794. Posh club with local bands, international recording acts, and DJ dance music.
- BaBalu, 654 Nelson St.; 604 6054343. Sophisticated club features live Swing and Latin musical acts.
- Lava Lounge, 1176 Granville St.; 604 688-8701. Popular gay club.
- Odyssey, 1251 Howe St.; 604 689-5256. Caters to a loyal gay crowd, features alternative dance music.
- Numbers Cabaret, 1098 Davie St.; 604 685-4077. Four split-levels and a pair of bars are crammed with a regular gay clientele
- Lotus, 455 Abbott St.; 604 602-0066. A lesbian bar at the convergence of Chinatown and downtown.

THEATRE:

- Arts Club Mainstage and Revue Theatre, 1585 Johnston St., Granville Island; 604 687-1644. Western Canada's largest regional theatre and a local institution.
- Doll & Penny's Café, 1167 Davie St.; 604 6853417. Entertaining weekly Drag show.
- Firehall Arts Centre, 280 East Cordova St.; 604 689-0926. Converted fire station specialising in alternative theatre, performance art and dance.
- Metro Theatre Centre, 1370 S.W. Marine Dr.; 604 266-7191. Attracts a loyal, mature audience looking for British comedy.
- Norman Rothstein Theatre, 950 West 41st Ave.; 604 257-5111. State-of-the-art theatre in the Jewish Community Centre.
- Presentation House Arts Centre, 333 Chesterfield Ave., North Vancouver; 604 990-3473. Terrific community theatre.
- Queen Elizabeth Theatre. 600 Block Hamilton St. (At Dunsmuir); 604 665-3050. Glitzy, glamourous Broadway-style productions.
- St. Andrew Wesley's Church (Tony & Tina's Wedding), 1012 Nelson St.; 604 280-3311 (Ticketmaster). Dinner theatre that begins in a real church and ends with the reception a short distance away.

- Stanley Theatre, 2750 Granville St.; 604 687-1644. The Arts Club's third stage in a former vaudeville venue and movie theatre.
- Urban Well Restaurant & Lounge, 1516 Yew St.; 604 737-7770. Adult improv comedy.
- Vancouver Playhouse. 600 Block Hamilton St. (At Dunsmuir); 604 873-3311. One of the best regional theatres in Canada.
- Waterfront Theatre, 1410 Cartwright St., Granville Island; 604 685-6217. Big stage in a small theatre where many Canadian works debut.

MUSIC:

- Chan Centre for the Performing Arts, 6265 Crescent Rd., University of B.C.; 604 822-9197. Best acoustics in town.
- The Commodore Ballroom, 868 Granville St.; 604 739-7469. Hosts an eclectic range of artists.
- Orpheum Theatre, 884 Granville St.; 604 665-3050. Old-time, elegant home of the Vancouver Symphony Orchestra.
- Performance Works, 1218 Cartwright St.; 604 6668139. A Granville Island stage for The popular KISS Project, among others.
- The Purple Onion Jazz Cabaret, 15 Water St.; 604 602-9442. Best place for jazz, with both lounge and large dance room.
- Vancouver East Cultural Centre (The Cultch), 1895 Venables St.; 604 251-1363. BC.'s most diverse performance space.
- Vogue Theatre, 918 Granville St.; 604 331-7909. Hosts top musical acts and film screenings during the Vancouver International Film Festival.
- The Yale, 1300 Granville St.; 604 681-9253. One of the world's best blues bars.

PARKS AND GARDENS

Mild in climate and outdoors-oriented, Vancouver and Victoria are rife with gardens. The following lists a few that shouldn't be missed:
- Beacon Hill Park, bounded by Dallas Rd. and Douglas, Southgate and Heywood Streets; 250 361-0364. Victoria's oldest and largest park with wading pool, swans, ducks, English-style rose garden and exotic trees.
- Butchart Gardens, Benvenuto Ave., Central Saanich; 250 652-5256, Website: www.butchartgardens.com Fifty acres of garden on the former site of a rock quarry.
- Century Gardens at Deer Lake Park, 6344 Deer Lake Ave., Burnaby. Rhododendrons are Burnaby's official flower, and flourish on the grounds of the Burnaby Art Gallery.
- Dr. Sun Yat-Sen Garden, 578 Carrall St.; 604 662-3207. Authentic, full-scale classical Chinese garden offering tours and a popular Enchanted Evening series.
- Park & Tilford Gardens, 440-333 Brooksbank Ave., North Vancouver; 604 984-8200, Website: www.northshore-online.com/park_tilford/main.html A garden oasis on the edge of a shopping centre.
- Queen Elizabeth Park and Bloedel Conservatory, West 33rd Ave. and Cambie St.; 604 872-5513. Quarry garden atop Little Mountain offers showy natural surroundings and a view of the city. The Conservatory encloses tropical birds and plants as well as desert and exotic plants.
- Riverview Lands Davidson Arboretum, 500 Lougheed Hwy., Coquitlam; 604 524-7120. Collection of 1800 trees on the Riverview Hospital grounds, for tree lovers.
- Stanley Park's gardens. Stanley Park; 604 257-8400 or 604 257-8544 for nature walks. Gardens flourishing in heavily forested Stanley Park include the Rose Garden and the Ted and Mary Grieg Rhododendron Garden.
- UBC Botanical Garden and UBC Gardens, 6804 S.West Marine Dr.; 604 822-9666, Website: www.hedgerows.com/UBCBotGdn/ A living teaching and research library spread over 30 hectares. Includes Alpine, Asian, Japanese Nitobe Memorial and BC Native gardens and nursery with unusual and new locally-developed plants.

- Vancouver Compost Demonstration Garden, 2150 Maple St.; 604 736-2250. The city's demonstration garden shows how effective composting can be.
- VanDusen Botanical Garden, 5251 Oak St.; 604 878-9274, Website: www.vandusengarden.org. Themed gardens on 55 acres of former golf course include Asian, Children's, Fragrance, Meditation, and Canadian Heritage gardens, a maze and fern dell. Many popular special events and sales.

SPORTS AND ACTIVITIES

Vancouver is the perfect destination for sports and outdoors enthusiasts in all seasons.

SPORTS

- Air Canada Championship Golf. Labour Day stop on the PGA Tour. Northview Golf and Country Club, 6857-168 St., Surrey; 604 574-0324.
- Alcan Dragon Boat Races. Colourful dragon boats compete as part of the Alcan Dragon Boat Festival. False Creek; 604 688-2382, Website: www.canadadragonboat.com
- B.C. Lions Football. Canadian Football League franchise. B.C. Place Stadium, 777 Pacific Blvd.; 604 661-7373 or 604 669-2300.
- Harness racing. Races from October to April. Fraser Downs Racecourse, 17740-62 Ave., Surrey; 604 576-9141.
- Horse racing. Thoroughbred and standardbred racing live or via satellite. Hastings Park Racecourse, Pacific National Exhibition Park; 604 254-1631.
- Molson Indy Vancouver. Championship Auto Racing Teams race in Vancouver. 765 Pacific Blvd.; 604 684-4639.
- Single A Canadians Baseball. Minor league baseball. Nat Bailey Stadium, Ontario St. and 29th Ave.; 604 872-5232.
- Telus Open Golf Tournament. An early June stop on the coast-to-coast Canadian Tour. Mayfair Lakes Golf and Country Club, 5460

#7 Rd., Richmond; 604 276-0585.
- Vancouver Canucks Hockey. National Hockey League franchise. General Motors Place, 800 Griffiths Way; 604 899-7889.
- Vancouver Eighty-Sixers Soccer. Mostly local talent play teams from around North America. Swangard Stadium, Central Park, Boundary Rd. and Kingsway, Burnaby; 604 435-7121.
- Vancouver Grizzlies Basketball. National Basketball Association franchise. General Motors Place, 800 Griffiths Way; 604 899-7889.

OUTDOOR ACTIVITIES

Cycling, hiking, swimming and lying on the beach can be done at will, almost anywhere. Beaches and parks in the city are the responsibility of the Vancouver Board of Parks and Recreation (604 257-8400). The following list provides useful information for a number of other recreational activities.

CYCLING

- Cycling British Columbia, 1367 West Broadway Ave.; 604 737-3034 or Cycling Hotline at 604 737-3165. Maps and information on routes and competitions.

SKIING AND SNOWBOADING

- Cypress Bowl. Great place for toboggans and inner tubes, with groomed trails for skiing. Weather and trail information: 604 926-6007. Programs: 604 926-5612.
- Grouse Mountain. Sleigh rides and outdoor ice-skating as well as downhill and cross-country skiing and snowboarding. Snow reports: 604 986-6262. Programs: 604 980-9311.
- Mount Seymour Provincial Park. Backcountry and downhill skiing, toboggans and inner tubes. Weather and conditions: 604 879-3999. Programs and special events: 986-2261.

BIRDWATCHING

- George C. Reifel Bird Sanctuary, 5191 Robertson St., Ladner; 604 946-6980. Wetlands environment is especially attractive to shorebirds.

CANOEING, KAYAKING, WINDSURFING

- Contact the Canoeing Association, Whitewater Kayaking Association and Sea Kayaking Association through the Outdoor Recreation Council of British Columbia, at 604 737-3058.

GOLFING

- Fraserview Golf Course, 7800 Vivian Ave.; 604 257-6923 (Pro Shop) or 604 280-1818 (Tee Time). A busy South Vancouver course.
- Furry Creek Golf and Country Club, 922-9461. For water views and a course carved from a mountainside.
- Langara Golf Course, 6706 Alberta St.; 604 713-1816 (Pro Shop) or 604 280-1818 (Tee Time). Popular city golf course.
- Mayfair Lakes Golf Course, 5460 #7 Rd., Richmond; 604 276-0505. Challenges the golfer with plenty of water hazards.
- Stanley Park and Queen Elizabeth Park Pitch-and-Putt. 604 874-8336. City operated courses in park settings.
- University Golf Club, 5185 University Blvd.; 604 822-1818. Beautiful, well-maintained course on the UBC grounds.

SWIMMING

- Beach Information: 738-8535 mid-May to mid-September; 604 665-3424 all other seasons.
- Kitsilano Pool, 2305 Cornwall Ave.; 604 731-0011. Gigantic outdoor saltwater pool.

KIDS' STUFF

INDOORS

- Alcan OMNIMAX Theatre, Science World. Runs documentaries to tremendous effect. 1455 Quebec St.; 604 443-7443, Website: www.scienceworld.bc.ca
- CN Imax Theatre, Canada Place. Film-viewing becomes an intense experience with big sound and bigger screens. Check with staff to determine if the film is too intense for young children. 999 Canada Place Way; 604 682-4629, Website: www.canadaplace.com

- H. R. MacMillan Planetarium and Pacific Space Centre. Hands-on galleries, interactive computer displays, multimedia and laser shows and live demonstrations bring space and the stars down to Earth. 1100 Chestnut St.; 604 738-7827, Website: www.pacific-space-centre.bc.ca
- Science World. Science and entertainment merge in creative, hands-on exhibits inside the mirrored geodesic dome. 1455 Quebec St.; 604 443-7443, Website: www.scienceworld.bc.ca
- Vancouver Aquarium Marine Science Centre. Brings the denizens of different dark sea habitats into close focus through aquatic displays, live shark dives, feedings and killer whale and dolphin shows. Also features the new Pacific Canada Pavilion, behind-the-scene tours, sleepovers and special animal encounters. Stanley Park; 604 659-3474, Website: www.vanaqua.org

OUTDOORS

- Capilano Suspension Bridge. Hang high above the forested Capilano River canyon on a swaying structure of sturdy steel cables; visit the totem poles and exhibits. 3735 Capilano Rd., North Vancouver; 604 985-7474, Website: www.capbridge.com
- George C. Reifel Bird Sanctuary. Feed the birds or view a wetlands ecosystem. 5191 Robertson St., Ladner; 604 946-6980.
- Greater Vancouver Zoo. Home to 126 animal species. 5048-264th St., Aldergrove; 604 856-6825.
- Harbour Cruises' train and boat excursion. To Squamish by steam locomotive and back on the MV Britannia. North Foot of Denman St.; 604 688-7246, Website: www.boatcruises.com
- Lynn Canyon Park. Begin a hike in Lynn Headwaters Regional Park with a visit to the Ecology Centre and brave the swinging footbridge high above the rapids of Lynn Creek. Lynn Canyon entrance on Park Rd.; 604 987-5922.
- Maplewood Farm. Five-acre petting farm with seasonal special events and weekend pony rides.

405 Seymour River Pl., North Vancouver; 604 929-5610.

- Pacific Spirit Regional Park. Experience B.C.'s coastal cedar and fir forests firsthand with an easy hike through the many trails. West 16th Ave. and Blanca (Visitor Centre); 604 224-5739.
- Playland. Outdoor amusement park rides, midway games and cotton candy from April to Labour Day. Pacific National Exhibition Park; 604 253-2311, Website: www.pne.bc.ca
- Stanley Park. Kids' attractions include the Children's Farm Yard and Miniature Railway, and the totem poles at Lower Brockton Oval. 2099 Beach Ave.; 604 257-8400.
- VanDusen Botanical Garden. Themed gardens on 55 acres include Children's Garden and Heritage and Elizabethan Hedge Maze. Many popular special events. 5251 Oak St.; 604 878-9274, Website: www.vandusengarden.org

WATERPLAY

- Canada Games Pool and Fitness Centre. Olympic-size pool and teaching/toddler pool. 65 East 6th Ave., New Westminster; 604 526-4281.
- Eileen Dailly Leisure Pool and Fitness Centre. Burnaby's best indoor pool and community centre. 240 Willingdon Ave., Burnaby; 604 298-7946.
- Granville Island Water Park. Wet adventure playground with water cannons, spouts, waterslide and wading areas. Near Sutcliffe Park, Granville Island; 604 666-5784.
- Kitsilano Pool. Gigantic outdoor saltwater pool. 2305 Cornwall Ave.; 604 731-0011.
- Newton Wave Pool. Metre-high waves for bodysurfing and waterslides. 13730 72nd Ave., Surrey; 604 594-7873.
- Second Beach Pool. Features three small waterslides. Stanley Park; 604 257-8371.
- Splashdown Park. Twisting waterslides, hot tubs and smaller sized equipment for little kids. 4799 Nu Lelum Way, Tsawwassen; 604 943-2251.

- Stanley Park Water Park. Wet adventure playground with equipment suitable for children with physical disabilities. Near Lumberman's Arch, Stanley Park; 604 257-8400.
- Vancouver Aquatic Centre. Olympic-size indoor and outdoor pools and toddler pool. 1050 Beach Ave.; 604 665-3424.
- Vancouver beaches. Second and Third Beach, English Bay, Sunset Beach, Kits Beach, Jericho Beach, Locarno Beach and Spanish Banks. Beach Information: 604 738-8535 mid-May to mid-September; 604 665-3424 all other seasons.

CHILDREN'S CULTURE

- Arts Umbrella. Classes in dance, acting, animation and filmmaking for those on longer stays. 1286 Cartwright St., Granville Island; 604 681-5268.
- Buschlen-Mowatt Gallery. Hosts annual visual art show by budding artists in May. 1445 West Georgia St.; 604 682-1234.
- Theatre Festival for Young Audiences. March performances by five companies at the Waterfront Theatre on Granville Island and Shadbolt Centre for the Arts in Burnaby. Waterfront Theatre, 1410 Cartwright St., Granville Island, Shadbolt Centre, 6450 Deer Lake Ave., Burnaby; 604 669-0631.
- Vancouver Art Gallery Super Sunday. Experiences in art for school age children on the third Sunday of each month. 750 Hornby St.; 604 662-4719, Website: www.vanartgallery.bc.ca
- Vancouver East Cultural Centre Kids Series. Saturday afternoon musical or dramatic performances monthly. Also a Youth Program discounting admission for youth to $2. 1895 Venables St.; 604 251-1363.
- Vancouver International Children's Festival. Week-long event featuring quality performances, roving entertainers, face painters and a multicultural community stage. Vanier Park, 1100 Chestnut St.; 604 708-5655, Website: www.youngarts.bc.ca

- Vancouver Public Library. Children's floor has CD-ROM stations, videos, books and displays of children's art. 350 West Georgia St.; 604 331-3600.
- Vancouver International Comedy Festival. Free and funny street entertainment and some ticketed family-oriented events. Granville Island; 604 683-0883, Website: www.comedyfest.com
- Vancouver International Writers Festival. Mid-October writers' festival has three days of children's events. Granville Island; 604 681-6330, Website: www.writersfest.bc.ca
- Vancouver Kidsbooks. Readings, book launches and book signings complement the huge variety of children's books. 3083 West Broadway Ave.; 604 738-5335.

HISTORY AND LIVING CULTURE

- B.C. Sports Hall of Fame and Museum. B.C.'s past professional and amateur sports and recreation history. Displays, hands-on exhibits, a Participation Gallery and multimedia. Gate A, BC Place Stadium, 777 Pacific Blvd. S.; 604 687-5520.
- Burnaby Village Museum and Carousel. Recreation of a 1920s village with hands-on activities, restored carousel and special events. 6501 Deer Lake Ave., Burnaby; 604 293-6501.
- Cedar Cottage/Trout Lake Pow Wow. Mother's Day event featuring intertribal dancing, drumming, hoop dancing, pageant and displays presents the cultural traditions of Canada's First Nations people. Trout Lake Community Centre, 3350 Victoria Dr.; 604 874-4231.
- Fort Langley National Historic Park. Sample life as it was in the last century in this reconstructed Hudson's Bay Company post. 23433 Mavis, Fort Langley; 604 888-4424.

VANCOUVER ANNUAL EVENTS

January

- Polar Bear Swim. A New Year's Day plunge into the Pacific. English Bay. 604 732-2304.
- Brackendale Winter Eagle Festival and Count. Just after the New Year begins, an eagle count is taken, and related events are hosted all month. Squamish-Brackendale area. 604 898-3333.
- Chinese New Year's Festival. Chinatown greets the first day of the lunar year (in January or February) with festivals and events. Chinatown. 604 687-0729.

February

- Vancouver International Boat Show. Consumer show featuring the latest in boating. B.C. Place Stadium, Coal Harbour Marina. 604 294-1313, Website: www.sportsmensshows.com
- B.C. Home and Garden Show. The largest consumer home show in Western Canada. BC Place Stadium. 604 433-5121.

March

- Festival du bois. Maillardville celebrates voyageur traditions and French-Canadian music, dance and food. Maillardville, Coquitlam.

April

- Vancouver Playhouse International Wine Festival. Week-long fundraising celebration of good wine and food. Vancouver Convention and Exhibition Centre. 604 872-6622, Email: winefest@bc.sympatico.ca Website: www.winefest.bc.sympatico.ca

May

- Granville Island Bluegrass Festival. A month of free outdoor weekend concerts. Granville Island; 604 215-0779.
- Vancouver International Marathon. Canada's largest marathon. Starts at the Plaza of Nations. 604 872-2928, Email: vim@istar.bc.ca Website: www.vanmarathon.bc.ca

- Vancouver International Children's Festival. A week of quality performances, roving entertainers, face painters and a multicultural community stage, all for kids. Vanier Park. 604 708-5655, Website: www.youngarts.ca

June

- Alcan Dragon Boat Festival. Dragon boats race in the largest dragon boat festival in North America. False Creek. 604 688-2382, Email: dragonb@axion.com, Website: www.canadadragonboat.com
- DuMaurier International Jazz Festival. Something for every jazz lover in the 400 or so performances held downtown. 604 682-0706, Website: www.jazzvancouver.com.
- Bard on the Beach. Shakespeare is staged in a backless tent to take advantage of the magical natural backdrop. Shows from June to September. Vanier Beach. 604 737-0625, Email: bardonthebeach@bc.sympatico.ca Website: www.faximum.com/bard

July

- Vancouver International Comedy Festival. Performances from a diverse mix of comic artists. Granville Island. 604 683-0883, Website: www.comedyfest.com
- Symphony of Fire Fireworks. Pyrotechnicians from different countries set fireworks to music in a four-day competition. English Bay. 604 738-4304.
- Illuminares Lantern Festival. A neighbourhood paper-lantern festival attracting thousands. Trout Lake Community Centre. 604 879-8611.
- Festival Vancouver. New festival featuring an array of opera, early music, jazz and world music. Various venues. 604 221-0080, Email: music@festivalvancouver.bc.ca Website: www.festivalvancouver.bc.ca
- Vancouver International Folk Music Festival. Hugely popular annual celebration of folk music. Jericho Beach. 604 681-0041, Website: www.thefestival.bc.ca

August

- Abbotsford International Airshow. Aerial displays and aerobatics. Abbotsford Airport; 604 857-1142.
- Pacific National Exhibition. Demolition derby, petting farm, Superdogs show, exhibits, midway games and amusement park rides. Win a house, win a car, eat candy floss and corndogs. Pacific National Exhibition Park. 604 253-2311, Website: www.pne.bc.ca
- Powell Street Festival. A celebration of Japanese-Canadian history and traditional Japanese food, music and entertainment. Oppenheimer Park, Powell Street. 604 682-4335.
- Squamish Nations Pow Wow, Aboriginal Cultural Festival. Traditional dancing and drumming and cuisine. Capilano Reserve, Squamish Territory, North Vancouver. 604 254-4844, Website: www.bcaafc.com

September

- Chilliwack Bluegrass Festival. Camp out for the bluegrass performances. 604 792-2069.
- Vancouver Fringe Festival. Alternative theatre performances by emerging and established companies. 604 257-0350, Email: thefringe@ultranet.ca, Website: www.vancouverfringe.com
- Molson Indy Vancouver. Championship Auto Racing in Vancouver. False Creek area. 604 684-4639.
- Vancouver International Film Festival. Over 250 innovative and accessible films from around the world. Various venues. 604 685-0260, Website: www.viff.org

October

- Vancouver International Writers (and Readers) Festival. One week of readings, talks and other events surrounding local and international writers. Granville Island. 604 681-6330, Website: www.writersfest.bc.ca

December

- Christmas Carol Ships Parade. Carollers sail on musical ships decked out with lights. Vancouver Harbour. 604 682-2007.

EXCURSIONS
WHISTLER

- Tourism Whistler, 4010 Whistler Way, Whistler BC V0N 1B4; 604 664-5625, 1-800-944-7853 Canada and the U.S., Fax: 604 938-5758, Website: www.tourismwhistler.com Source for information on what to see and do, where to sleep and eat.
- Resort Reservations Whistler, 4545 Blackcomb Way, Whistler BC V0N 1B4; 604 932-3434, 1-888-284-9999, Website: www.whistler-blackcom.ca Bookings in hotels, condominiums, bed-and-breakfasts. Also puts together customized vacation packages.
- Whistler Activity and Information Centre, 604 932-2394. Provides information on recreation in Whistler.

THE GULF ISLANDS

- Tourism Vancouver Island, Old City Square, 203-335 Wesley Street, Nanaimo BC V9R 2T5; 250 754-3500, Fax: 250 754-3599, Website: www.islands.bc.ca

THE SUNSHINE COAST

- Big Pacific, 604 740-8812, 1-800-517-9378, Website: www.bigpacific.com. Provides information on the Sunshine Coast and helps visitors find accommodations, dining and entertainment.

SHOPPING
VANCOUVER
NEIGHBOURHOODS

GEORGIA AND GRANVILLE

- The Bay, Georgia & Granville, 604 681-6211.

- Bentall Centre, Burrard St. and Dunsmuir St.; 604 661-5656.
- Canadian Craft Museum, 639 Hornby St.; 604 687-8266.
- Pacific Centre, 700 West Georgia St.; 604 688-7236
- Royal Centre, 1055 West Georgia St.; 604 689-1711.
- Vancouver Art Gallery Shop, 750 Hornby St.; 604 662-4706.

ROBSON STREET

- Banana Republic, 1098 Robson St.; 604 331-8285.
- The Gap, 9-1125 Robson St.; 604 683-0906.
- Mexx, 1119 Robson St.; 604 801-6399.
- Roots, 1001 Robson St.; 604 683-4305.

GASTOWN

- Art in Handmade Rugs, 20 Water St.; 604 605-8990.
- Calico Cat, 121-131 Water St.; 604 685-5643.
- Deluxe Junk, 310 W. Cordova St.; 604 685-4871.
- Hill's Native Art, 165 Water St.; 604 685-4249.
- Inuit Gallery, 345 Water St.; 604 688-7323.
- Miki House, The Landing, 375 Water St.; 604 681-6454.
- Rossilini, The Landing, 375 Water St.; 604 682-7348.
- Salmegundi West, 321 W. Cordova St.; 604 681-4648.
- The Edinburgh Tartan Gift Shop, The Landing, 375 Water St.; 604 646-3915.

GRANVILLE ISLAND

- Edie's Hats, 11-1666 Johnston St.; 604 683-4280.
- El Greco Jewellery, 1660 Johnston St.; 604 681-0942.
- Granville Island Public Market, 1689 Johnston St.; 604 666-5784.
- Kids Only Market (Kids Market) 1496 Cartwright St.; 604 689-8447.
- Nancy Lord, 4-1666 Johnston St.; 604 689-3972.

ANTIQUES AND COLLECTIBLES

- Ages Ago Used Furniture and

Antiques, 3243 Main St.; 604 876-3055.
- Baker's Dozen, 3520 Main St.; 604 879-3348.
- Blue Heron, 3516A Main St.; 604 874-8401.
- Canada West Antique Co., 4430 West 10th Ave.; 604 222-9190.
- Carmen Boré, 3036 Granville St.; 604 738-3677 and 1867 Marine Dr., West Vancouver; 604 925-3151.
- Deeler's Antiques, 4391 Main St.; 604 879-3394 and 810 Park Royal North, West Vancouver; 604 922-0213.
- Farmhouse Collections, 2915 Granville St.; 604 738-0167.
- Folkart Interiors, 3651 West 10th Ave.; 604 731-7576.
- Forest Hills Antiques, 4329 West 10th Ave.; 604 222-4992.
- Hampshire Antiques, 3007 Granville St.; 604 733-1326.
- Second Time Around, 4428 Main St.; 604 879-2313.
- William Robert Antiques, 1529 W.14th Ave.; 604 731-0808.

BOOK STORES

- Banyen Books and Sound, 2671 West Broadway Ave.; 604 732-7912.
- Chapters, 788 Robson St.; 604 682-4066. Additional locations: 4700 Kingsway, Burnaby; 604 431-0463 and 2505 Granville St.; 604 731-7822.
- Duthie Books, 2239 West 4th Ave.; 604 732-5344.
- Granville Book Company, 850 Granville St.; 604 687-2213.
- Little Sister's Book Store, 1238 Davie St.; 604 669-1753, 1-800-567-1662.
- Vancouver Kidsbooks, 3083 West Broadway Ave.; 604 899-8675 and 3040 Edgemont Blvd., North Vancouver; 604 899-8526.

CANADIAN CLOTHING DESIGNERS

- A-Wear Clothing, 350 Howe St.; 685-9327 and Lansdowne Park Shopping Centre; 604 276-1850.
- Dorothy Grant, 250-757 West Hastings St.; 604 681-0201.
- Jacqueline Conoir Boutique, 3035 Granville St.; 604 732-4209

- Margareta Design, 2448 West 41st Ave.; 604 264-4625.
- Nancy Lord, 4-1666 Johnston St.; 604 689-3972.
- Tilley Endurables, 2401 Granville St.; 604 732-4287.
- Zonda Nellis Design, 2203 Granville St.; 604 736-5668.

CHILDREN'S STORES

- Bobbit's for Kids, 2951A West 4th Ave.; 604 738-0333.
- Bratz, 2828 Granville St.; 604 734-4344.
- Isola Bella Design, 5692 Yew St.; 604 266-8808.
- Kaboodles Toy Store, 1496 Cartwright St., Granville Island; 604 684-0066.
- Kids Only Market (Kids Market), 1496 Cartwright St., Granville Island; 604 689-8447.
- Please Mum, 2041 W.41st Ave.; 604 264-0366 and 2951 West Broadway Ave.; 604 732-4574. Also in many malls.
- The Toybox, 3002 West Broadway Ave.; 604 738-4322.
- Toys R Us, 1154 West Broadway Ave.; 604 733-8697.

CHINA AND CRYSTAL

- Atkinson's, 1501 West 6th Ave.; 604 736-3378.
- Chintz and Company, 950 Homer St.; 604 689-2022.
- W.H. Puddifoot & Co., 2350 West 41st Ave.; 604 261-8141.

DESIGNER BOUTIQUES

- Bacci Design, 2788 Granville St.; 604 732-7317.
- Boboli, 2776 Granville St.; 604 257-2300.
- Boutique Zolé, 287-650 West 41st Ave.; 604 266-8221.
- Cabbages & Kinx, 315 West Hastings St.; 604 669-4238.
- Chanel, 103-755 Burrard St.; 604 682-0522.
- E.A. Lee for Men and Women, 466 Howe St.; 604 683-2457.
- Edward Chapman's Ladies Shops, 2596 Granville St.; 604 732-3394. Also at 750 West Pender St.; 604 688-6711 and Oakridge Centre; 604 261-8161.

- Enda B Fashion, 4346 West 10th Ave.; 604 228-1214 and 2625 Granville St.; 604 733-2000.
- Escada Plaza Escada, 757 West Hastings St.; 604 688-8558.
- Gianni Versace Boutique, 757 West Hastings St.; 604 683-1131.
- Instante, 769 Hornby St.; 604 669-8080.
- Leone Fashions, 757 West Hastings St.; 604 683-1133.
- Romeo Gigli, 773 Hornby St.; 604 669-8398.

FIRST NATIONS ART AND JEWELLERY

- Eagle Spirit Gallery, 1814 Maritime Mews, Granville Island; 604 801-5205.
- Hill's Native Art, 165 Water St.; 604 685-4249.
- Inuit Gallery, 345 Water St.; 604 688-7323.
- Leona Lattimer, 1590 West 2nd Ave.; 604 732-4556.
- Marion Scott Gallery, 481 Howe St.; 604 685-1934.
- Museum of Anthropology, 6393 N.W. Marine Dr. (University of BC campus); 604 822-5087.

FINE ART GALLERIES

- Art Beatus, M1-888 Nelson St.; 604 688-2633.
- Bau-Xi Gallery, 3045 Granville St.; 604 733-7011.
- Buschlen-Mowatt Fine Arts, 1445 West Georgia St.; 604 682-1234.
- Graham Sayell Gallery, 2416 Granville St.; 604 738-3521.
- Harrison Galleries, 2932 Granville St.; 604 732-5217 and 1471 Marine Dr., West Vancouver; 604 926-2615.
- Heffel Gallery, 2247 Granville St.; 604 732-6505.
- Ramsay John Gallery, 2423 Granville St.; 604 737-8458.
- Simon Patrich Galleries, 2329 Granville St.; 604 733-2662.
- Uno Langmann Limited, 2117 Granville St.; 604 736-8825.

GIFT SHOPS

- Bookmark - Vancouver Public Library Gift Shop, 350 West Georgia St.; 604 331-4040.
- Chachkas Design, 1075 Robson St.; 604 688-6417.
- Circle Craft Co-op, 1-1666 Johnston St., Granville Island; 604 669-8021.
- Lightheart and Co., 100-535 Howe St.; 604 684-4711.
- Moulé, 1944 West 4th Ave.; 604 732-4066.
- The Museum Company, 53D-701 West Georgia St.; 604 688-1502.
- Vancouver Art Gallery Shop, 750 Hornby St.; 604 662-4706.
- Vancouver Craft Museum Gift Shop

HOME FURNISHINGS

- Abode Designs, 555 West Broadway Ave.; 604 872-0303 and 2887 West Broadway Ave.; 604 738-9488.
- Country Furniture, 3097 Granville St.; 604 738-6411 and 980 Marine Dr., North Vancouver; 604 985-3359.
- Industrial Revolution, 2306 Granville St.; 604 734-4395.
- Jordan's Interiors, 1470 West Broadway Ave.; 604 733-1174.
- Sofa So Good, 2219 Cambie St.; 604 879-4878.
- Sofas à la Carte, 909 West Broadway Ave.; 604 731-9020.
- UpCountry, 2210 Cambie St.; 604 875-9004.

JEWELLERY

- Birks Jewellers, 698 West Hastings St.; 604 669-3333 and 118-650 West 41st Ave.; 604 266-2301.
- Georg Jensen, 701 West Georgia St.; 604 688-3116.
- Karl Stittgen Goldsmiths, 2203 Granville St.; 604 737-0029.
- Martha Sturdy Originals, 3039 Granville St.; 604 737-0037.
- Tiffany in Holt Renfrew, 633 Granville St.; 604 681-3121.

LEATHER

- Castle Milano, 248-757 West Hastings St.; 604 647-0202.
- Danier Leather, 1018 Robson St.; 604 689-7330. Also in Pacific Centre; 604 683-6846 and Eaton Centre Metrotown; 604 430-3881. Factory outlet, 3003 Grandview Hwy.; 604 432-6137.

- Mack's Leathers, 1043 Granville St.; 604 688-6225.
- Marquis of London Manufacturing Ltd., 526 Beatty St.; 604 688-2201.
- Neto Enterprises, 54 East 4th Ave.; 604 875-8474.

MALLS

- Aberdeen Centre, 4400 Hazelbridge Way, Richmond; 604 273-1234.
- Arbutus Village Square, 4255 Arbutus St.; 604 732-4255.
- Bentall Centre, Burrard St. and Dunsmuir St.; 604 661-5656.
- City Square, 555 West 12th Ave.; 604 893-3229.
- Eaton Centre Metrotown & Metropolis, 4700 Kingsway, Burnaby; 604 438-4715.
- Guildford Town Centre, 2695 Guildford Town Centre, Surrey; 604 585-1565.
- Lougheed Mall Shopping Centre, 9855 Austin St./Ave.?; 604 421-2882.
- Oakridge Centre, 650 West 41st Ave.; 604 261-2511.
- Pacific Centre, 700 West Georgia St.; 604 688-7236.
- Park Royal Shopping Centre, 2002 Park Royal South, West Vancouver; 604 925-9576.
- Richmond Centre, 6551 No. 3 Rd., Richmond; 604 713-7467.
- Royal Centre, 1055 West Georgia St.; 604 689-1711.
- Surrey Place Shopping Centre, 102 Ave. and King George Hwy., Surrey; 604 588-6431.
- Vancouver Centre, 650 West Georgia St.; 604 688-5658.
- Yaohan Centre, 3700 No. 3 Rd., Richmond; 604 231-0601.

MUSIC

- A & B Sound, 556 Seymour St.; 604 687-5837. Also at 3433 East Hastings St.; 604 298-0464 and 732 S.West Marine Dr.; 604 321-5112.
- Black Swan Records, 3209 West Broadway Ave.; 604 734-2828.
- D & G Collectors Records, 3580 East Hastings St.; 604 294-5737.
- Highlife Records & Music, 1317 Commercial Dr.; 604 251-6964.
- HMV Canada, Robson St.; 604 685-9203 and Eaton Centre Metrotown; 604 430-1699.

- Magic Flute Record Shop, 2203 West 4th Ave.; 604 736-2727.
- Sam the Record Man, 568 Seymour St.; 604 684-3722.
- Virgin Megastore, 788 Burrard St.; 604 669-2289.
- Zulu Records, 1869 West 4th Ave.; 604 738-3232.

MEN'S CLOTHING

- Boboli, 2776 Granville St.; 604 257-2300.
- Boys' Co., 1044 Robson St.; 604 684-5656. Also at Oakridge Centre, 604 266-0388; Metrotown Centre, 604 431-1866 and Richmond Centre, 604 303-0374.
- Chevalier Creations, 620 Seymour St.; 604 687-8428 or 604 687-4643.
- E.A. Lee, 466 Howe St.; 604 683-2457.
- Eddie Bauer Centre, Metrotown; 604 436-3441; Guildford Town Centre; 604 589-5666; Oakridge Centre; 604 261-2621; Pacific Centre; 604 683-4711; Park Royal Centre; 604 925-0858.
- Harry Rosen Men's Wear, 700 West Georgia St.; 604 683-6861 and Oakridge Centre, 604 266-1172.
- Holt Renfrew, 633 Granville St.; 604 681-3121.
- Mark James, 2941 West Broadway Ave.; 604 734-2381.
- Roots, 1001 Robson St.; 604 683-4305; Eaton Centre Metrotown; 604 435-5554; Guildford Town Centre; 604 583-0689; Grandview Factory Outlet, 3695 Grandview Hwy.; 604 433-4337; Oakridge Centre; 604 266-6229; Pacific Centre; 604 683-5465; Richmond Centre; 604 244-9113; Park Royal Shopping Centre; 604 925-2166.
- S. Lampman, 2126 West 41st Ave.; 604 261-2750.
- Tilley Endurables Adventure Clothing, 2401 Granville St.; 604 732-4287.

SECOND-HAND CLOTHING

- The Comeback, 3122 Edgemont Blvd., North Vancouver; 604 984-2551.
- Kisa's of Kerrisdale Consignment Boutique, 2352 West 41st Ave.; 604 266-2885.
- MacGillycuddy's for Little People,

4881 Mackenzie St.; 604 263-5313.
- Turnabout Collections, 3060 West Broadway Ave.; 604 731-7762.
- Value Village, 1820 East Hastings St.; 604 254-4282 and 6415 Victoria Dr.; 604 327-4434.

SHOE STORES

- John Fluevog Boots and Shoes, 837 Granville St.; 604 688-2828.
- Salvatore Ferragamo, 918 Robson St.; 604 669-4495 or 604 669-2218.
- Simard & Voyer Shoes, 1047 Robson St.; 604 689-2536 and Oakridge Centre, 604 263-1080.
- Stephane de Raucourt Shoes, 1067 Robson St.; 604 681-8814 and Oakridge Centre, 604 261-7419.

VICTORIA

EMPRESS HOTEL AND VICTORIA CONVENTION CENTRE

- Art of Man Gallery, 721 Government St.; 250 383-3800.
- Collections by Madison Avenue, 736 Douglas St.; 250 380-0697.
- Stephen Lowe Art Gallery, 752 Douglas Rd.; 250 384-3912.

GOVERNMENT STREET

- British Importers, 138 Victoria Eaton Centre; 250 386-2133.
- Christmas House, 1209 Wharf St.; 250 388-9627.
- Copithorne and Row, 901 Government St.; 250 384-1722.
- Victoria Eaton Centre Mall, 1000 block Government St.; 250 389-2228.
- Harbour Trading Company, 811 Wharf St.; 250 381-1022.
- Irish Linen Stores, 1019 Government St.; 250 383-6812.
- Original Christmas Village, 1323 Government St.; 250 380-7522.
- Purdy's Chocolates, 102 Victoria Eaton Centre; 250 361-3024.
- Rogers Chocolates, 913 Government St.; 250 384-7021, 1-800-663-2220.
- Sydney Reynolds, 801 Government St.; 250 383-2081.
- The Spirit of Christmas, 1022 Government St.; 250 385-2501.
- W&J Wilson Clothiers, 1221 Government St.; 250 383-7177.

YATES STREET AREA

- Cowichan Trading Company, 1328 Government St.; 250 383-0321.
- English Sweet Shop, 738 Yates St.; 250 382-3325.
- Grandpa's Antique Photo, 1252 Wharf St.; 250 920-3800.
- Hill's Indian Crafts, 1008 Government St.; 250 385-3911.
- Sa-Nuu-Kwa Gallery, 606 Johnson St.; 250 480-5515.
- Starfish Glassworks, 630 Yates St.; 250 388-7827.
- The British Candy Shoppe, 635 Yates St.; 250 382-2634.

MARKET SQUARE

- Fat Phege's fudge Factory, 560 Johnson St.; 250 383-3435.
- Foxglove Toys, 162-560 Johnson St.; 250 383-8852.
- Griffin Books, 168-560 Johnson St.; 250 383-0633.
- La Cache, 562 Johnson St.; 250 384-6343.
- Marigold Galleria, 101-560 Johnson St.; 250 386-5339.
- Out of Hand, 566 Johnson St.; 250 384-5221.

CHINATOWN

- Chinatown Trading Company, 551 Fisgard St.; 250 381-5503.
- Fan Tan Gallery, 541 Fisgard St.; 250 382-4424.
- Quonley's, 1628 Government St.; 250 383-0623.

ANTIQUE ROW

- Charles Baird, 1044A Fort St.; 250 384-8809.
- Faith Grant, 1156 Fort St.; 250 383-0121.
- Maggie Dove, 1032 Fort St.; 250 383-7722.
- Old Vogue Shop, 1034 Fort St.; 250 382-4493.
- Recollections Antiques and Collectibles Mall, 817A Fort St.; 250 385-1902.
- The Glass Menagerie, 1036 Fort St.; 250 475-2228.

INDEX

Abbotsford International Airshow, 84
Aberdeen Centre, 54
Aerie Resort, 153
Ages Ago, 51
Air Canada Championship, 72
Alcan Dragon Boat Festival, 82
Alcan OMNIMAX Theatre, 27
Alexandra Park, 95-96
Alhambra Hotel, 99
Ambleside Beach, 13, 72, 74
Anna Wyman Dance, 60
Annual Boat Show, 81
Annual events
  spring, 82
  summer, 82-84
  winter, 81-82
Annual Festival of the Written Arts, 168
Annual International Wine Festival, 82
Annual Winter Eagle Festival, 81
Antolin, Neil, 154
Appleton Gallery, 63
Art Beattus, 53, 63
Art Emporium, 61
Art of Man, 151
Arts Club Theatre, 56-57
Arts Umbrella, 79, 109
Artspeak, 63
Atelier Gallery, 62
Atkinson's, 52
Authors à la Carte, 84

B.C. Electric, 18
BC Lions, 70
BC Place Stadium, 70, 80
B.C. Sports Hall of Fame, 80
BaBalu's, 60
Baby Gap, 50
Bacchus Restaurant, 47
Bacci's, 52
Baker's Dozen, 51
Ballantyne Pier, 35
Ballet British Columbia, 60
Banyen Books, 51
Barb's Fish & Chips, 155
Barclay Heritage Square, 94
Bard on the Beach, 83
baseball, professional, 69
basketball, professional, 70
Bastion Square, 127
Bau-Xi Gallery, 53, 61
Beach House, 45, 120
Beach Side Cafe, 45
beaches, 23, 74, 77-78, 121
Beaconsfield building, 93
Beckwoman's, 106
Bentall Centre Mall, 50, 54
bicycle routes, 73
Block 17, 101-2
Blodel Conservatory, 67
Boboli, 52, 55
Bonniebrook beach, 167
Borgo Antico, 44
Boys' Co., 55
Brennan, Sean, 154
British Candy Shoppe, 151
British Pacific Properties, 18
Brockton Point Lighthouse, 23
Brockton Point Totem Park, 23
Bukowski's, 106
Burnaby Art Gallery, 68
Burnaby Village Museum & Carousel, 80
Buschlen Mowatt Gallery, 53, 62, 80
Butchart Gardens, 144-46, 156
Byrnes Block, 98

C., 46
Canada Games Pool, 78
Canada Place, 35-36, 45
Canada West Antiques Co., 51
Canadian Craft Museum, 50, 63
canoeing, 72
Canton alley, 102
Capers, 120
Capilano Suspension Bridge, 13, 35, 75-77
Carillon Tower, 129
Carnegie Library, 32
Carr, Emily, 30-31, 128, 136, 140-41
Cedar Cottage/Trout Lake Pow Wow, 80
Century Gardens, 68
Chachkas, 53
Chan Centre for the Performing Arts, 59
Chanel, 52
Charles Baird, 152
Charles H. Scott Gallery, 62, 109
Chartwell, 47
Chevalier Creations, 55
Chic Pea, 161
Children
  bookstores, 51
  Children's Maritime Discovery Centre, 35
  clothing stores, 52, 55
  culture, 78-80
  history and living culture, 80
  outdoor attractions, 75-77
  summer activities at Whistler, 162
  water play, 77-78, 162
Chilliwack Bluegrass Festival, 84
Chinatown, Vancouver
  free walking tours, 14
  stores and associations, 103-4
  walking tour, 101-3
Chinatown, Victoria, 134-35
Chinese Benevolent Association, 104
Chinese Cultural Centre, 103
Christ Church Cathedral, 88
Christmas, 80, 81, 110
Christy, Jim, 168
Clove, 106
CN IMAX Theatre, 36
Commercial Drive
  cafes and eateries, 106
  Italian neighbourhood, 105-6

Commodore Ballroom, 59
Concourse Gallery, 62
Contemporary Art Gallery, 63
Craigdarroch Castle, 143-44
Creek Restaurant and Brewery and Bar, 48
Creekhouse Gallery, 109
Crystal Gardens, Victoria, 131
cycling, 73
Cypress Bowl, 74
Cypress Park Market, 121
Cypress provincial park, 73, 124

D & G Collectors, 55
David C. Lam Asian Garden, 64
Davie Village, 96
Davis Bay, 167
de Cosmos, Amor, 128, 129
Deadman's Island, 21, 24
Deeler's, 51
Deep Cove, 72
Deep Cove Canoe and Kayak Centre, 123
Deep Cove Cultural Centre, 122
Deep Cove Heritage Association and Arts, 123
Deep Cove Lookout, 123
Deer Lake Park, 68
Deighton, John "Gassy Jack," 15-16
Descanso Bay, 166
Dining, Vancouver
    Chinese, 41-43
    cultural diversity, 40-41
    family, 48
    First Nations, 37-38, 45
    French, 44
    Italian, 44
    Japanese, 42-43
    Mediterranean, 44-45
    Pacific Northwest, 45-46
    South Asian, 44
    southeast Asian, 45-46
    upscale, 46-47
    vegetarian, 47
dining, Victoria
    bistros, cafes, 155
    brew pubs, 156
    ethnic eateries, 156
    fine dining, 153-55
    seafood, 156
    tea, 156
Dionisio Point Park, 166
Diplomat Cake, 48
Diva, 45-46, 46-47
Dogwood Princess, 168
Douglas, James, 128, 129, 130
Dr. Sun Yat-Sen Classical Chinese Garden, 38-39, 67-68
Dr. Vigari Gallery, 106
dragon boat racing, 72
Drumberg Provincial Park, 166
du Maurier International Jazz Festival, 82-83
Dundarave Pier, 45, 120
Dundarave Print Workshop, 62
Dundarave village, 120
Dunsmuir residence, 143-44

Eaton Centre Mall, 150
Eileen Dailly Pool, 78
El Greco Jewellery, 51
Elizabethan Hedge Maze, 76
Emily Carr House, 140-41
Emily Carr Institute of Art & Design, 62, 109
Empress Hotel, 129, 130, 133-34, 156
English Bay, 72, 74, 77, 81, 94-96
English Sweet Shop, 151
Entertainment
    clubs, 60
    dance, 59-60
    music, 58-59
    theatre, 56-58, 79, 123
Equinox Gallery, 61-62
Erickson, Arthur, 18
Europe Hotel, 98
Everything Garlic, 123
Excalibur Base II Station, 161
Excalibur Village Station, 161

Fairweather, 50
False Creek, 72, 73
False Creek-Point Grey bike route, 73
Fan Tan Alley, 135
Farmhouse Collections, 51
Festival Vancouver, 83
Firehall Arts Centre, 57
football, professional, 70
Forest Hills, 51
Fort Langley National Historic Park, 80
Four Seasons Hotel, 47
Fraser Downs, 71
Frederic Wood Theatre, 117
Freschi, Bruno, 18
Fresco Inn, 96
Fulford Harbour, 165
Furry Creek golf course, 73

Gabriola Island, 166
Galiano Island, 165-66
galleries, Vancouver, 53
    alternative, 63
    Art Gallery of Greater Victoria, 135-37
    downtown, 62-63
    First Nations, 63
    Gastown, 99
    Granville Island, 62, 109 North, 123
    South Granville ("The Row"), 61-62, 63
    UBC, 117
    Vancouver Art Gallery, 29-31
Gallery of B.C. Ceramics, 62
Gambier Island, 168
Ganges, 165
Garden Bay, 168
Gastown
    attractions, 97-98
    free walking tours, 14
    historic past, 15-16, 98
    shopping, 50-51
    steam clock, 99
    walking tour, 98-100
gay and lesbian

scene, 106
clubs, 60
Davie Village, 96
General Motor Place, 70
Georg Jensen, 54
George C. Reifel Bird Sanctuary, 77
Gibsons, 167
Gibsons Harbour, 167
Glacier Bite, 162
Glacier Creek, 162
golf courses, 73-74, 167-68
golf, professional, 71-72
Granville Island, 13
    Bluegrass Festival, 82
    children's attractions, 79-80
    ferries, 96
    galleries, 62, 63
    industrial past, 107-8
    Market, 48, 51, 108, 121
    Performance Works on, 60
    theatre, 57, 79
    walking tour, 109-10
    Water Park and Adventure playground, 78
Greater Vancouver Zoo, 76
Grouse Grind, 73, 124
Grouse Mountain, 73-74, 124
Grunt Gallery, 63
Guildford Mall, 54
Guinness Brewing Company, 18
Gulf Islands 164-66

H.R. MacMillan Pacific Space Centre, 33
H.R. MacMillan Planetarium, 33-34
Hadden Park, 111
Halfmoon Bay, 168
Hamburger Mary's, 96
Hampshire Antiques, 51
Harbour Centre, 90-91
Harbour Centre Tower, 14
Harbour Cruises, 76
Harbourside Hotel, 156
Harrison Festival of the Arts, 83
Hastings Park

Racecourse, 71
Helmcken House, 141
Henry Hudson Elementary School, 111
Highview Lookout, 124
hiking, 74
    Baden Powell trail, 123
    Cliff Gilker Park, 167
    Cypress Mountain, 124
    Grouse Grind, 37, 124
    Yew Lake trail, 124
hockey, 70-71
Hollyburn Lodge, 124
Holy Rosary Cathedral, 91
Home and Garden Show, 81
Hon's, 41-42, 47
Horne Block, 100
horseracing, 71
Horstman Glacier, 158
Hotel Vancouver, 17-18, 87-88
Howe Sound, 72
Hudson's Bay Company, 49, 128, 130
Hunt, Henry, 111

Illuminares Lantern Festival, 83
Images for a Canadian Heritage, 63
Inuit and Spirit Wrestler, 63
The Inuit Gallery, 53
Irvines Landing, 168
Isola Belia, 52

Jericho Bank, 74
Jericho Beach, 77, 83
Jewish Community Centre, 58
Johnson, Pauline, 23
Juan de Fuca Strait, 127

Keats Island, 168
Kennedy, Arthur, 128
Kids Only Market, 51, 52, 108
Killarney, 113-14
Kirin Mandarin, 42
KISS Project, 60
Kitsilano

architecture, 114
beach, 74, 77, 112-14
restaurants, 47
shopping, 114
Vanier Park, 31
walking tour, 111-13
Kitsilano Pool, 74, 78, 113
Kitsilano Showboat, 113
Koerner Library, 117
Koffel, Pierre, 155
Kokoro Dance, 60

Lansdowne (mall), 54
Latin Quarter, 106
Leckie Building, 100
Li Ka-Shing, 18
library, central branch, 80
Library Square, 91
Lightheart and Co., 53
Lighthouse Park, 73, 124
Lions Gate Bridge, 18
Literary Cabaret, 84
Little Mountain (Queen Elizabeth Park), 46, 66-67
Little Sister's Book Store, 51
Locarno Beach, 78
Lonsdale Quay Hotel, 123
Lonsdale Quay Market, 51, 123
Lost Lagoon, 22, 23
Loughheed Mall, 54
Lower Seymour Conservation Reserve, 73

M.V. Britannia, 14
MacMillan Bloedel Building, 18
McPherson Playhouse, 127
Madeira Park, 168
Le Magasin building, 100
Magic Flute, 55
Main Library, 116
Malkin Bowl, 22
Manhattan Building, 93
Maple Tree Square, 98
Maplewood Farm, 77
Marine Building, 88-89
Market Square, 152

Martha Sturdy, 54
Martin, David, 111
Martin, Mungo, 111
Masonic Grand Lodge, 100
Mason's Deep, 114
Mayfair Lakes Golf and Country Club, 72, 73
Mayne Island, 166
Memorial Library, 120
Metro Theatre, 58
Metrotown, 54
Mission Folk Festival, 83
Molson Indy Vancouver, 72, 84
Mon Keong School, 104
Montague Harbour Park, 166
Mori, Kannosouke, 65
Morris, William, 68
Mount Seymour, 74, 124
Mount Seymour Parkway, 122
Mountain Grill, 161
The Museum Company, 53
The Museum Store, 50
MV Britannia, 76

Nat Bailey Stadium, 69
Newton Wave Pool, 78
Nitobe Memorial Garden, 66
Norman Rothstein Theatre, 58
Norris, George, 32
North Shore
    North Vancouver, 122-24
    Porteau Cove, 123-24
    West Vancouver, 119-22
    Whytecliff Park, 123
Northview Golf and Country Club, 72

Oak Bay, 148
Oak Bay Beach Hotel, 148
Oak Bay Marina, 148
Oak Bay Marina Restaurant, 156
Oakridge, 54
O'Brien, Mel, 156
Ocean Towers, 95
O'Reilly residence, 141-43

Orpheum Theatre, 58

Pacific Coliseum, 71
Pacific Mall, 49-50, 54
Pacific National Exhibition (PNE), 84
Pacific Spirit Regional Park, 73, 74, 76
Pakenham, Alma, 131-32
Pan Pacific Hotel, 35
Park & Tilford Gardens, 68
Park Royal, 54, 119
Parliament Buildings (Victoria), 129, 130-32
Pastis, 44
Pear Tree, 46
Pender Harbour, 168
planetarium. See H.R. MacMillan Planetarium
Playland, 77
Plumpers Cove, 168
Poetry Bash, 84
Point Atkinson Lighthouse, 114, 124
Point Ellice House, 141-43
Polar Bear Swim, 81
Porteau Cove, 123-24
Presentation House, 58, 123
Presentation House Gallery, 123
Presidio building, 94
Princess Marguerite, 132
Queen Elizabeth Theatre, 58

Radisson President Hotel, 41
Rainbow Lodge, 159
Ramsay John Gallery, 53
Rattenbury, Francis Mawson, 129, 131-32
Raven's Cry Theatre, 167
Recollections, 152
Reid, Bill, 29
Revue Theatre, 57
Richmond Centre, 54
Richmond dike system, 73, 74
Riverview Lands Davidson Arboretum, 68

Roberts Creek, 167
Rockwood Lodge, 168
Roedde House Museum, 94
Rogers, Benjamin Tingley, 17
Roger's House, 96
Royal British Columbia Museum, 129, 137-39
Royal Centre Mall, 50, 54
Royal Hudson steam locomotive, 14, 76, 119
Ruby Lake Resort, 168

Saltspring Island, 165
Sandwell Provincial Park, 166
Sandy Cove, 121
Sasamat Lake, 78
Saturna Island, 166
Science World, 26-27
Sea Village, 109
Sea Walk, West Vancouver, 119-20
SeaBus, 51, 123
Seasons in the Park, 46
Sechelt, 168
Second Beach, 74, 77
Second Beach Pool, 78
Second Time Around, 51
Secret Cove, 168
Seymour Art Gallery, 123
Seymour Demonstration Forest, 74
Shadbolt Centre for the Arts, 79
Shanghai alley, 102
Shanghai Bistro, 42
Shaughnessy
    "The Crescent," 68
    VanDusen Botanical Garden, 65-66
Shaughnessy, William, 17
Shaw Theatre, 123
Simard & Voyer Shoes, 55
Simon Patrich Gallery, 53, 62
Sinclair Centre, 89-90
skiing, 73-74
    Blackcomb Mountain, 158-59, 161-62
    Cypress Provincial Park, 124

Grouse Mountain, 37-38, 124
Mount Seymour, 124
Whistler Mountain, 158-59, 160-61
Skookumchuk Narrows, 168
snowboarding, 158, 160, 161
soccer, 72
Sooke Harbour House, 153, 154
space centre. See H.R. MacMillan Pacific Space Centre
Spanish Banks, 74, 78
Spencer residence, 135
Splashdown Park, 78
sports
recreational, 73-74, 82
spectator, 69-71
Stanley Park, 13
amusements, 22
beaches, 23
Brockton Point Lighthouse, 23
Brockton Point Totem Park, 23
Children's Farm Yard, 76
Deadman's Island, 21, 24
gardens, 68
getting around, 20
Girl in a Wetsuit sculpture, 22-23
Hollow Tree, 21
interior, 23-24
Lost Lagoon, 23
Lumberman's Arch, 21
Malkin Bowl, 22
miniature train, 76
Nine-O'Clock Gun, 23
Prospect Point, 23
recreation facilities, 22
restaurants and concessions, 22, 46
seawall, 21-23
Siwash Rock, 21
Water Park, 78
Stearman Beach, 121
Sunset Beach, 77, 96
Sunshine Coast, 168-69
Sunshine Coast Golf and Country Club, 167-68

Surrey Centre, 54
Sutton Place Hotel, 47, 60
Suze Restaurant and Lounge, 155
Swangard Stadium, 72
Swans, 156
swimming
beaches, 74, 77-79
indoor pools, 78
Sydney Reynolds, 150
Sylvia Hotel, 95
Symphony of Fire Fireworks Festival, 83

Taylor, L.D., 17
Ted and Mary Grieg Rhododendron Garden, 68
Telus Open, 71-72
Terrain Park, 160, 161
Theatre Festival for Young Audiences, 79
Theatre Under the Stars, 22
Third Beach, 74, 77
Tiffany, 54
tours, Vancouver, 14
The Toybox, 52
Trower, Peter, 168
Turnabout Collections, 55

UBC
Aquatic Centre, 118
Astronomical Observatory, 118
C.K. Choi building, 118
Chan Centre for the Performing Arts, 59
First Nations Longhouse, 118
Forest Sciences Building, 118
gardens, 64-68
Geophysical Observatory, 118
history, 115-16
Main Library, 116
Main Mall, 117
Opera Society, 59
Student Recreation Centre, 118
Student Union Building, 118
walking tour, 116-17
War Memorial Gym, 118
UBC Museum of

Anthropology, 18, 53
architecture, 28
artifacts, 27-28
Great Hall, 28, 29
Rotunda, 29
Uno Langmann Limited, 53
Upper Levels Highway, 122
Upper Village Blackcomb Base (Daylodge), 161
Urban Well Restaurant and Lounge, 57

Van Horn, William, 17, 86
Van Norman, C.B.K., 18
Vancouver Aquarium Marine Science Centre, 24-25
Vancouver Aquatic Centre, 78, 96
Vancouver Art Gallery, 50, 53, 79
architecture, 29-30
concerts, 31
Emily Carr collection, 30-31
Vancouver Canadians, 69
Vancouver Cantata Singers, 59
Vancouver Canucks, 70-71
Vancouver Central Library, 80
Vancouver Centre, 54
Vancouver Convention and Exhibition Centre, 82
Vancouver East Cultural Centre, 59-60, 79, 106
Vancouver Eighty-Sixers, 72
Vancouver Fringe Festival, 84
Vancouver Grizzlies, 70
Vancouver International Children Festival, 78, 82
Vancouver International Comedy Festival, 79, 83
Vancouver International Film Festival, 84
Vancouver International Folk Music Festival, 83

Vancouver International Marathon, 82
Vancouver International Writers Festival, 79-80, 84
Vancouver Maritime Museum, 34-35
Vancouver Opera Company, 58-59
Vancouver Playhouse Theatre Company, 56
Vancouver Public Library, 53
Vancouver rowing and yacht clubs, 22
Vancouver Symphony Orchestra, 58, 59
Vancouver Trade and Convention Centre, 35
Vancouver Trolley Company, 14
VanDusen Botanical Garden, 65-66
Vesuvius, 165
Vicious Cycle Laundro & Leisurama, 106
Victoria
early beginnings, 128-31
economic development, 129
Inner Harbour, 132-33
Village Walk, 120

Waterfront Station, 89
Waterfront Theatre, 79
Wedgewood Hotel, 47
West Bay, 121
West End Vancouver boundaries, 92
Davie Village, 96
diversity, 92
English Bay, 94-96
walking tour, 93-94
Western Front, 63

Whistler, 158-61
Whistler golf courses, 73
Whyte Islet, 123
William Robert, 51
Willows Beach, 148
windsurfing, 72
Wing Sang Building, 103
WISE Hall, 106
Wreck Beach, 74

Yale (blues bar), 59
Yaohan, 54

Zoo, Greater Vancouver, 76-77

PHOTO CREDITS

Legend: Top – T; Centre – C; Bottom – B

Photography by Hamid Attie, except for those listed below.

Formac Publishing Company Limited acknowledges the support of the Cultural Affairs Section, Nova Scotia Department of Tourism and Culture. We acknowledge the financial support of the Government of Canada through the Book Publishing Industry Development Program (BPIDP) for our publishing activities.